THE CAMBRIDGE COMPANION TO CAMUS

Albert Camus is one of the iconic figures of twentieth-century French literature, one of France's most widely read modern literary authors and one of the youngest winners of the Nobel Prize for Literature. As the author of *L'Etranger* and the architect of the notion of 'the Absurd' in the 1940s, he shot to prominence in France and beyond. His work nevertheless attracted hostility as well as acclaim and he was increasingly drawn into bitter political controversies, especially the issue of France's place and role in the country of his birth, Algeria. Most recently, postcolonial studies has identified in his writings a set of preoccupations ripe for revisitation. Situating Camus in his cultural and historical context, this Companion explores his best-selling novels, his ambiguous engagement with philosophy, his theatre, his increasingly high-profile work as a journalist and his reflection on ethical and political questions that continue to concern readers today.

THE CAMBRIDGE
COMPANION TO
CAMUS

EDITED BY

EDWARD J. HUGHES

Queen Mary, University of London

CAMBRIDGE
UNIVERSITY PRESS

CAMBRIDGE UNIVERSITY PRESS
Cambridge, New York, Melbourne, Madrid, Cape Town, Singapore,
São Paulo, Delhi, Dubai, Tokyo

Cambridge University Press
The Edinburgh Building, Cambridge CB2 8RU, UK

Published in the United States of America by Cambridge University Press, New York

www.cambridge.org
Information on this title: www.cambridge.org/9780521549783

© Cambridge University Press 2007

First published 2007

A catalogue record for this publication is available from the British Library

ISBN 978-0-521-84048-4 Hardback
ISBN 978-0-521-54978-3 Paperback

Transferred to digital printing 2010

CONTENTS

NOTES ON CONTRIBUTORS

DAVID CARROLL is Professor of French and Director of European Studies at the University of California, Irvine. His books include *The Subject in Question: The Languages of Theory and the Strategies of Fiction* (1982); *Paraesthetics: Foucault, Lyotard, Derrida* (1987); and *French Literary Fascism: Nationalism, Anti-Semitism, and the Ideology of Culture* (1995). He is also editor of a collection of essays entitled *The States of 'Theory'* (1989, 1994). He has recently completed a book entitled *Albert Camus, The Algerian: Colonialism, Terrorism, Justice* (forthcoming).

MARTIN CROWLEY is Senior Lecturer in French at the University of Cambridge. His publications include: *Duras, Writing, and the Ethical: Making the Broken Whole* (2000); *Robert Antelme: Humanity, Community, Testimony* (2003); and *Robert Antelme: L'Humanité irréductible* (2004). He is currently writing a book on conceptions of the human in post-1945 French thought.

COLIN DAVIS is Professor of French at Royal Holloway, University of London. His research falls principally in the area of post-war French fiction and thought, with a particular interest in the connections between ethics and literature. His principal publications are *Michel Tournier: Philosophy and Fiction* (1988); *Elie Wiesel's Secretive Texts* (1994); *Levinas: An Introduction* (1996); *Ethical Issues in Twentieth-Century French Fiction: Killing the Other* (2000); *French Fiction in the Mitterrand Years: Memory, Narrative, Desire* (co-authored with Elizabeth Fallaize, 2000); and *After Poststructuralism: Reading, Stories and Theory* (2004).

PETER DUNWOODIE is Professor of French Literature and Head of the Department of English and Comparative Literature, Goldsmiths, University of London. His most recent book-publications are *Writing French Algeria* (1998) and *Francophone Writing in Transition* (2005). He is currently working on the subject of colonialism and proselytism in the work of Louis Bertrand.

DAVID R. ELLISON is Professor of French and Comparative Literature at the University of Miami. He is the author of *The Reading of Proust* (1984);

Understanding Albert Camus (1990); *Of Words and the World: Referential Anxiety in Contemporary French Fiction* (1993); and *Ethics and Aesthetics in European Modernist Literature: From the Sublime to the Uncanny* (2001).

CHARLES FORSDICK is Professor of French at the University of Liverpool. He is the author of *Victor Segalen and the Aesthetics of Diversity: Journeys between Cultures* (2000) and *Travel in Twentieth-Century French and Francophone Cultures: the Persistence of Diversity* (2005), and co-editor of *Francophone Postcolonial Studies: a Critical Introduction* (2003). He is currently co-editing a volume on *Postcolonial Thought in the Francophone World* (2008), and completing a typescript entitled *Representing the Revolutionary: the Afterlives of Toussaint Louverture*. His critical editions of Victor Segalen's *Equipée* and *Essai sur l'exotisme* are forthcoming.

TOBY GARFITT is Fellow and Tutor in French at Magdalen College, Oxford. He is the author of *The Work and Thought of Jean Grenier (1898–1971)* (1983), and of numerous articles on Grenier, Mauriac, Green, La Tour du Pin, Camus and Makine, among others. His edited volumes include one entitled *Daniel Halévy, Henri Petit et les Cahiers Verts* (2004), and another devoted to the contemporary writer Sylvie Germain (*Sylvie Germain: rose des vents et de l'ailleurs*, 2003). He has recently completed a full-scale biography of Jean Grenier, *La Discrétion d'un maître* (forthcoming).

MARGARET E. GRAY is Associate Professor in the Department of French and Italian at Indiana University, Bloomington, Indiana. She is the author of *Postmodern Proust* (1992), and of articles on Proust, George Sand, Beckett, Camus, Simone de Beauvoir and the Belgian writer Jean-Philippe Toussaint. Her current typescript, entitled *Stolen Limelight: Gender, Display, and Displacement in Twentieth-Century French and Francophone Narrative*, is under review for publication.

JEANYVES GUERIN is Professor of French at the University of Paris III (La Sorbonne Nouvelle). His main areas of research are twentieth-century French theatre (Audiberti, Ghelderode, Ionesco, Claudel) and *la littérature engagée* (Camus, Malraux, Sartre). He is the author of *Le Théâtre d'Audiberti et le baroque* (1976); *Camus, portrait de l'artiste en citoyen* (1993); *Audiberti. Cent ans de solitude* (1999); and *Art nouveau ou homme nouveau. Modernité et progressisme dans la littérature française du xxe siècle* (2002). He is the editor of several collective volumes, including the *Dictionnaire des pièces théâtrales françaises du xxe siècle* (2005).

EDWARD J. HUGHES is Professor of French Studies at Queen Mary, University of London. He is the author of *Marcel Proust: a Study in the Quality of Awareness* (1983); *Albert Camus: 'La Peste'/'Le Premier Homme'* (1995); and

Writing Marginality in Modern French Literature: from Loti to Genet (2001). He is co-editor, with Peter Dunwoodie, of *Constructing Memories: Camus, Algeria and 'Le Premier Homme'* (1998).

DEBRA KELLY is Professor of French and Francophone Literary and Cultural Studies at the University of Westminster and Director of the Group for War and Culture Studies. She is an Associate Fellow of the Institute of Germanic and Romance Studies, University of London. She has published widely in the fields of Text and Image Studies (especially the early twentieth-century Parisian avant-garde), War and Culture Studies focusing on France in the twentieth century, and Francophone Postcolonial Studies. Her major publications are *Pierre Albert-Birot. A Poetics in Movement, A Poetics of Movement* (1997) and *Autobiography and Independence. Selfhood and Creativity in Postcolonial North African Writing in French* (2005).

CHRISTINE MARGERRISON is a Tutor in French Studies at Lancaster University. She is the author of a number of articles on Camus and is currently completing a book on him, *'Ces forces obscures de l'âme': Women, Race and Origins in the Writings of Albert Camus* (forthcoming). She is also joint editor of a forthcoming volume on post-independence Algeria, *L'Algérie: quarante ans après*.

DANIELLE MARX-SCOURAS is Professor of French at Ohio State University, Columbus, Ohio. She is co-editor of the review *Research in African Literatures* and edited that review's special number on 'Dissident Algeria' (1999). She is the author of *The Cultural Politics of 'Tel Quel': Literature and the Left in the Wake of Engagement* (1996); *La France de Zebda: 1981–2004* (2005); and of numerous articles on French, Francophone and Italian literature.

IEME VAN DER POEL is Professor of French Literature at the University of Amsterdam. Her books include: *Traveling Theory: France and the US* (1999, with Sophie Bertho), and *Congo-Océan: un chemin de fer colonial controversé* (2006). She was appointed 'Chevalier dans les Arts et les Lettres' by the French government in 2004 for her work in the field of Francophone literature, and has published widely on Francophone Maghrebin literature, French Modernist writing and colonialism. She is currently directing a research project, funded by the Netherlands Organisation for Scientific Research (NWO), on the new Moroccan literatures in French, Spanish and Dutch.

ACKNOWLEDGEMENTS

My first thanks go to the contributors to this volume. They have shown a commitment to the project that has been immensely encouraging throughout, as has their engagement with Camus's work and the issues it raises. I want to thank in particular Charles Forsdick for his excellent advice on a number of issues. I also thank Mike Routledge for his translation of chapter 6 and the French Department of Royal Holloway, University of London for its very generous help. Warm thanks go to the staff of Cambridge University Press, in particular to Linda Bree, Rachel de Wachter, Maartje Scheltens, Joanna Breeze and Audrey Cotterell, who combined to guide me through the various planning and delivery stages of the book. Thanks are also due to Eamonn Hughes for his help with the Index. The acknowledgement of indebtedness would not be complete without a sincere expression of gratitude to the anonymous readers at Cambridge University Press. In suggesting many excellent modifications to my initial volume proposal, they have greatly influenced and improved the shape of this book. Needless to say, any limitations in its overall conception remain my own responsibility.

7 November 1913	Birth of Albert Camus. His working-class parents, Catherine Hélène Sintès and Lucien Auguste Camus, are living in the village of Mondovi near Constantine, in Algeria. A French colony between 1831 and 1962, Algeria had been declared French national territory by the French government in the mid nineteenth century and was administered as three departments of the French nation.
August 1914	Camus's family move to Algiers, living in the working-class district of Belcourt.
11 October 1914	Death of Camus's father as a result of wounds received at the Battle of the Marne. He is buried in a French war cemetery in Saint-Brieuc in Brittany.
May 1920	Camus and his brother Lucien acquire the official status of 'pupilles de la nation' or war orphans.
October 1924	Camus begins his secondary education at the Grand Lycée in Algiers and thus enters a culturally very different world from that of his 'petit colon' (working-class colonial) background.
1930–1	French celebrations to mark the centenary of the colonial occupation of Algeria.
December 1930	Camus, diagnosed as having tuberculosis, is forced to interrupt his studies at the Grand Lycée. His life will be blighted by intermittent ill-health.
1931–4	Key period in Camus's intellectual development. His teacher and mentor, the writer Jean Grenier, opens up the world of philosophical ideas for him.

16 June 1934	Camus marries Simone Hié. The marriage will end two years later.
1935	Camus joins the Algerian Communist Party.
1936	Outbreak of the Spanish Civil War. Camus will prove an outspoken supporter of the Spanish Republican cause over the years. Publication of *Révolte dans les Asturies*. Camus involved in amateur theatre in Algeria with the Théâtre du Travail. He will go on to found the Théâtre de l'Equipe in 1937.
Summer 1936	Camus travels to central Europe and Italy.
1937	Camus delivers the opening address at the launch of the new *Maison de la Culture* in Algiers (8 February). His first book, *L'Envers et l'Endroit*, dedicated to Jean Grenier, is published in Algiers by Editions Charlot. Camus is expelled from the Algerian Communist Party for opposing the Party's ending of its campaign for indigenous civil rights. In November, he begins work at the Institute of Meteorology in Algiers and will work there until September 1938.
September 1938	The writer Pascal Pia, editor-in-chief of a new newspaper, *Alger républicain*, hires Camus as an editorial secretary. The paper runs from 6 October 1938 to 28 October 1939.
20 October 1938	Camus's review of Sartre's *La Nausée* (*Nausea*) appears in *Alger républicain*.
23 May 1939	Publication of collection of lyrical essays, *Noces*.
5–15 June 1939	Camus publishes a series of ground-breaking newspaper articles, 'Misère de la Kabylie'. Although his work is not anti-colonialist, it lays bare the catastrophic economic impact of colonialism on the Kabylia region of Algeria. His critique comes at a time when metropolitan France shows no interest in the state of affairs in Algeria.
September 1939	Pascal Pia and Camus found a second newspaper, *Le Soir républicain*.
10 January 1940	Following conflict with the censors, *Le Soir républicain* is suspended by the French authorities.

March 1940   Camus arrives in Paris to work for *Paris-Soir* as a '*secdac*', or editorial secretary. Although he does not publish in this paper, he finds out how a big popular newspaper works. He will spend the war years partly in France, partly in Algeria.

December 1940   Camus remarries. His second wife is Francine Faure.

1940–2   Camus working on texts that will establish his reputation as one of the most important writers of his generation: the novel *L'Etranger* (published May 1942), the essay *Le Mythe de Sisyphe* (December 1942). The play *Caligula*, written substantially in the late 1930s, is published in 1944.

1942   Camus suffers a relapse of tuberculosis.

1943   Sartre's very positive review of *L'Etranger* appears in the Resistance periodical *Les Cahiers du Sud*. Camus is actively engaged with the *Combat* group of the Resistance movement. He becomes editor-in-chief of the clandestine newspaper *Combat*. Publication of the first of the *Lettres à un ami allemand*. Camus begins working for the Gallimard publishing house.

1944   The play *Le Malentendu* receives an indifferent reception.

1944 to 1947   Writing for *Combat*, Camus plays an influential role in public debate in France. He is now a prominent figure in Parisian intellectual circles. He writes of the journalist as a historian of the day-to-day (*Combat*, 1 September 1944).

May 1945   Thousands of indigenous Algerians are killed by the French army in Sétif in retaliation for the killing of Europeans. Coincidentally a trip Camus made as a reporter to Algeria ended immediately prior to the massacres.

8 August 1945   Camus writes an outspoken condemnation of the bombing of Hiroshima in *Combat*. He is one of the few journalists in France to do so.

September 1945   First performance of *Caligula*. The play is a success.

March–June 1946   Camus travels to the United States and Canada.

November 1946	Camus publishes eight articles, reflecting on revolt, revolution and violence, under the heading *Ni victimes ni bourreaux*. Camus's position will contrast markedly with the views expressed by the philosopher Maurice Merleau-Ponty in *Humanisme et terreur* (*Humanism and Terror*), published in 1947.
10 June 1947	*La Peste*, written mainly during the last years of the war, is published. 22,000 copies are sold in just two weeks.
October 1948	First performance of *L'Etat de siège*. The play closes after only seventeen performances.
Summer 1949	Camus travels to South America.
December 1949	First performance of *Les Justes*. The play is a success.
1950	A carefully chosen selection of Camus's editorials appear in a volume entitled *Actuelles I*.
18 October 1951	Publication of *L'Homme révolté*.
1952	Francis Jeanson's hostile review of *L'Homme révolté* appears in *Les Temps modernes*. The ensuing acrimonious exchanges involving Sartre and Camus acquire the status of a national dispute. In the wake of the *Les Temps modernes* quarrel and given Camus's anti-communism, he becomes an increasingly isolated figure in French intellectual milieux of the 1950s.
December 1952	Camus visits Laghouat in the Algerian hinterland. The landscape will provide the setting for 'La Femme adultère'.
1953	Publication of *Actuelles II*.
1954	Publication of *L'Eté*. In October, Camus makes a brief trip to The Hague and Amsterdam.
1 November 1954	Outbreak of what was to become the Algerian War of Independence.
1955	Camus becomes a columnist at *L'Express*.
January 1956	Camus visits Algeria and calls for a civil truce there. The move fails and his position becomes further marginalised.

February 1956	He leaves *L'Express*.
May 1956	Publication of *La Chute*.
September 1956	Camus's adaptation of Faulkner's *Requiem for a Nun* (*Requiem pour une nonne*) is performed.
November 1956	Soviet invasion of Hungary to suppress Hungarian uprising. Camus will cite this example of totalitarian repression in his dispute with Marxist-leaning intellectuals in France.
15 March 1957	Speaking at the Salle Wagram in Paris, Camus expresses solidarity with Hungarian intellectuals and workers. He dismisses Stalinist culture as repressive and propagandising.
1957	Publication of *L'Exil et le Royaume*.
December 1957	Camus receives the Nobel Prize for literature in Stockholm. He dedicates his acceptance address to his primary-school teacher, Louis Germain. At a press conference, when pressed about French Army violence in the Algerian War, he makes the controversial statement that he will defend his mother before justice.
1958	Camus draws together his journalistic writings on Algeria in *Actuelles III: Chroniques Algériennes (1939–1958)*. He publishes 'Algérie 1958', justifying his position on the situation there. He opposes colonial oppression but at the same time underscores the rights of Algeria's 1.1 million Europeans.
1959	Camus is working on what will remain his unfinished novel, *Le Premier Homme*.
4 January 1960	Camus and his publisher friend Michel Gallimard die in a car crash south of Paris in Villeblevin.
July 1962	Algeria becomes independent.
1970	Conor Cruise O'Brien's reading of Camus as a colonial author takes Camus studies in a new direction. Subsequent, postcolonial readings of his work will extend this critique.
1990s	Camus's reputation is in some measure restored in the wake of the decline of communism. In France, Bernard-Henri Lévy endorses his work. A bloody civil war is waged in Algeria between the military government and Islamic fundamentalists

(the F.I.S.). The gruesome violence indirectly prompts a favourable reappraisal of Camus's work by a number of Algerian Francophone women writers, among them Assia Djebar. Djebar links Camus to the victims of assassinations carried out by Algerian fundamentalists (*Le Blanc de l'Algérie* (*The White of Algeria*), 1995).

1994   Publication of Camus's unfinished novel, *Le Premier Homme*. The work is an international publishing success.

Two French terms regularly used in the pages of this book derive from the context of colonial French culture that Camus knew well. The first of these, *petit colon*, literally 'small colonial', means a member of the colonial European working class. The second term, the *pieds-noirs* (literally 'black feet'), historically designated the stokers on a coal-powered boat who would have worked barefoot – many of the stokers on French boats in the Mediterranean in the early twentieth century were in fact indigenous Algerians. But from the mid 1950s on, *pieds-noirs* came to mean the French Algerians and particularly those who steadfastly considered Algeria as their homeland (for some observers, the term indeed carried connotations of complicity with colonial militarism). It was not a designation that Camus himself chose to use. With Algerian independence in 1962, *les pieds-noirs* came to signify the French Algerians repatriated to France.

Titles and translations

Quotations from Camus's published works are given both in the French original and in English translation, with page references to both sources indicated. Where published translations have been modified, this is signalled in the text. Occasionally, contributors have provided their own translations; where translations are not attributed, this is always the case.

Readers will find full bibliographical details of Camus's published work in the 'Guide to Further Reading' at the end of this volume, but they may find it helpful to have a summary list here of those main works by Camus that are cited in the volume, together with the English translations. The list is set out in alphabetical order, the exception being that the titles of individual texts within a larger text (for example individual section titles within a collection such as *L'Exil et le Royaume*) are located together as a sub-category at that point in the list). The original date of publication of the French texts is indicated in parenthesis.

Actuelles I (1950)	*Current Chronicles I*
Actuelles II (1953)	*Current Chronicles II*
Actuelles III (Chroniques algériennes) (1958)	*Current Chronicles III (Algeria)*

(The three volumes of *Actuelles* are partly translated in *Resistance, Rebellion, and Death*)

'Algérie 1958' (1958)	'Algeria 1958'
'Appel pour une trêve civile' (1956)	'Appeal for a Civil Truce'
Caligula (1944)	*Caligula*
Camus à 'Combat' (2002)	*Camus at 'Combat'*
Carnets I: mai 1935-février 1942 (1962)	*Notebooks I*
Carnets II: janvier 1942-mars 1951 (1964)	*Notebooks II*
La Chute (1956)	*The Fall*
'Crise en Algérie' (1945)	'Crisis in Algeria'
L'Envers et l'Endroit (1937)	*Betwixt and Between*
'L'Ironie'	'Irony'
'Entre oui et non'	'Between Yes and No'
'La Mort dans l'âme'	'Death in the Soul'
'Amour de vivre'	'Love of Life'
'L'Envers et l'Endroit'	'Betwixt and Between'
L'Etat de siège (1948)	*State of Siege*
L'Eté (1954)	*Summer*
including	
'Le Minotaure ou la halte d'Oran'	'The Minotaur or the Halt at Oran'
'L'Exil d'Hélène'	'Helen's Exile'
'Retour à Tipasa'	'Return to Tipasa'
L'Etranger (1942)	*The Outsider* (also translated as *The Stranger*)
L'Exil et le Royaume (1957)	*Exile and the Kingdom*
'La Femme adultère'	'The Adulterous Woman'
'Le Renégat'	'The Renegade'
'Les Muets'	'The Silent Men'
'L'Hôte'	'The Guest'
'Jonas ou l'Artiste au travail'	'The Artist at Work'
'La Pierre qui pousse'	'The Growing Stone'
Fragments d'un combat, 1938–1940 (1978)	*Fragments of a Combat, 1938–1940*

L'Homme révolté (1951)	*The Rebel*
Les Justes (1949)	*The Just* (also translated as *The Just Assassins*)
Lettres à un ami allemand (1945)	*Letters to a German Friend*
Le Malentendu (1944)	*Cross Purpose*
'Misère de la Kabylie' (1939)	'Poverty in Kabylia'
La Mort heureuse (1971)	*A Happy Death*
Le Mythe de Sisyphe (1942)	*The Myth of Sisyphus*
Ni victimes ni bourreaux (1946)	*Neither Victims nor Executioners*
Noces (1939)	*Nuptials*
'Noces à Tipasa'	'Nuptials at Tipasa'
'Le Vent à Djémila'	'The Wind at Djemila'
'L'Eté à Alger'	'Summer in Algiers'
'Le Désert'	'The Desert'
La Peste (1947)	*The Plague*
Le Premier Camus (1973)	*Youthful Writings*
Le Premier Homme (1994)	*The First Man*
'Réflexions sur la guillotine' (1957)	'Reflections on the guillotine'

French editions used

For the original French texts by Camus, the two-volume Pléiade edition of his work has been used: vol. I: *Théâtre, Récits, Nouvelles*, Paris, Bibliothèque de la Pléiade, 1962; vol. II: *Essais*, Paris, Bibliothèque de la Pléiade, 1965. This edition contains the bulk of his fictional works and political and philosophical essays (the first two volumes of a new, substantially extended Pléiade edition of Camus's complete works appeared in 2006).

For works not contained in the Pléiade edition, the *Companion* makes use of the available Gallimard editions.

Abbreviations

The following abbreviations of French and English editions of Camus's works are used throughout the volume, with accompanying page references. Full bibliographical details of these editions can be found in the 'Guide to Further Reading' at the end of the volume.

BB   *Betwixt and Between* (contained in *Albert Camus: Lyrical and Critical*)

BHR	*Between Hell and Reason*
CAC	Cahiers Albert Camus
CC	*Camus à 'Combat'*
C*I*, C*II*, C*III*	*Carnets, vols. I, II* and *III*
COP	*Caligula and Other Plays: Caligula, Cross Purpose, The Just, The Possessed*
Corr	*Correspondance Albert Camus/Jean Grenier*
EK	*Exile and the Kingdom*
Ess	*Essais*
F	*The Fall*
FC	*Fragments d'un combat, 1938–1940*
FM	*The First Man*
HD	*A Happy Death*
MH	*La Mort heureuse*
N*I*, N*II*	*Notebooks, vols. I* and *II*
MS	*The Myth of Sisyphus*
O	*The Outsider*
P	*The Plague*
PH	*Le Premier Homme*
R	*The Rebel*
RRD	*Resistance, Rebellion, and Death*
SEN	*Selected Essays and Notebooks*
TRN	*Théâtre, Récits, Nouvelles*
YW	*Youthful Writings*

EDWARD J. HUGHES

Introduction

Albert Camus was a writer who emerged from social obscurity to become a best-selling author and post-war icon in France and beyond, winning the Nobel Prize for literature in 1957. His premature death in January 1960 – he and the publisher Michel Gallimard were killed in a car crash at Ville-blevin, south of Paris – did nothing to diminish that iconic status. Yet behind this tidy, poverty-to-celebrity-to-tragedy narrative, a more complex life story and body of writing beckon. In his Nobel acceptance speech at Stockholm in December 1957, he points out that his life story is part of the collective history of his generation, which has lived through 'une histoire démentielle' ('an insane history'), one that has had to contend with 'le mouvement destructeur de l'histoire' (*Ess*, 1072, 1074) ('the destructive movement of history'). Born on the eve of the First World War, Camus continues, he and his contemporaries reached adulthood as Hitler obtained power and as the first of the revolutionary trials got under way in the Soviet Union. And just to round off the education of his generation, a string of confrontations follow – with civil war in Spain, the Second World War and the concentration camps. Meanwhile the children of this generation face the spectre of nuclear destruction. Camus's conclusion is that a death instinct is at work in the collective history of his times as tyranny's 'grands inquisiteurs' (*Ess*, 1073) ('grand inquisitors') hold sway.

In addition, however, Camus's Europeanness and more particularly his Frenchness was in an important sense atypical, skewed by the fact that he was born into the working-class poor of colonial Algeria, thereby joining the ranks of the so-called *petits colons* or small-time colonisers. This marginal position – adrift not only from metropolitan France but also from the French colonial bourgeoisie who ruled Algeria and an under-class of native Algerians whose plight he nevertheless highlighted[1] – was to remain central to his sense of identity. A French colony since 1831, Algeria had been declared French national territory by the French government of the 1848 revolution. In demographic terms, it was to become France's most French colonial possession, so that by 1936 there were a million Europeans living there, mostly French but also Spanish, Italians and Maltese. By the beginning of the Algerian War of Independence in 1954, Europeans made up about one-ninth of the overall population. As a contested social site, Algeria was to provide the setting for the unfolding of complex cultural tensions that manifest themselves in Camus's own life, in his public pronouncements and positions and in his fictional creations. Significantly it was specifically as a French Algerian that he chose to designate himself when thanking the Nobel Committee for their recognition of his work (*Ess*, 1892).

Camus was also, then, a child of empire, of what French colonial culture had learned to call 'la plus grande France' or greater France. These two dimensions in Camus's life, captured by Conor Cruise O'Brien in his suggestive book-title, *Albert Camus of Europe and Africa*, were to remain inseparable.[2] They generate tensions and dilemmas that go to the heart of his work and that shape and energise readers' varying responses to it. Certain events were crucial in bringing these tensions into acute focus. The Algerian War of Independence was an obvious example. Well before that, in May 1945, we find another troubling point of intersection on the European and North African axes. While the defeat of Nazism was being celebrated in France and much of Europe, Algeria saw an unleashing of French military repression in the form of the Sétif massacres, the French colonial army inflicting massive casualties on native Algerians in retaliation for the killing of Europeans by Algerian insurgents. Faced with these events, Camus appeared unable to appreciate that colonial structures themselves were fundamental to the problem. Wedded to a policy of benign colonial assimilation, he believed that the solution lay in the implementation of democratic French republican structures. His formulations of that belief were sometimes couched in a language that was uncomfortably close to the triumphal language of empire: 'L'Algérie est à conquérir une seconde fois' ('Algeria is to be conquered a second time') was how he exhorted French metropolitan readers of *Combat* a week after the massacres. In fairness, what he meant when he said that this second conquest would be even more difficult to achieve than the first (that is, the military conquest of Algeria in the nineteenth century) was that delivering wholesale political and economic reform would be a tall order. Yet his calls for social amelioration remain within the colonial paradigm and he appears unable to think his way beyond it: 'En Afrique du Nord comme en France, nous avons à inventer de nouvelles formules et à rajeunir nos méthodes si nous voulons que l'avenir ait encore un sens pour nous' ('In North Africa as in France, we must come up with new formulae and update our way of doing things if we wish to ensure that the future has a meaning for us').[3] Consistent with his urging of reform, Camus remains outspoken in his opposition to metropolitan French voices who call for what Camus condemns as 'une répression aveugle' ('a blind repression').[4] Ultimately, then, Camus's sincerely held reformist beliefs failed to encompass the sheer scale of social polarisation and colonial militarism signalled by the massacres in Sétif. Nevertheless, as Conor Cruise O'Brien forthrightly observed, for many North Africans, French Algeria was every bit as 'repugnant as the fiction of Hitler's new European order was for Camus'.[5] Yet as O'Brien concedes, Camus was most probably oblivious to any such analogy, as were many left-wing intellectuals at the time. Camus was most likely still a communist in 1937 when he developed a conception of Mediterranean culture which to all intents and purposes legitimised the French domination of Algeria.[6] In the longer term and particularly in the mid to late 1950s with the Algerian War of Independence in full spate, Camus remained fundamentally ill equipped to adapt to the nascent postcolonialism in the country of his birth. Indeed, he failed to give any credence to the logic of anti-colonialism.

Camus's rootedness in Frenchness was deep. He was, if we are to heed the semantic charge of the French term for a war orphan, a child or ward of the French nation, a 'pupille de la nation'. Belonging to the ranks of countless orphans of parents killed in the First World War (his father died from wounds received at the Battle of the Marne), he and his brother Lucien were placed, as it were both symbolically and, in a very restricted sense, economically, under the protection of the nation.[7] His conception of Frenchness was strongly coloured by historical memory of the service his French Algerian antecedents had paid to the nation. His unfinished novel, *Le Premier Homme* (*The First Man*), posthumously published in 1994, is a eulogy both of those nineteenth-century, small-time colonial settlers who uprooted and moved to North Africa and of the settlers' descendants (as well as indeed their Algerian Arab contemporaries), who in 1914 crossed the Mediterranean to fight in defence of France. By preserving the memory of these loyal predecessors, Camus implicitly shows his distaste for France's programme of post-war decolonisation. Indeed, he saw French equivocation in respect of Algeria as a form of betrayal. Camus remained deeply sensitive to the patriotic discourse that evoked memories of earlier struggles. He was both inspired and troubled by the memory of military sacrifice in the First World War. In the pages of *Le Premier Homme*, we are offered, as an exemplary tale of that sacrifice, Roland Dorgelès's patriotic war novel, *Les Croix de bois* (*The Wooden Crosses*), from which the primary school teacher Monsieur Germain (to whom Camus incidentally dedicated his Nobel Prize address) reverently reads to his pupils (*PH*, 139; *FM*, 114). In this way, the lessons of patriotism and the French educational system were mutually reinforcing.

As a ward of the nation, so to speak, Camus had entitlement to a school bursary. French colonial culture was such that his academic formation was that provided by the national lycée system and Toby Garfitt sets out in detail the nature of the education Camus received (chapter 2). Reading about Camus's literary tastes in his brief essay on the aesthetics of the novel, 'L'Intelligence et l'Echafaud' (1943) – his enthusiasm for Mme de Lafayette, the Marquis de Sade, Stendhal and Proust – we could be forgiven for forgetting that his background was very unlike that of bourgeois, metropolitan France. Yet in his fiction, life as a *petit colon* is central. It is actively celebrated in the pages of *L'Etranger*, where the young shipping clerk Meursault, working in the port of Algiers, is unexcited by his boss's plans to open up an office in Paris and have Meursault work there. The reason Meursault gives is that 'toutes (les vies) se valaient et que la mienne ici ne me déplaisait pas du tout' (*TRN*, 1156) ('one life was as good as another and . . . I wasn't at all dissatisfied with mine here' (*O*, 44)).

Yet notwithstanding Meursault's stay-at-home, *petit colon* ways, for decades many readers saw in Meursault not, to put it crudely, a specific by-product of European colonial rule in North Africa but rather a largely innocent, indeed martyr-like figure falling foul of an unjust, Absurd world. As Danielle Marx-Scouras points out (chapter 10), Meursault became the rebellious hero of the post-war and Vietnam eras. Not surprisingly, given the resonance enjoyed by the text and the accompanying 'literature of the Absurd' tag, Camus tended to become synonymous, for many readers, with his Absurd fictional progeny, Meursault. If the runaway success of the novel largely obscured the cultural seedbed from which *L'Etranger* emerged, Peter Dunwoodie crucially restores the French Algerianist backdrop in his examination of the origins of Camus's literary formation (see chapter 11).

On the back of the success of *L'Etranger*, Camus became a cult figure whose reputation came to be entwined with an array of conditions, causes and concerns: the world of youth, impulsiveness and rebellion; existential angst and the struggle with evil; the deadening impact of social hypocrisy, the dread of conformism, and the individual's struggle to locate himself in society. But if one of the challenges in this *Companion* is to account for and situate historically the iconic status that Camus's work acquired for millions across national boundaries during his lifetime and after, our situation of his work needs to assume other dimensions too. We need to understand not just the adulation but also the acrimony his work aroused, particularly in the last decade of his life and in the era of postcolonialism. This entails a repositioning of Camus's work, the hope being that we will open up new ways of reading and contextualising the corpus.

Camus continues to attract critical attention, both negative and appro-
batory. As Ieme van der Poel reminds us in chapter 1, Bernard-Henri Lévy,
writing in 1991 against the backdrop of the decline of communism, accords
Camus a special place in his account of French intellectual history; by contrast, Edward Said, writing around the same time, sees in Camus's work a
strong exemplification, indeed a 'clarification', of the culture of empire.[8] In
postcolonial Algeria, as Charles Forsdick and Debra Kelly both demonstrate,
forty years on from the acrimonious War of Independence, a new generation
of Algerian Francophone women writers, alienated by post-independence
violence, has reclaimed Camus as an adoptive brother. These fluctuations
in the reception given to his work provide their own period-specific and
situation-specific cultural barometers. Likewise, the varying perspectives on
Camus collected in this volume necessarily reflect modes of analysis and
appreciation operating at a particular historical juncture.

By the same logic, if we wind back rapidly to the generation of the 1940s in
France, we find a different set of circumstances and a contrasting reception.
In that particular decade, which was dominated by the Second World War
and the bleak post-war period, the young Camus was seen as the embodiment
of a mindset, an outlook that he branded 'the Absurd'. At the heart of
the Absurd lay what Camus saw as the confrontation between the human
desire for a rational account of the world and a world that resisted any
such explanation. Humanity craves clarity, Camus argues in *Le Mythe de
Sisyphe*, and the world appears gratuitous and irrational. While the term
enjoyed prominence particularly in French intellectual life, the Absurd came
to suggest more a widespread feeling of human malaise than of any tightly
argued philosophical system.

Camus was writing in a context of crisis in twentieth-century values
prompted by the loss of religious belief, by totalitarianism and by war being
waged on a global scale. As David Carroll explains in chapter 4, the mood in
France (which Camus saw at first hand and wrote about) was one of abject
desolation and hopelessness after national defeat and collaboration with the
Nazis. For Camus personally, it was also a time of serious illness. Yet however urgent the term's application in that particular set of circumstances, the
'Absurd' label has come to be no less dated, no less historically specific than
the events of the war itself. As Carroll demonstrates, Camus himself asserted
in the mid 1950s that the Absurd was a phase which, however important,
he had by then worked beyond. As with many forms of intellectual pack-
aging or badging, the Absurd tag has persisted. It leaves us with a vestigial
reminder of 1940s gloom. Yet if we overplay it, we risk obscuring not only
the evolution in Camus's writing career but also, no less importantly, contrasting generational responses to his works. The progressive interpretations

of Camus's output have led to a mythologisation of his work that has delivered both ringing endorsement and hostile critique. Thus exegesis of his work provided by French Camusians has been broadly accommodating and sometimes even hagiographic. In an Anglophone context, on the other hand, postcolonial readers of French literature often gravitate towards Camus (his language, characterisation and fictional settings) in their search for an exemplary incarnation of the colonial mindset. The complexity and internal contradictions of his work would suggest it can usefully be read in nuanced ways that neither adulation nor demonisation can adequately account for.

A high-profile opinion-former in war-torn France, Camus also played a central role in post-war cultural and political debate. As an internationalist, he was able to look well beyond metropolitan France and French Algeria. He engaged powerfully with issues such as dictatorship in Franco's Spain and other forms of totalitarianism, both fascist and communist, elsewhere in Europe. In an outspoken editorial published in *Combat* two days after the bombing of Hiroshima on 6 August 1945, Camus vigorously attacked the seductive presentation of the atomic bomb as a triumph of scientific genius in the French, American and British press. Rejecting as especially objectionable the 'picturesque literature' used to prettify and obscure the horror of atomic destruction, Camus concluded that a 'mechanical civilisation' had reached its point of ultimate savagery.[9] In a post-war France where communist influence was strong, he became increasingly sceptical, especially when news began to emerge of brutal Stalinist repression. He remained unconvinced by revolutionary ideology, arguing from a position of social reformism. As Martin Crowley draws out (chapter 7), Camus placed the figure of the human at the heart of a fundamentally moral politics; such a politics would work, to use Camus's terminology, in the service of man.

This volume attempts, then, to give a full account of Camus's situation socially, politically and culturally. At the same time, it seeks to guard against any exclusive focus on the circumstantial. For Camus's appeal as a writer draws us back to, but also takes us beyond, the conditions in which he lived and worked. He did not conceal his claim to be a writer of the human condition. His appeals to a mythological figure such as Sisyphus, a deranged ancient ruler such as Caligula, a dehistoricised type such as Don Juan, show that he did not restrict himself to fictional situations couched in mid twentieth-century actuality. In *L'Homme révolté*, he dismisses the revolutionary interpreters of Hegel's *Phenomenology of the Spirit* who argue that in a reconciled social order there would no longer be a need for art since – in Camus's disbelieving formulation – 'la beauté sera vécue, non plus imaginée' (*Ess*, 658) ('beauty will be lived and no longer only imagined' (*R*, 220)).

Likewise, he refuses to accept Marx's thesis that art is determined by the epoch in which it is produced and that it expresses the privileged values of the dominant class (*ibid.*). In the same essay, perhaps with Sartre, the exponent of the idea that literature has to be understood in terms of its social situation, also in his sights, Camus delights in telling the story about Balzac, who remarked at the end of a long conversation about politics and the fate of the world that it was now time to get down to serious business, by which he meant talking about his novels (*Ess*, 663; *R*, 226).

The reader repeatedly senses Camus's urge to get beyond constricting political and social circumstance. In negotiating the connection between the world and art, he regularly prefers to foreground acutely personal dilemmas. If life's circumstances for the individual are often conveyed as being restrictive and sordid, emotions as overwhelming, grief as disabling, Camus encourages his reader to see art, by contrast, as a form of compensation, of correction. Appealing to what he characterises as a tradition transcending historical periods, Camus writes enthusiastically about Madame de Lafayette's seventeenth-century novel, *La Princesse de Clèves*. Here, the princess's crippling if ultimately successful struggle against the temptation of adultery has disastrous consequences for her and her husband. Camus heaps praise on the husband prince who, even though he will die of grief, uses a contained, measured language that does not entertain despair and madness. Camus is mesmerised by this exercise of control. He sees the greatness of the French classical novel lying in its obdurate containment of life's miseries, in its refusal of what he terms 'bavardage' or chatter (*TRN*, 1896): 'Aucun de nos grands romanciers', he asserts, 'ne s'est détourné de la douleur des hommes, mais il est possible de dire qu'aucun ne s'y est abandonné et que par une émouvante patience, ils l'ont tous maîtrisée par les règles de l'art' (*TRN*, 1902) ('None of our great novelists has turned away from human suffering but it could be said that none of them has given way to it, that, by exercising a moving patience, they have dominated it through the rules of art'). Camus draws these same characteristics into his own fiction, where, be it Meursault's self-containment, the resignation of the mother in *Le Premier Homme* or of Sisyphus, or Rieux's understatement in *La Peste*, a premium is put on stoic detachment, on an acceptance of one's destiny.

If in Camus's estimation the containment of intense suffering is a key attribute of the French classical novel, he sees other ways too in which art works against life. As he conceives of it, art is a form of utopia, to the extent that it appeals to and placates the human desire for unity. Be it art, crime or religion, Camus argues, each responds to human kind's 'désir déraisonnable' ('unreasonable desire'), which is to 'donner à la vie la forme qu'elle n'a pas' (*Ess*, 666) ('give life a form it does not have' (*R*, 228)). The novel, then, corrects the world by providing finality: its characters run, in Camus's image, to their meeting with destiny, thereby experiencing a resolution, a completion that in real life remains unavailable. In delivering a sense of unity, the work of art responds, in Camus's judgement, to a metaphysical need (*Ess*, 668; *R*, 229).

The aesthetic preferences that Camus is voicing here connect with the humanist perspective which holds at its centre the affirmation of human endeavour as ultimately affirmative. But like the volume more generally in which they appear, *L'Homme révolté*, these views would be subject to contestation. Thus post-humanist readings of Camus have mapped out a different critical terrain in which his often unapologetically moralising accounts of the creative life are often viewed with suspicion. More broadly, European humanism's socio-cultural legacy was itself called into question with the emergence of postcolonialism. In particular, Europe's failure to export to its colonies the humanist value-systems on which it prided itself is a leitmotif of postcolonial contestation. Notwithstanding Camus's own campaigning on behalf of Algerian rights in *Misère de la Kabylie*, for example, his position and work have come to be the objects of close scrutiny.[10]

This *Companion to Camus* is designed to convey something of the energy, variety and generic range of Camus's work and to counter the narrowing of his corpus that has tended to follow on from the iconic Camus. It seeks to explore the circumstances of his life and writing career, to gauge his literary achievements, and to examine the exposure to public controversy that he attracted. Aiming not to fall into Camus worship, it picks up on the unevenness in his published work, acknowledging how his literary achievements helped preserve corners of his writing that might otherwise have fallen from view. The celebrity Camus secured on the strength of successes such as *L'Etranger*, *La Peste* and *La Chute* – landmarks of twentieth-century world literature that have sold in their millions of copies and been translated around the world – was indeed considerable. But as Jeanyves Guérin points out (chapter 6), critical interest in his journalism, for example, persists largely as a derivative of that literary success. Likewise, and even allowing for Camus's keen commitment to the theatre, his plays, as Christine Margerrison demonstrates in chapter 5, have had mixed success. Certainly they have not enjoyed collectively the sustained resonance and impact of the work of a contemporary such as Samuel Beckett, whose more accomplished technical dramatisation of an absurd human condition has attracted justifiably fuller critical attention. Nevertheless, as Danielle Marx-Scouras argues in chapter 10, Camus's puzzling over competing ethical imperatives feeds centrally into the debate about justice and love in *Les Justes*.

The first two of the three chapters of Part I combine biographical overview and an account of the cultural and intellectual influences that shaped Camus's outlook. Chapter 3 complements these by exploring Camus's early collection of essays *L'Envers et l'Endroit* and gleaning evidence of the author's cautious moves towards autobiographical writing. Part II begins by exploring the generic range to be found in the corpus: his ambiguous engagement with philosophy and the cult of the Absurd in *Le Mythe de Sisyphe* (chapter 4); his work in the world of theatre (chapter 5); his increasingly high-profile work as a journalist, writing and often campaigning in the hard-edged circumstances of colonial life in Algeria, the Second World War and that war's aftermath (chapter 6). The section then moves on to explore Camus's very public and sometimes controversial contributions to ethical and political debate: chapter 7 looks at Camus's attempt to articulate a pragmatic theory of meaningful social responsibility in an age of genocide and global conflict; chapter 8 addresses the temptation of violence that Camus wrestles with through fictional protagonists such as Caligula, Meursault and Kaliayev; and chapter 9 re-evaluates an emblematic moment in Cold War cultural debate in 1950s France, namely the quarrel between Camus and Sartre in the wake of Camus's controversial essay which attacked both fascist and communist forms of totalitarianism, *L'Homme révolté*. Chapter 10 explores the love/justice paradigm in Camus and considers specifically how fictional heroines such as Janine and Dora work for a reconciliation of spheres that are deemed irreconcilable in Western political thought, namely the private and the public. The four chapters in Part III, finally, are devoted to the fictional texts that are central to Camus's literary legacy and reputation: chapter 11 charts the cultural genesis of Camus's fiction, taking the reader through some of the early prose work, principally *Noces* and *L'Etranger*; chapter 12 explores the incremental accumulation of meaning in *La Peste*; chapter 13 unpacks the complex baggage of evasiveness and garrulousness that makes up *La Chute*; and chapter 14 approaches Camus's last text, *Le Premier Homme*, in the light of concerns about legacy and collective memory.

NOTES

1. See chapter 6, where Jeanyves Guérin discusses Camus's reporting on famine in Kabylia in 1939.
2. Conor Cruise O'Brien, *Albert Camus of Europe and Africa* (New York, The Viking Press, 1970).
3. *Camus à 'Combat'*, ed. Jacqueline Lévi-Valensi (Paris, Gallimard, 2002), p. 501. For a sense of the scale of the French army reprisals against local Algerians, see Olivier Todd, *Albert Camus: une vie* (Paris, Gallimard, 1996), pp. 378–9.
4. *Camus à 'Combat'*, p. 502.

5. Conor Cruise O'Brien, *Camus* (Glasgow, Collins (Fontana), 1970), p. 48.
6. See *ibid.*, p. 13. For a detailed consideration of Camus's conception of Mediterranean culture, see Peter Dunwoodie's discussion in chapter 11.
7. See Todd, *Albert Camus: une vie*, p. 24. The status of 'pupille de la nation' entailed a modest entitlement to medical care and a school bursary.
8. Edward Said, *Culture and Imperialism* (London, Vintage, 1994), p. 224.
9. *Camus a 'Combat'*, pp. 569–71.
10. Frantz Fanon, for example, writing in *Les Damnés de la terre* (*The Wretched of the Earth*), complains: 'Cette Europe qui jamais ne cessa de parler de l'homme, jamais de proclamer qu'elle n'était inquiète que de l'homme, nous savons aujourd'hui de quelles souffrances l'humanité a payé chacune des victoires de son esprit' ('This Europe which never stopped talking about man and proclaiming that man was its sole, anxious concern, we know today with what sufferings humanity has paid for each of the victories of the European mind'), Fanon, *Les Damnés de la terre* (Paris, Gallimard, 1991), p. 372.

PART I

Biography and influences

I

IEME VAN DER POEL

Camus: a life lived in critical times

The life of Albert Camus (1913–60) was profoundly affected by the three major tragedies which dominate the history of twentieth-century France: the Great War (1914–18), World War II (1939–45) and the Algerian War of Independence (1954–62). It is unusual that Camus's destiny should have been so closely bound up with that of metropolitan France. As a French *petit colon* born in Algeria, he spent most of his life outside France. It was not until he was in his late thirties that, as a celebrated writer, Camus settled in France permanently. After the very successful publication of *La Peste* in 1947, he was able to set up house in the sixth *arrondissement* in Paris, near the premises of his editor, Gallimard.

Camus was born on 7 November 1913, on the eve of the First World War, in the little village of Mondovi near Constantine, one of the major cities of what was then French Algeria. His mother was of Spanish origin, his father a so-called *pied-noir*, a Frenchman born in the colony and whose family had lived there for several generations. In his last and unfinished work, the autobiographical novel *Le Premier Homme*, Camus claims that his forebears had fled from Alsace after the French defeat in the Franco-Prussian war of 1870–1. According to Camus's biographer Olivier Todd, however, the Camus family came from the Bordeaux region in the south-west of France. This would make it more probable that it was economic rather than political reasons that led them to try their fortune in Algeria.[1]

In terms of social class, Camus's parents belonged to the colony's poor whites, who occupied an intermediate position between the French ruling class (*les colons*), and the indigenous population, which consisted mainly of Arabs and Berbers. When Camus was eight months old, his father was drafted into the French army and shipped to France, to become one of the first victims at the Battle of the Marne. He died on 11 October 1914 and was buried in Saint-Brieuc in Brittany. In *Le Premier Homme*, Camus draws a striking portrait of the father he never knew, showing him as one of the countless, nameless soldiers from the colonies who, immediately on their arrival in a foreign country they were supposed to consider as their homeland, were thrown into the battle:

> On n'avait pas eu le temps de leur trouver des casques, le soleil n'était pas assez fort pour tuer les couleurs comme en Algérie, si bien que des vagues d'Algériens arabes et français, vêtus de tons éclatants et pimpants, coiffés de chapeaux de paille, cibles rouges et bleues qu'on pouvait apercevoir à des centaines de mètres, montaient par paquets au feu, étaient détruits par paquets. (*PH*, 70)

> There was no time to find them helmets; the sun was not strong enough to erase colours as it did in Algeria, so that waves of Arab and French Algerians, dressed in smart shining colours, straw hats on their heads, red-and-blue targets you could see for hundreds of metres, went over the top in droves into the fire, were destroyed in droves. (*FM*, 55)

Camus here criticises the seemingly casual way in which metropolitan France disposed of the lives of its colonial subjects during the Great War. It is also worth noting that the Arab and French soldiers are depicted here as brothers in arms, dying together on the same battlefield. From the author's point of view, this is not a coincidence: both the Arab masses and the poor whites from Algeria were victims of oppression and social injustice, united, so to speak, in their communal suffering and in their profound attachment to their native soil. One sees the theme's prominence in Camus's late fictional writings, such as *L'Exil et le Royaume* (1957) and *Le Premier Homme* (still unfinished when he died in 1960), at a time when the Algerian War of Independence was bitterly tearing apart the Arabs and the working-class Europeans. Yet this should not blind one to the fact that the same theme may also be detected in some of Camus's earliest stories, making it one of the more permanent preoccupations in his life and art.

Camus found the inspiration for his first book, *L'Envers et l'Endroit*, published in Algiers by Charlot in 1937, in Belcourt, the working-class quarter in east Algiers where he spent his early childhood. This also explains its initial title: *Voix du quartier pauvre* (*Voices from the Poor Quarter*). In the preface to the second edition published in 1958, Camus claims that, in spite of its 'forme maladroite' (*Ess*, 5) ('clumsiness'), he considers this small volume to be the source that sustained all his later life and work. It is about poverty and the Algerian sunlight, which, according to Camus, makes the misery of the inhabitants of southern locations less grim than the grey skies of the north; moreover, the author professes his love for the sparsely furnished Arab and Spanish houses, preferring them to the apartments of the wealthy Parisian bourgeoisie that he became familiar with after he had grown to be one of the most successful writers of his time. Finally, he concludes that if he had to rewrite the original text, he would again centre it on 'l'admirable silence d'une mère et l'effort d'un homme pour retrouver une justice ou un amour qui équilibre ce silence' (*Ess*, 13) ('the admirable silence of a mother and a man's effort to find a kind of justice or love that would counterbalance that silence').

The figure of the resigned, older woman, as she appears in several of the sketches collected in this volume, was modelled, no doubt, on Camus's own mother, a partially deaf and taciturn figure. She belongs to the women who find themselves 'au bord de la vie' ('on the edge of life'), as Maïssa Bey puts it, thus symbolising Camus's humble origins, which he never denied and which laid the foundations for a political and social engagement that lasted a lifetime.[2] Moreover, in one of the stories, entitled 'Entre oui et non' ('Between Yes and No'), the mother's silence is juxtaposed with that of the owner of a Moorish café, where the narrator muses upon his past. In fact, there is a continual intermingling of the two spaces: the deserted café that is about to close, and the humble lodgings where the narrator lived with his mother as a child. In both, people sit together in total silence, which opens up the possibility for another, more corporeal kind of 'communication'. It consists in a sharing, next to one another, but not jointly, of the same, strong, sensory perceptions, which are bound up with the Mediterranean: its smells, its sounds, its light, its starry nights. The three silent figures, then, of the mother, the owner of the Moorish café and the child, can be seen as the embodiment of an all-encompassing, Mediterranean culture, glossing over all ethnic and linguistic differences. In *L'Envers et l'Endroit*, the geographical and other 'continuities' of the Mediterranean basin are also evoked in a series of colourful evocations of the Italian landscape, the small harbours along the coast of Ibiza and the smiles of the Genoese women.

Around the time that Camus was working on his first book, he became increasingly involved in politics. In this respect also, the idea of a Mediterranean culture was of great concern to him, as is made clear by the text of a lecture that he gave at the Algiers Cultural Centre on 8 February 1937: 'Nous sommes d'autant mieux préparés que nous sommes au contact immédiat de l'Orient, qui peut tant nous apprendre à cet égard . . . Le rôle essentiel que pourraient jouer les villes comme Alger et Barcelone, c'est de servir pour leur faible part cet aspect de la culture méditerranéenne qui favorise l'homme au lieu de l'écraser.'[3] (We are all the better prepared for this because we are in immediate contact with the Orient, from which we can learn so much in this regard . . . the cities of Algiers and Barcelona could play a small though essential part in the process of restoring the idea of a Mediterranean culture that defends human values, instead of crushing them.) Camus opposed Italian fascism's call for a new Rome that would emulate ancient Roman imperial grandeur by once again radiating greatness across the Mediterranean, the *Mare Nostrum* ('Our Sea'). By dismissing Mussolini's revivalism, he exhorted his fellow citizens to save the Mediterranean from the Italian fascists. Instead of Mussolini's dream of the supremacy of a Latin culture which would match that of Hitler's *Germania*, Camus invited his audience to recall yet another aspect of a glorious past: that of *al-Andalus*, in which the different ethnic and religious groups from Spain and the Arab-Muslim Mediterranean had been united. In this way, Camus made it very clear that he was not only opposed to fascism, but that he also looked upon Arab culture as a substantial part of the Mediterranean heritage.

From 1935 until 1937, Camus was a member of the Algerian Communist Party. In his choice of membership, he was certainly influenced by his former teacher and mentor, the writer Jean Grenier. It is less obvious why, after a relatively short period of time, Camus was struck off the party's register. His fall from grace took place against the background of growing political tension between the communists and the nationalists in Algeria. Although the communists had already fought against colonialism since the beginning of the 1920s, they were unhappy that Messali Hadj, the leader of the newly created Algerian Popular Party (PPA), should hark back to certain traditional values in order to reinforce the notion of an Algerian identity. This was also the reason why Messali rejected the Blum–Violette plan (1937), according to which the French socialist government planned to offer full French citizenship to 22,000 Algerians. In Messali's view, this plan, to which the Algerian communists were also fiercely opposed, would increase the gap that already existed between the assimilated Algerian elite and the impoverished masses from the countryside.[4]

Camus's support for the PPA is also illustrated by his work as a reporter. In September 1938 he met Pascal Pia, the journalist and former Surrealist, who had recently arrived from France to become editor-in-chief of the newly created newspaper *Alger républicain*. Pia hired Camus as an editorial secretary and it was in this position that he first worked as a journalist. He wrote several book reviews, including an article about Sartre's first novel *La Nausée*, which had come out in the autumn of 1938. But central to Camus's contributions to the newspaper were the articles he produced about current developments in Algeria itself, which seem to have preoccupied him more at this time than the growing threat of war in Europe or the civil war in Spain.

Camus was very critical of the way in which the French-Algerian government handled the rise of nationalism. In the summer of 1939, several leading members of the PPA were arrested and died of ill treatment in Algerian prisons.[5] In an article published in *Alger républicain*, Camus commented:

'La montée du nationalisme algérien s'accomplit sur les persécutions dont on le poursuit' (*Ess*, 1370) ('The rise of Algerian nationalism is brought about by the persecution directed against it'). In Camus's view, the repressive measures taken by the French authorities against nationalist political leaders were not the only reason for the growing discontent among native Algerians. Between 5 and 15 June 1939, he published the ten instalments of *Misère de la Kabylie*. In this travel report, consisting of articles about the terrible famine that had struck the Kabylia region, Camus questioned the impact of colonialism on the native inhabitants of Algeria. He accused his fellow citizens of systematically exploiting the local population, by refusing them equal pay and by providing them with insufficient schools and medical care.

With the publication of *Misère de la Kabylie*, Camus became one of the first French intellectuals to criticise overtly the French colonial enterprise in its overseas territories. But in Camus's case, his denunciations of the ill treatment of the Algerian peasants by their colonial oppressors did not have the same impact on the French public as, somewhat earlier, André Gide's protest against the excesses of colonial rule in the French Congo, or Andrée Viollis's condemnation of the atrocities that were being perpetrated in Indochina. In France, all public attention was now focused on the impending war in Europe.

Meanwhile, in Algeria, Pia and Camus had founded a second newspaper, *Le Soir républicain*. The outbreak of the war had made the distribution of *Alger républicain* more difficult and it saw an important decrease in the number of copies sold. By launching a new paper, the editors hoped to make up for this loss, but after a few months, *Alger républicain* folded. The impact of the war was not limited to economic matters; it also affected the ethics of journalism. Although the press in Algeria was placed under censorship, this did not prevent Camus from exercising his right to freedom of speech. In favour of neither Hitler nor Stalin, he and Pia were, above all, convinced pacifists: they protested against the rounding up of communists after the German–Russian non-aggression pact had been concluded and they published extensively on the historical background of the then current situation, as well as on the possibilities of restoring peace. After many altercations with the censors, *Le Soir républicain* was eventually suspended by the French authorities on 10 January 1940.[6]

The years 1940–2 constituted a turning point in Camus's career as a writer, profoundly affecting both his political and philosophical views. Living in occupied France part of the time (and at other times in the Algerian city of Oran), Camus wrote the three texts that would establish his reputation as one of the most important writers of his generation: the novel *L'Etranger*

(1942), the philosophical essay *Le Mythe de Sisyphe* (1942) and the play *Caligula* (1944). These texts, together with the articles that he wrote for *Le Soir républicain*, and the *Lettres à un ami allemand*, which appeared in the underground press during the German occupation, give a clear picture of the way in which the experience of war and oppression affected the development in Camus's way of thinking.

Time and again, Camus confesses his all-encompassing love of life. His writings abound with images that represent the physical world. The pleasurable experience of swimming and sunbathing is present in both *L'Etranger* and 'La Guerre' ('War'), an article he wrote for *Le Soir républicain* in 1939. The *Lettres à un ami allemand* praise the beauty of the European landscape, as embodied by 'les pigeons se détach[ant] en grappes de la cathédrale de Salzbourg' ('the clusters of pigeons taking off from the cathedral of Salzburg'), and 'les géraniums rouges [qui poussent] inlassablement sur les petits cimetières en Silésie' (*Ess*, 236) ('the red geraniums that grow with tireless energy in the small cemeteries of Silesia'). In 'La Guerre', however, these images of a physical world that seems absurdly unaffected by the atrocities of war and destruction are relegated to an irretrievable past. From this, the author draws the conclusion that 'c'est bien là peut-être l'extrémité de la révolte que de perdre sa foi dans l'humanité des hommes' (*Ess*, 1377) ('losing one's faith in the humanity of men may perhaps be the ultimate form of revolt'). This hint of pessimism recalls the answer that Meursault, in *L'Etranger*, gives to his boss, when the latter asks him if he would like to change his way of life: 'J'ai répondu qu'on ne changeait jamais de vie, qu'en tout cas toutes se valaient et que la mienne ici ne me déplaisait pas du tout' (*TRN*, 1155–6) ('I replied that you could never change your life, that in any case one life was as good as another and that I wasn't at all dissatisfied with mine' (*O*, 44)).

But these texts also reflect Camus's struggle with the absurdity of a world in which God is no longer present. In *Caligula*, the main character's lawless behaviour calls to mind the Surrealists' idea of revolt against a civilisation seen as fundamentally restrictive. It is a behaviour also reminiscent of the sense of revolt as articulated by the marquis de Sade in the eighteenth century. In a similar way, Caligula claims the right to exercise his individual freedom, even at the expense of the lives and happiness of his fellow men, and totally rejects human law. But in the last scene of the play the tyrant is killed by his best friend, Cherea. Although the latter shares Caligula's conviction about the overall absurdity of human destiny, he is revolted by the pointless sacrifice of human lives that results from it.

If *Caligula* marks the beginning of a major change in Camus's philosophical insights, this becomes even more apparent from the first of the *Lettres à un ami allemand*, published in 1943: 'C'est beaucoup que de se battre en méprisant la guerre, d'accepter de tout perdre en gardant le goût du bonheur, de courir à la destruction avec l'idée d'une civilisation supérieure' (*Ess*, 222) ('It demands a lot to fight when one despises war, and to accept to lose everything while keeping a taste for happiness, to run headlong towards destruction while being guided by the idea of a superior civilisation'). In Camus's view, it is precisely because we cling to life so much that we find the strength to sacrifice it for a future of which we ourselves will no longer be part. In a world in which God is no longer present, solidarity provides the only possible answer to the absurdity of human destiny. In this respect, Camus's idea of revolt has developed from the contesting of the legitimacy of any human law, as illustrated by Caligula, to laying claim to a human order in which all answers are human. Or, as Camus puts it in *L'Homme révolté*: 'L'homme révolté, c'est l'homme jeté hors du sacré et appliqué à revendiquer un ordre humain où toutes les réponses soient humaines' (*Ess*, 1688) ('The rebel is man thrown outside the sacred and keen to lay claim to a human order in which all answers are human').

The *Lettres à un ami allemand* also read like a declaration of love to European culture. Contrary to the Germans, it is not out of patriotism or to gain supremacy over 'cet espace cerclé de mers et de montagnes' (*Ess*, 234) ('this space surrounded by seas and mountains') that the author of the letters wants to fight. He is prepared to sacrifice his life in order to defend a set of spiritual values that represent to his mind 'Europe', and which he considers to be 'ma plus grande patrie' (*Ess*, 236) ('my wider fatherland').

Camus spent the war years partly in Algeria, partly in France. In 1942, he suffered a relapse of the tuberculosis that he contracted in his adolescent years and was advised to spend some time in the mountains in France. He stayed in Le Chambon sur Lignon, a Huguenot village in the Vivarais region. After the war, its inhabitants were the only community in occupied Europe to be awarded collectively the Yad Vashem decoration for their support of Jewish refugees during the German occupation. It is not unlikely that during his stay in the mountains Camus got involved with the French Resistance. It is equally possible, though, that it was through his friend Pascal Pia (living in nearby Lyons), that he became engaged in the Combat group of the Resistance movement in 1943.

Soon after settling in Paris, Camus became the editor-in-chief of the clandestine newspaper *Combat*, which drew together a number of Resistance groups. By this time, Camus had come to be a prominent figure in Parisian intellectual circles. He had made friends with Jean-Paul Sartre and Simone de Beauvoir, as well as with his editor, Gaston Gallimard, and had also become involved with the world of theatre. On 21 August 1944, *Combat* celebrated the Liberation of France with a leading article, 'De la Résistance à la Révolution' ('From Resistance to Revolution'), written by Camus. It already contains the core of the paper's programme for the next few years which was to stand for political renewal and freedom of speech, while keeping its independence from any political party.[7] Nevertheless, *Combat* had to operate under various restrictions. Printing paper was scarce and censorship continued, since the war in Europe had not yet ended. Moreover, *Combat* and the other newspapers that had been founded during the days of the Resistance had to compete with new titles, such as *Le Monde*, which published its first issue on 19 December 1944.[8]

From 1944 to 1947, Camus as *Combat*'s editor-in-chief played a major role in public debate in France. In the direct aftermath of World War II, the former Resistance divided into two groups which strongly disagreed about the country's political future, the communists and the adherents of General Charles de Gaulle. This controversy was deeply influenced by the dramatic events in Greece, where, after the defeat of the German army, a bloody battle was unleashed between the adherents of the former government, now returned from exile, and the former partisans who had fought the Germans.

Another matter of discontent involved the purges taking place across France in the aftermath of the war. Camus wrote a series of polemical articles against his fellow writer and journalist, François Mauriac. The latter, opposing the general climate of hatred and vengefulness, had pleaded for clemency to be shown to former collaborators. Camus, in turn, argued that justice, not Christian charity, should guide the French in dealing with the darker side of their recent history: 'Si nous consentons à nous passer de Dieu et de l'espérance, nous ne nous passons pas si aisément de l'homme. Sur ce point, je puis bien dire à M. Mauriac que nous ne nous découragerons pas et que nous refuserons jusqu'au dernier moment une charité divine qui frustrerait les hommes de leur justice' (*CC*, 442) ('If we agree to manage without God and hope, we can't so easily do without man. On this point, I say to Monsieur Mauriac that we will not be discouraged and that we will refuse right to the last a divine charity that would deprive mankind of its justice'). As in *La Peste* (1947) and *La Chute* (1956), Camus here shows himself to be a humanist at heart.

It was also due to this humanist stance that Camus definitively broke with Sartre and the *Les Temps modernes* group in 1951. To understand this controversy, one should be aware of the highly polarised atmosphere which dominated intellectual life in France during the post-war years. This situation was to last until the second half of the 1970s, when Marxism finally lost its attraction for the majority of the French intelligentsia. In *L'Homme révolté* (1951), Camus reproaches Marxism for sacrificing the defence of universal human values to historical relativism. He draws a clear distinction between the Marxist *prophecy*, that is, the generous and universal ambition to secure a certain quality of life for the destitute masses, and the revolutionary *practice* which resulted from it and which made everything dependent on, as Camus termed it, history and nothing else.

Camus's criticism of Marxism also implied a condemnation of Sartrian existentialism, which valued the idea of 'taking action', 'making political choices', at any cost, even if it later turned out that one had supported a political system that was most repressive (as was the case with Sartre and Simone de Beauvoir's support for the new China in the 1950s). It is, therefore, quite understandable that *Les Temps modernes*, with Sartre as its director, should publish an unfavourable review of Camus's *L'Homme révolté*. This led to a long-lasting polemic between Camus and Sartre's influential literary review, and resulted in the final break between the two leading intellectuals (see below chapter 9). Sartre became a fellow traveller (as sympathisers were called) of the French Communist Party, whereas Camus turned away from communism altogether after the existence of the Gulag – the concentration camps created under Stalin's regime – was made public in the West. As illustrated by the fictional works he wrote during these years, including the play *Les Justes* and his most famous novel *La Peste*, the concept of revolution and the bloodshed it implied, even if it was meant to create a better world, became intolerable to Camus. As a result of his humanist stance and firm anti-communism, he became a somewhat lonely figure on the French intellectual post-war scene, where communist sympathies held such sway.

By 1954 the Algerian War of Independence had become inevitable. In France, Sartre and a number of other influential intellectuals immediately gave their support to the Algerian nationalists, but Camus's position was more ambiguous. At this point, a noticeable difference also emerges between the articles he wrote for *L'Express* and other news media, on the one hand, and his fictional writings on the other. In his 1957 essay 'Réflexions sur la guillotine', Camus condemned the severe French repression of the FLN (Front de Libération Nationale), the Algerian resistance movement. But, in spite of his long-lasting criticism of French colonial rule in Algeria, Camus was also opposed to the idea of an independent, Arab nation. In fact, even when the hostilities among the three main parties involved – the Algerian nationalists from the FLN, the French army and the right-wing 'secret army' or OAS ('Organisation d'Armée Secrète'), which wanted to keep Algeria French – had reached a point of no return, Camus continued to foster the hope of a federal state reuniting France, Algeria and the two former French protectorates, Tunisia and Morocco.

From 1952 until his untimely death in a car crash in 1960, Camus's home-land served as the major locale in two of the fictional works he was working on, *L'Exil et le Royaume* and *Le Premier Homme*. A careful reading of these texts uncovers a more subtle approach to the Algerian tragedy and all it encompassed than that provided by Camus's journalistic texts, which were, of course, written on the spur of the moment.[9] In his last, unfinished novel as well as in two of the short stories collected in *L'Exil et le Royaume*, 'L'Hôte' and 'La Femme adultère', Camus elaborates on what he sees as the main problem of Algerian society: the impossibility of communication between the French and Arab populations, because they speak a different language and do not mix socially. ' "C'est toi le juge?" ' (*TRN*, 1618) (' "Are you the judge?" ') the Arab prisoner in 'L'Hôte' asks the French schoolteacher, who has been obliged by the French authorities to guard him for the night. These four words contain the nightmarish situation in which the Arab pris-oner finds himself caught, in his native land and yet in a social system that is utterly alien to him. As a writer, Camus reveals that he is aware of the anomaly of the system but – as the half-hearted attempt of the schoolteacher to save the prisoner at the end of the novel shows – he is unable to solve the problem. Therefore, one does more justice to Camus as a colonial writer by stressing his fundamental pessimism about the final outcome of the Algerian tragedy, in which the underprivileged Europeans of Algeria would be among the principal victims. In Camus's view, their fate was universal in the sense that they resembled all the other ethnic groups who, as a consequence of war and political conflicts, had been deprived of their native soil.

This is also the main theme of *Le Premier Homme*. In this novel, as we have seen, Camus tried to reconstruct the unknown history of his own forebears, the poor settlers from France, who, from their arrival in the colony during the nineteenth century, toiled and suffered, from one generation to the next, on what is presented as an inhospitable African soil. But in spite of the fact that they shared this life of hardship and poverty with the large majority of the Arab population, Camus also shows the deep rift that existed between the two races. The wary stand-off between them, as Christiane Chaulet-Achour has so rightly argued, could switch all of a sudden to bloody conflict.[10]

It is an irony that in 1957, as Camus was achieving worldwide recogni-tion as the winner of the Nobel Prize for literature, he was becoming increas-ingly isolated from his fellow writers in France. Neither his anti-communism nor his refusal to back the cause of Algerian nationalism had made him popular with those who set the tone in Parisian intellectual circles at that time. His famous but awkward remark made to an Algerian interlocutor in Stockholm – 'Je crois à la justice, mais je défendrai ma mère avant la jus-tice' (*Ess*, 1882) ('I believe in justice, but will defend my mother before justice') – dealt a final blow to his already damaged reputation as a progressive intellectual. What Camus had really meant to say was that, for him, there existed no excuse for acts of terrorism on any side. In an article published in *L'Express* on 23 July 1955, he had given a very perceptive analysis of the spiral of violence as it had developed and grown under French colonial rule in Algeria:

> L'oppression, même bienveillante, le mensonge d'une occupation qui parlait toujours d'assimilation sans jamais rien faire pour elle, ont suscité d'abord des mouvements nationalistes, pauvres en doctrine, mais riches en audace. Ces mouvements ont été réprimés.
>
> Chaque répression, mesurée ou démente, chaque torture policière comme chaque jugement légal, ont accentué le désespoir et la violence chez les militants frappés. Pour finir, les policiers ont couvé les terroristes qui ont enfanté eux-mêmes une police multipliée. (*Ess*, 1868)

> (Oppression, even if benevolent, and the lie of an occupation that always talked about assimilation without ever doing anything to bring it about, have given rise to various nationalist movements, which were ideologically weak but certainly audacious. These movements have been repressed.
>
> Every instance of repression, whether measured or demented, every act of police torture, every legal judgement has increased the despair and the violence of the militants affected by them. In the end, the police have bred terrorists, who have in turn multiplied the number of police.)

But the time for peace negotiations of the kind Camus had wanted had long passed. Algeria was to obtain its independence in 1962, after a long and bloody battle, and about a million French were to leave the country immediately afterwards.

In the novel *La Chute* (1956), one can sense the feeling of isolation and loneliness that Camus as an intellectual experienced during the last years of his life. Clamence, the protagonist, is not to be identified with his creator, Albert Camus, of course, yet some of the reflections on his personal life seem close to Camus's own: 'Ah! mon ami, savez-vous ce qu'est la créature solitaire, errant dans les grandes villes? . . .' (*TRN*, 1536) ('Oh, my friend, do you know what it means to be a solitary figure, wandering around in our big cities? . . .'), asks the narrator, without even expecting an answer from his silent interlocutor. And he concludes his soliloquy with the observation that it is neither possible to ignore one's very existence nor to escape from it: 'Que faire pour être un autre? Impossible' (*TRN*, 1550) ('What does one do to be another? Impossible').

In 1954 Camus received an invitation to give a lecture in Holland and on this occasion he also visited Amsterdam, which he would choose as the grey and drizzly setting for Clamence's confession in *La Chute*. In his lecture, Camus spoke on the subject of 'The Artist and his Time', the text of which has only recently been rediscovered. Although written in French, the lecture was aimed at a non-French, non-Parisian audience. It was an opportunity for Camus, no doubt, to speak more freely about his own situation as an engaged intellectual. The writer should share the fate of his fellow men, he said, but should refrain from foretelling the future, sticking instead to that part of history he knows from personal experience; he must not be afraid to position himself in the midst of the public debate: 'The only peace that is attainable for an artist is the peace that resides in the heat of the battle. "Each wall is a door", as Emerson put it so rightly. Let us not seek a door or an exit, except in the wall that surrounds us.'[11]

In the decade that followed his death, Camus's intellectual heritage was considered out of date. The 1960s saw the spectacular rise of the social sciences in France. Leading intellectuals were no longer writers or philosophers like Camus or Sartre; they were to be found among anthropologists, psychoanalysts and social scientists. It was only after Marxism had definitively ceased to be a main point of reference within intellectual circles in France that a younger generation of French intellectuals, generally known as 'les Nouveaux Philosophes' (the 'New Philosophers'), turned to universalism again and started rereading Camus.

Bernard-Henri Lévy gave Camus a special place in his essay on French intellectual history, *Les Aventures de la liberté* (*The Adventures of Freedom*) (1991). Lévy not only praises Camus for his humanist stance, but also considers him to be one of the first opponents of colonial rule in France. Around the same time, Edward Said, writing in *Culture and Imperialism* (1993), defended an attitude that was radically opposed to that of Lévy. Said characterised Camus as one of the last colonial writers whose writings consolidate an imperialist vision of the relationship between the Orient and the Occident. However, given the fact that France has only just begun to come to terms with its colonial heritage, in particular with the traumatic years of the Algerian War of Independence, we are only beginning to gauge the full significance of French colonial rule and its legacy.

NOTES

1. Olivier Todd, *Albert Camus, A Life*, trans. Benjamin Ivry (New York, Carroll & Graf, 2000), p. 4.
2. Maïssa Bey, 'Femmes au bord de la vie', *Albert Camus et les écritures algériennes. Quelles traces?* (Aix-en-Provence, Edisud, 2004), pp. 127–33.
3. Emile Temime, *Un rêve méditerranéen* (Arles, Actes Sud, 2002), p. 140.

4. Jean-Pierre Biondi, *Les Anticolonialistes (1881–1962)* (Paris, Laffont, 1992), p. 216.
5. *Ibid.*, p. 228.
6. Todd, *Albert Camus, A Life*, pp. 90–4.
7. See Jacqueline Lévi-Valensi's comments in *Camus à 'Combat'*, ed. J. Lévi-Valensi (Paris, Gallimard, 2002), pp. 42–5.
8. *Ibid.*, pp. 59–60.
9. See Ieme van der Poel, 'Albert Camus, ou la critique postcoloniale face au "rêve méditerranéen" ', *Francophone Postcolonial Studies* 2.1 (Spring/Summer 2004), 70–9.
10. Christiane Chaulet-Achour, *Albert Camus et l'Algérie* (Algiers, Barzakh, 2004), p. 98.
11. Albert Camus, 'De kunstenaar en zijn tijd', trans. Liesbeth van Nes, *Raster* 108 (2004), 154–70 (169).

2

TOBY GARFITT

Situating Camus: the formative influences

When speaking of formative influences on Camus, it would be a mistake to concentrate exclusively on the 'great' names: Nietzsche, Dostoyevsky, Gide, and so on. Like any French boy with a passion for reading, the young Albert Camus lived largely on a diet of adventure stories, among which the historical series about the swashbuckling hero Pardaillan by Michel Zévaco took pride of place (Sartre acknowledges his own debt to this series in his autobiographical text, *Les Mots* (*Words*)). Well before he was a confident reader himself, he was moved by Roland Dorgelès's First World War novel of the trenches *Les Croix de bois* (*The Wooden Crosses*), which his revered primary teacher Louis Germain used to read to the pupils at the end of term and on other special occasions: it introduced him to a different form of heroism from that of Pardaillan, and provided an essential link with his own father, who had died before Albert was two, from wounds received at the Battle of the Marne.

At the Grand Lycée in Algiers, where Camus discovered a totally different world from that of the rough working-class district of Belcourt where he grew up, the author who appealed most to him was probably Molière. The implications of that are still to be explored, both for his dramatic practice and for his often unrecognised humour. By the age of sixteen, in the *classe de première*, he was beginning to explore outside the school syllabus, and that was the year his uncle Gustave Acault lent him André Gide's *Les Nourritures terrestres* (*Fruits of the Earth*). Gide's lyrical celebration of heady, sensual pleasure did not immediately speak to him. 'A Alger, à seize ans, j'étais saturé de ces richesses; j'en souhaitais d'autres, sans doute' (*Ess*, 1117) ('In Algiers, at sixteen, I was saturated with these riches; no doubt I was looking for something else'). It was in the following year, 1930–1, that Camus encountered the man who was to unlock the world of books and ideas for him. That man was Jean Grenier, who at the age of thirty-two arrived back in Algiers (where he had already taught for a year in 1923–4) to teach philosophy at the Lycée. But Grenier was not only a teacher of philosophy and a practising philosopher himself: he had recently begun to publish essays in the *Nouvelle Revue française* (*NRF*), and he had even worked for a while for the publishers Editions de la *NRF* (Gallimard), so that he brought with him all the prestige of the Parisian literary world. His aim was less to teach the official syllabus than to open his pupils' minds to culture in a broad sense. He had also recently visited Spain, and his enthusiasm for the culture of that country (evident in his essays of the next few years) may well have encouraged Camus to explore his own Spanish heritage: the figure of Don Juan, discussed in one of Grenier's essays, was to be of particular importance to Camus, who devoted a chapter to 'Le Don Juanisme' in *Le Mythe de Sisyphe*.

Grenier was generous about lending books, and the first that he passed on to Camus in the autumn of 1931 (on restarting the *classe de philosophie* after a year of illness) was a slim novel by an obscure writer whom Grenier had met only just before coming to Algiers, André de Richaud. *La Douleur* (*Grief*) was a revelation to Camus. This book was

> le premier à me parler de ce que je connaissais: une mère, la pauvreté, de beaux soirs dans le ciel . . . Je venais d'apprendre que les livres ne versaient pas seulement l'oubli et la distraction. Mes silences têtus, ces souffrances vagues et souveraines, le monde singulier qui m'entourait, la noblesse des miens, leur misère, mes secrets enfin, tout cela pouvait donc se dire!   (*Ess*, 1117–18)

> (the first to speak to me of what I knew: a mother, poverty, beautiful evening skies . . . I discovered that books offered more than just escapism. My moody silences, those unclear but imperious sufferings, the strange world around me, the nobility of my family, their poverty, my own secrets, all of that could be acknowledged and expressed!)

He found something similar in Louis Guilloux's account of his father's syndicalist (trades union) past in *La Maison du peuple* (*The House of the People*) (Guilloux was a friend of Grenier's from his adolescence in Saint-Brieuc). These affirmations of the value of his personal identity set him free to explore in writing what he later called the 'part obscure' (*Ess*, 1925) ('the hidden side'), a term which also covers his strongly physical appreciation of the natural environment, and defines his distinctive form of *algérianité*. Another writer that Grenier greatly admired and recommended to his pupil was Proust; and given his passion for sport, this period may well have found Camus reading *Les Olympiques* (*Olympics*), by Grenier's friend Henry de Montherlant, with the preface exalting sport as a means of escape from oppressive sociological definition.

During the year, of course, there were philosophical texts that the whole class had to read, some of them on the official syllabus, and others chosen by the teacher to complement their studies. Schopenhauer, Nietzsche and Bergson were three on whom Grenier particularly insisted, as well as the Greek thinkers that he knew so well, including both Plato and Plotinus (Camus's interest in the Greeks was to be further encouraged by René Poirier during his university studies). Schopenhauer had been at the source of Grenier's own vocation as a philosopher, while Nietzsche had been central to the analysis of modern nihilism that he had published in *Philosophies* in 1924. It was Nietzsche's *Birth of Tragedy* that he made his pupils read, with its reinterpretation of the Greek tradition and its message of heroic optimism in the face of despair: Grenier's portrayal of Suetonius's Caligula as 'un Nietzsche barbare' ('a barbarian Nietzsche')[1] was to make a profound impact on Camus. Already between March and June 1932 several essays that Camus had originally written for Grenier and other teachers in the *classe de philosophie* appeared in the local monthly review *Sud*, culminating in a longer piece on music (in relation to Schopenhauer and Nietzsche: the full title of Nietzsche's work is *The Birth of Tragedy from the Spirit of Music*) which Grenier had corrected with great care. If all his pupils benefited from this level of attention, they were indeed fortunate. One of them reminded Grenier many years later of 'vos admirables . . . corrigés de dissertation sur l'unité profonde du moi' ('your wonderful . . . comments on our essays on the deep unity of the self').[2] He was a harsh marker, in a good French tradition; but this rigorous training left Camus with a love for philosophical investigation and a desire to take it further.

By October 1932, when he did at last enter the *khâgne* (or *classe préparatoire* for the prestigious Parisian *grandes écoles*; this had been created two years before by Pierre Martino, Dean of the Faculty of Arts, but covered just one year rather than the normal two, with some pupils going on to do a second year of preparation at one of the big Paris lycées), Camus was beginning to write seriously, which consolidated the burgeoning friendship with Grenier. Although the class was small, numbering only a dozen, quite a few of the pupils found Grenier's classes incomprehensible. Their teacher was also fairly frequently absent through illness. Camus and two or three others, on the other hand, found him immensely stimulating. Germaine Blanchet (Mme Blasi) describes a typical lesson, which might have to do with ideas of freedom:

> Au début, c'était construit . . . Grenier est en train de faire son exposé, il écrit au tableau . . . et tout d'un coup, on ne sait pas d'où cela est parti, on s'envole . . . on plane, on plane . . . c'est une espèce de délire . . . c'était inspiré . . . De ce fait, il y avait des élèves qui ne pouvaient pas l'encaisser.

(To begin with, there was a clear structure . . . Grenier would be giving his lecture, writing on the blackboard . . . and suddenly, without warning, it just took off . . . we were soaring high . . . in a kind of delirium . . . it was inspired . . . So of course some of the pupils couldn't cope with it at all.)[3]

Grenier introduced his students to all sorts of heterodox material, not least the Eastern traditions of Hinduism, Buddhism and Taoism, Western mystics, and the radical Russian Jewish philosopher Chestov, whose existential irrationalism was inspired by the Old Testament prophets and by Dostoyevsky. Dostoyevsky was one of the more mainstream authors he recommended, along with Stendhal and Malraux, whose *La Condition humaine* (*The Human Condition*) came out in instalments in the *NRF* throughout the first half of 1933. Dostoyevsky was one of Grenier's heroes: when he and Louis Guilloux were starting out as writers in the early 1920s, Guilloux aimed to be the new Tolstoy, and Grenier the new Dostoyevsky. As with Schopenhauer, it was Dostoyevsky's exploration of evil that first spoke to Grenier, in relation to human freedom. He later noted that Dostoyevsky's analysis, in *Notes from the Underground*, of man's awareness of his total impotence within a blind, even absurd world, was very similar to that found in *L'Etranger*:[4] it may well have been his own teaching that got Camus thinking along those lines. It was certainly the personal rather than the historical implications of Dostoyevsky's thought that touched Camus initially, although he came to see him as an earlier and more reliable prophet of nihilism than Nietzsche. Dostoyevsky revealed the hidden depths of human nature, characterised by the tragic conflict between the desire for truth and the almost irresistible desire for unlimited freedom (represented by Ivan in *The Brothers Karamazov*), in relation to which Camus was to comment that Dostoyevsky's 'souffrance personnelle est d'y participer et de le refuser à la fois' (*TRN*, 1888) ('own personal suffering comes from sharing in it and at the same time refusing it'). Meursault will find that the compatibility of truth and personal freedom is problematic, and the extension of the debate in Camus's later works to include justice will keep it firmly in a Dostoyevskian perspective. He and Grenier often discussed Dostoyevsky in their correspondence; and in 1950, when Grenier was writing a series of articles on 'le mal' ('evil'), Camus approved enthusiastically, saying that it was 'le sujet contemporain et, d'une certaine manière, le seul' (*Corr*, 168) ('the subject of the day, and in a sense the only subject'), and immediately referring to *The Brothers Karamazov*. Meanwhile Paul Mathieu, who taught French literature in the *khâgne*, lost no opportunity to share his enthusiasm for Nietzsche with his pupils, alongside the more traditional Racine and Pascal (the second of whom both Camus and Grenier later held to be the greatest of the French stylists, together with Chateaubriand). Faced with these very diverse examples of heroism in literature and thought, Germaine Blanchet remembered that Grenier's main advice to Camus was 'qu'il fallait *dominer*' ('you must be *in control*').[5]

Camus was producing creative texts of his own now. It is indeed clear from his first surviving letter to Grenier, dated 20 May 1932 (*Corr*, 11),[6] that he looked for guidance and probably specific comments on his early literary efforts, and at a later stage Grenier would provide these in quite extensive detail on many of his most important manuscripts. Camus was naturally drawn to the kind of lyrical essays that Grenier was now publishing regularly. 'Les Iles Kerguelen' ('The Kerguelen Islands') had appeared in the *NRF* in May 1931, and in 1932 he was working on 'Les Iles Fortunées' ('The Fortunate Isles'). Although starting from Grenier's experience of a recent trip to Spain, with early evocations of Barcelona and Toledo, this essay focusses on the more general point that 'il existe quelques lieux, quelques moments privilégiés où la vue d'un pays agit sur nous, comme un grand musicien sur un instrument banal qu'il *révèle*, à proprement parler, à lui-même' ('there are certain places, certain privileged moments, in which the sight of a landscape acts on us like a great musician playing on a very ordinary instrument and truly *revealing* it to itself'). For Grenier, such moments of intense recognition, of consonance with self and the world, are also tragic reminders of the *solitude* and indeed *néant* (nothingness) of ordinary human existence. Grenier's writing achieves lyrical and emotional heights in this essay, while retaining a remarkable classical sobriety:

> Qu'on travaille à Paris, à Londres, passe encore. Mais partout où règnent perpétuellement le soleil et la mer, il faut se contenter de jouir, de souffrir et d'exprimer. A quoi bon remuer la boue de la planète quand on demeure au centre des choses? Et lorsque lentement sonnaient les coups de midi et que tonnait le canon du Fort Saint-Elme, un sentiment de plénitude, non pas un sentiment de bonheur, mais un sentiment de présence réelle et totale, comme si toutes les fissures de l'être étaient bouchées, s'emparait de moi et de tout ce qui était autour de moi. De tous côtés affluaient des torrents de lumière et de joie qui de vasque en vasque tombaient pour se figer dans un océan sans bords. En ce moment (le seul) je m'acceptais par la seule adhésion de mes pieds au sol, de mes yeux à la lumière. Et au même moment sur tous les rivages de la Méditerranée . . . des milliers d'hommes étaient comme moi, retenant leur souffle et disant: Oui. Et je pensais que si le monde sensible n'est qu'un tissu léger d'apparences, un voile de chimères changeantes que la nuit nous déchirons et que notre douleur essaie en vain de balayer, il est pourtant des hommes qui, les premiers à en souffrir, reforment ce voile, reconstruisent ces

apparences et font rebondir la vie universelle qui sans cet élan quotidien se tarirait quelque part comme une source perdue dans la campagne.[7]

(If you work in Paris or London, that is one thing. But wherever the sun and the sea reign perpetually, one must be content with enjoying life, with suffering and expressing. What is the use of stirring up the mud of the planet when one is at the centre of everything? And when the clock slowly struck midday and the cannon fired from the fort of Sant' Elmo, a sense of plenitude, not a sense of happiness, but of real, total presence, as if all the cracks were now filled, took hold of me and everything around me. From all sides came torrents of light and joy, cascading down and down and eventually coming to rest in a limitless ocean. In that moment (alone) I accepted myself by virtue of the simple contact between my feet and the ground, between my eyes and the light. And at the same moment on every shore of the Mediterranean . . . thousands of others like me were holding their breath and saying Yes! And I reflected that if the external world is only a frail tissue of appearances, a veil of changing chimeras that we tear aside at night and that our suffering attempts in vain to banish for good, there are yet those who, while being the first to suffer from it, reinstate the veil, rebuild the appearances, and set life going again – that universal life that would otherwise trickle away and dry up like a spring in the depths of the countryside.)

Passages like this were to have a major impact on the first readers of *Les Iles* (*Islands*), among them Camus. By November Grenier was working on a third essay, 'L'Ile de Pâques'. The story of the dying butcher, feeling increasingly vulnerable, isolated, and at the same time guilty, and of his young friend's well-meaning but clumsy attempts to comfort him, is a powerful and largely depressing parable of the human condition, and it lacks the compensating luminosity of Grenier's earlier essays. But it was deliberately conceived as a foil to the previous two 'islands'. Camus, for one, was to find 'L'Ile de Pâques' ('Easter Island') at least as suggestive as the others, and it contains the seeds of both *Caligula* (in the reference to the narrator reading Suetonius's life of Caligula to the butcher) and *La Chute* (in the episodes where the butcher behaves as a kind of *juge-pénitent*). The essays of *Noces*, with their double emphasis on the intense present-ness of the natural environment and the inescapability of death, are of course deeply indebted to those of *Les Iles*, and to others that Grenier published in the local press.[8]

For Grenier, the island is a place of inevitable confrontation with the self, in the absence of all other distractions, and is therefore in its essence metaphysical. One is confronted with the truest image of oneself, and it is that experience that can then release one's inner song. The experience of the island, then, as Deleuze was later to argue,[9] gives rise to both philosophy and artistic creation. Camus's initial response to *Les Iles* was written down for his own purposes as soon as he had finished the book, and communicated to Grenier only later, in a letter (*Corr*, 13–14). There is a genuine desire to understand, a sense of almost surprised recognition, and at the same time a fair amount of resistance to Grenier's line of thought, which is strongly influenced by Indian philosophy and is constantly pulling away from the human, relegating it to the periphery. Camus is struggling with Grenier's essentially metaphysical and potentially antisocial approach, and wanting to assert the possibility of a definitive commitment to the values of the here-and-now. *Noces* will be the fullest statement of that response. What Camus says about *Les Iles* in his 'Notes de lecture' is less combative, more appreciative (CAC2, 204). In a letter of 1938 he would bring together the combative and the appreciative sides, recognising that 'Ce que vous me dites me révolte toujours pendant quelques heures. Mais cela me force à réfléchir et à comprendre. Après, je ne sens plus que ma gratitude et mon amitié pour vous' (*Corr*, 28) ('What you say always revolts me for a few hours. But it makes me think, and understand. Afterwards, I feel nothing but gratitude, and my friendship for you'). Camus is drawn despite himself to the tragic recognition that true satisfaction is ultimately unattainable, and in the preface he wrote much later for a new edition of *Les Iles* in 1959 he gave Grenier the credit for initiating him and his hedonistic Algerian contemporaries into *désenchantement* (disenchantment with the here-and-now) and hence into an appreciation of the less materialistic values of culture. He was avidly reading Gide at the same time, but not for the sensual awakening experienced by so many Northern European readers, and which was simply part of his Algerian heritage: rather, he saw in Gide the model of the creative artist, and in his writing, 'l'évangile de dénuement dont j'avais besoin' (*Ess*, 1118) ('the gospel of asceticism that I needed'). Grenier thus acted as a catalyst for the lasting influence that Gide was to have on Camus.

In the summer of 1933 Grenier and his family moved up to the 'Parc d'Hydra', on the hills above Algiers, where Camus and his first wife Simone would also live for a short while after their marriage in 1934. It was not always easy for teachers and pupils to get to know each other socially, but Grenier's writing offered a discreet invitation to dialogue, and so provided an opening. The responses of Camus and others encouraged Grenier to take the initiative in establishing more of a social relationship, and the new, bigger house at Hydra made it possible for him to invite some of his pupils round on a Sunday. This soon became a regular feature, and was remembered with warmth and gratitude, for instance by Charles Dufourcq, later a distinguished historian of medieval Spain and North Africa.[10] Many others came, including Max-Pol Fouchet, the future editor of the poetry review *Fontaine*, André Belamich, who was to translate Lorca, the architect Jean de

Maisonseul, the sculptor Louis Bénisti, and several painters. Edmond Charlot, whom Grenier later helped to set up his own bookshop and publishing house, and who would be Camus's first publisher, joined them before long. It was to be Charlot who, with Camus, formed the nucleus of the revived Ecole d'Alger. The colonial tradition launched by Louis Bertrand (*Le Sang des races* (*The Blood of the Races*), 1899; *Nuits d'Alger* (*Algiers Nights*), 1930) was no longer dynamic, and the way was open for these two to gather round them not only the elite group whose collective intellectual adventure was later celebrated by Fouchet,[11] but other significant writers such as Emmanuel Roblès and the slightly older Gabriel Audisio. Ideas of all kinds were discussed on those Sundays at Hydra, and books recommended and lent: Proust, Chestov (the Russian Jewish philosopher) and many others.

Grenier was certainly someone whose advice was worth listening to. From 1934 onwards, his contributions to the *NRF* often addressed current political topics, if from an unconventional angle. Camus recognised that he had something important to say. 'Le monde d'aujourd'hui est un dialogue M(alraux) G(renier)' (*C II*, 214) ('The world of today is a dialogue between M(alraux) and G(renier)'): when Camus jotted down this observation in 1947, it was not new to him. Already in 1934, according to Olivier Todd,[12] he had identified two visions of the world, represented by Grenier and Malraux. He was well aware that the communists, with whom Malraux was closely associated, put man at the centre, while the Oriental philosophers saw 'the all' at the centre, with man round the edge. Despite the powerful lyrical expressions of humanism that can be found in *Les Iles*, particularly in the essay 'Les Iles fortunées', the attraction of the Indian metaphysical systems focussed on the Absolute is dominant in the volume, and Camus was not wrong to identify in Grenier's thought an implicit challenge to the philosophy of action represented by Malraux, most notably in *Les Conquérants* (*The Conquerors*) and *La Voie royale* (*The Royal Way*).

In the following year, 1935, Grenier published an article entitled 'Le cas Malraux' ('The case of Malraux'), in which he dealt not with *La Condition humaine* but with an article by Malraux that had appeared much earlier, 'D'une jeunesse européenne' ('On European youth') (1927).[13] In this article Malraux had already defined the dilemma in which Camus now found himself, in terms of what Nietzsche called European nihilism. For Malraux, this nihilism showed itself as an actual appetite for 'le néant' ('nothingness'), experienced as 'intensité' ('intensity') and indeed 'grandeur' ('greatness, grandeur'), for the conquest of which the countries of the Far East offered almost unlimited scope. It is hardly surprising that Camus was more receptive to this kind of Orientalism (explored also in *La Tentation de l'Occident* (*The Temptation of the Occident*), 1926) than to that offered by Grenier. In terms of his own writing, the Nietzschean adventurer-hero favoured by Malraux was to form the subject of a chapter in *Le Mythe de Sisyphe*, and also, in conjunction with the figure of Caligula (discussed by Grenier in class and in 'L'Ile de Pâques'), to give rise to the eponymous protagonist of Camus's first play, the first version of which displays stronger Nietzschean elements, most notably the fascination with extreme self-assertion, than the subsequent rewritings. In terms of political commitment, Camus was under pressure in 1934 to join the Communist Party, but he wanted to keep his eyes open and avoid being 'aveuglé par de courtes certitudes' (*Ess*, 1159) ('blinded by short-term convictions'); in the course of the next year, Grenier was to encourage his pupil to follow his natural inclinations and join the Party. In October 1935, Grenier's article 'La Porte fermée' in the *NRF* argued for the freedom to choose according to one's own 'profonde exigence' ('deep imperatives'), and while for himself that meant a philosophical and indeed metaphysical imperative, he recognised that in the case of Camus there were different imperatives. Grenier's advice will have been based on Camus's own deep needs at the time and the appropriateness of expressing them in terms of the current social and political climate, rather than on any belief that communism (or any other 'ism' for that matter) was the only legitimate creed. Like the rest of humanity, Camus needed 'un élan vers quelque chose qui la dépasse' ('an aspiration towards something that transcends the human'), as Grenier said in his lecture to the Algiers branch of the 'Amis d'*Esprit*' (a nationwide 'third-way' movement founded by the left-wing Catholic intellectual Emmanuel Mounier), which Camus may indeed have attended.[14] Both workers and intellectuals needed to work for justice, but Grenier interpreted that in terms of human dignity in a broad sense rather than in terms of a specific political programme.

Grenier and Malraux enjoyed a long and good friendship, but their differences of approach and emphasis were marked. These stem essentially from their analyses of modern nihilism, and the conclusions they draw. Grenier had got in on the act earlier than Malraux, with his two-part article in *Philosophies* in 1924 entitled 'Le Nihilisme européen et les appels de l'Orient' ('European Nihilism and the Call of the East'). This article, published under the pseudonym 'Jean Caves', already contains a number of themes that will run through Grenier's subsequent work. There is an acute awareness of the climate of nihilism in both Europe and Russia, stemming from an analysis of European civilisation that owed much to Nietzsche and Spengler on the one hand and a pessimism derived from Schopenhauer on the other.[15] If Grenier's preferred solution is to heed what he calls 'les appels de l'Orient' ('the call(s) of the East'), he does not recommend an uncritical Orientalism (such as that of the Theosophists, who tried to combine Western spiritualism with Hinduism, or the devotees of Gandhi's creed of non-violent resistance to imperialism). His analysis of the heritage of nihilism, and his disquiet at the cult of action, were to be confirmed by the political events of the 1930s: the rise of the fascist threat across Europe, the attempted right-wing *coup d'état* of 6 February 1934 in Paris, the disputes over the French Popular Front coalition of 1936–8 and the prospect of renewed world conflict.

In April 1936 Grenier published an important article in the *NRF*, 'L'Age des orthodoxies'. The problem with modern Western society, Grenier argues, is that there has been a loss of faith in principles, while the necessity of action has become imperious. Action, once performed, is then used to furnish principles for thought. He gives credit to Malraux for exploring this paradox so effectively in *L'Espoir* (*Hope*), as is clear from his open letter to Malraux dated 30 January 1938 and included in his *Essai sur l'esprit de l'orthodoxie*. Both of them recognise that there is an unbridgeable gap between thought and action. The choice of particular forms of action is just that, a choice, and not an 'évidence' ('an obvious, logical conclusion'), and it will inevitably involve a 'déchirement' ('agonising decision'). That of course is precisely the dilemma that Camus will explore in *Les Justes* and *L'Homme révolté*, and in very much the same terms that Grenier uses here:

> Vaut-il mieux être un enfant ou un bourreau? Voilà ce que peut se demander un révolutionnaire . . . Mais voici un cas particulier, celui des gens qui attachent tant d'importance à des choses (qu'il faut bien se résigner à appeler des vieux noms de Justice et de Vérité) qu'ils ont toutes sortes de scrupules (même quand ils sont lancés en pleine action) à faire quelque chose qui aille contre ces abstractions . . . tel un de nos aviateurs qui trouve par moments son métier degoûtant et se sent à la fois justicier et assassin.[16]

> (Is it better to be a child or an executioner? That is a question that a revolutionary may well ask . . . But here is a particular case, that of people who attach such importance to certain things (that one must resign oneself to calling by the old names of Justice and Truth) that they have all sorts of scruples (even when in the thick of action) about doing anything that goes against those abstract ideas . . . such as one of our airmen who at times finds his job revolting and feels himself to be a righter of wrongs and a murderer rolled into one.)

Grenier offered no practical solutions. In the face of the Absolute, that which is relative is indeed 'mensonger' ('deceitful, a lie'). But such a conclusion is untenable, because inhuman. Nevertheless, Camus was deeply sympathetic to Grenier's desire to find an alternative to Prometheus, and his own choice of Sisyphus may have been partly inspired by a historical reflection in 'Le cas Malraux', where Grenier had written: 'Notre époque de progrès matériel indéfini a aboli le rocher de Sisyphe: l'œuvre d'une génération s'ajoute à l'autre: mais elle a instauré la pensée de Sisyphe depuis la ruine de la méthode d'autorité par Descartes.' ('Our age of unlimited material progress has done away with the rock of Sisyphus: the work of the next generation carries on where the previous one left off: but in the realm of thought, Sisyphean thinking has dominated since the destruction of the old system of authority by Descartes.')[17] Camus's instinctive reaction to Grenier's *Essai sur l'esprit d'orthodoxie* will again have been negative, but he was generous enough to recognise the validity of its arguments. He pinpoints Grenier's main contention in a footnote in *L'Homme révolté* as being the need to preserve 'la liberté de l'intelligence' in the face of 'le principe d'autorité' which seeks to reduce it to conformity (*Ess*, 626). That is a message that is always relevant, and so Camus can hail the *Essai* as still being pertinent fifteen years later, even though Grenier had made it quite clear in the preface that the individual essays that constituted it 'n'ont pas eu pour objet l'actualité . . . puisqu'ils ont été écrits contre elle' ('they were not about current affairs, indeed they were written in conscious reaction against current trends').[18] For his part, Grenier indicated later that what Camus had appreciated in the *Essai* was simply 'l'amour de la vérité' ('the love of truth'):[19] truth, as a bulwark against all kinds of 'mensonge' ('lies'), was very important to both of them.

In a letter to Camus in 1945, in the context of Camus's forthcoming 'Remarque sur la révolte' ('A Comment on Revolt') (which Grenier had commissioned for a volume he was editing), Grenier warns him against the dangers of following Malraux and undoing the positive achievements of the Nietzschean revolt against values:[20] 'Pourtant les valeurs sont des choses qui enchaînent l'homme; et à chaque fois qu'il en crée il se forge de nouveaux liens' (*Corr*, 111) ('But values are things that put men in chains; and each time they create values, they are forging new shackles for themselves'). Grenier nevertheless considered Malraux to be 'le meilleur reflet de ce qui a fait la grandeur et la misère de l'époque' ('the best reflection of what has gone to make the greatness and the wretchedness of our age').[21] To that extent Camus was right to take Malraux as the representative of one major current in the modern world, although by 1947, with his Resistance episode behind him, Malraux had chosen a different (Gaullist) kind of *engagement*. Grenier, on the other hand, represented for Camus the uncompromising intellectual, upholding an ideal that his pupil would always aspire to. Camus's division of the world into a Malraux-camp and a Grenier-camp was of course artificial. The post-war world was indeed becoming polarised, but Malraux was no longer the left-wing activist of the Spanish Civil War, and Grenier was certainly no Americanised liberal intellectual. The two of them represented two very different yet also uncannily similar ideals that Camus admired but never felt himself able to emulate; pivotal figures, on the borderline between the human and the supra-human, the 'plein' ('fullness', 'plenitude') and the 'vide' ('emptiness', 'the void'). It may have been the half-realisation of their underlying similarity that influenced the choice of the name Victor Malan for the character in *Le Premier Homme* who is explicitly identified with 'J.G.' (Grenier) in the manuscript (*PH*, 33): Victor = 'conquérant' (cf. Malraux's novel *Les Conquérants*), Malan = Malraux?

The period 1931–4 was crucial for Camus's intellectual development, and it is clear that many of the elements that he absorbed in those three years were introduced to him, and mediated, by Grenier. Their conversations continued, in person and by letter, for the rest of Camus's life. There were brief interruptions (and a certain cooling between 1935 and 1938 during Camus's communist phase), which had a positive value in helping Camus to establish his intellectual independence: he and Grenier would now be equal partners in a relationship that continued to be fruitful for both of them. Camus, for his part, was now equipped with his major literary and philosophical interlocutors, of whom Dostoyevsky and Nietzsche were probably the most important, with Grenier himself, Malraux and Gide coming close behind. Others, such as the idealist Jewish/Christian thinker Simone Weil, would appear later (although Grenier had already introduced Camus to the work of Rachel Bespaloff, which has much in common with that of Weil). Camus's collaboration with Edmond Charlot kept him anchored in the Ecole d'Alger; and the continuing importance of the 'part obscure' (*Ess*, 1925) ('dark side'), which is considered in chapter 3, should not be overlooked.

NOTES

1. See Jean Grenier, *Albert Camus. Souvenirs* (Paris, Gallimard, 1968), p. 59.
2. Unpublished letter from Jean Granarolo to Jean Grenier, 24 November 1967.
3. Conversation with Mme Blasi.
4. See Jean Grenier, *L'Existence malheureuse* (Paris, Gallimard, 1957), p. 176.
5. Conversation with Mme Blasi.
6. Internal evidence, however, suggests that this may be a misreading for 20 September – 5 and 9 can look very similar – and therefore the second letter, dated 25 August, in fact comes first.
7. Jean Grenier, *Les Iles* (Paris, Gallimard, 1959 (original edition 1933)), pp. 89–90.
8. Some of these were collected in *Santa-Cruz* (Algiers, Charlot, 1937) and then in *Inspirations méditerranéennes* (Paris, Gallimard, 1941), others were never reprinted.
9. See Gilles Deleuze, 'L'Ile déserte' (1953), in *L'Ile déserte et autres textes*, ed. David Lapoujade (Paris, Minuit, 2002).
10. Unpublished letter from Charles Dufourcq to Grenier, 11 February 1964.
11. Max-Pol Fouchet, 'Mémoire parlée', *Magazine littéraire* 8 (June 1967), 6, quoted by Jacqueline Lévi-Valensi, *Albert Camus ou la naissance d'un romancier (1930–1942)* (Paris, Gallimard, 2006, édition établie par Agnès Spiquel), pp. 28–9.

12. Olivier Todd, *Albert Camus, une vie* (Paris, Gallimard, 1996), p. 69.
13. Jean Grenier, 'Le cas Malraux', *Les Cahiers du Plateau* 3 (1935), 45–7; André Malraux, 'D'une jeunesse européenne', in André Chamson, André Malraux, Jean Grenier, Henri Petit and Pierre-Jean Jouve, *Ecrits* (Paris, Grasset, 1927).
14. Reprinted in Jean Grenier, *Essai sur l'esprit d'orthodoxie* (Paris, Gallimard, 1967 (original edition 1938)).
15. Oswald Spengler had published the two volumes of his *Der Untergang des Abendlandes* (*The Decline of the West*) in German in 1917 and 1922: Grenier's analysis came well before the French translation of the book appeared in 1931. Schopenhauer's *Die Welt als Wille und Vorstellung* (*The World as Will and Representation*) was published in 1818.
16. Grenier, *Essai*, p. 172.
17. Grenier, 'Le cas Malraux', p. 45.
18. Grenier, *Essai*, p. 11.
19. Grenier, *Albert Camus*, p. 30.
20. See Nietzsche, *Also sprach Zarathustra* (*Thus Spake Zarathustra*), 1883–5; *Jenseits von Gut und Böse* (*Beyond Good and Evil*), 1886.
21. Jean Grenier, *Sous l'occupation* (Paris, Claire Paulhan, 1997), p. 223.

3

EDWARD J. HUGHES

Autobiographical soundings in *L'Envers et l'Endroit*

Le même vertige qui avait saisi l'enfant que j'étais a obscurci mes
yeux d'homme.
(*TRN*, 1423–4)

[I] felt the same horror sweep over me now I was a man as I had
previously felt as a child.[1]
(*P*, 193)

The collection of five brief essays that go to make up *L'Envers et l'Endroit* were first published by Charlot in Algiers in 1937 in a limited print run of 350 copies. Written by Camus in his early twenties, the essays, which he dedicated to his mentor Jean Grenier, include a sometimes raw account of family life for a child growing up in real poverty in working-class colonial Algiers. In his preface to the second edition published two decades later, Camus accounts for his reluctance over many years to authorise a new edition.[2] While insisting that he denies nothing of the portrait of life contained in the collection, he expresses doubts about the writing, which he sees as being maladroit and in places unnecessarily high-flown. Yet in spite of their aesthetic limitations, these early essays stand, he argues with hindsight, as potent testimony to a childhood that involved not only prolonged poverty but also what he claims to have been genuine happiness. In a letter to the poet René Char in October 1953, he writes of a legacy that he cannot ignore: 'Oui, renoncer à l'enfance est impossible. Et pourtant, il faut s'en séparer un jour, extérieurement au moins . . . j'ai grandi dans les rues poussiéreuses, sur les plages sales. Nous nagions et, un peu plus loin, c'était la mer pure. La vie était dure chez moi, et j'étais profondément heureux, la plupart du temps' (*Ess*, 1180) ('Yes, renouncing childhood is impossible. And yet one has to separate oneself from it, at least externally . . . I grew up in dusty streets, on dirty beaches. We used to swim and, a bit further out, the sea was so pure. Life at home was hard, and I was deeply happy, most of the time.')

The autobiographical evidence that we glean from *L'Envers et l'Endroit* does not necessarily square with the largely positive balance-sheet which the letter to Char conveys. Moreover, *Noces*, Camus's other collection of early essays much more widely available in his day than *L'Envers et l'Endroit*, preached an exuberant celebration of life that masked the darker side explored in the latter collection.[3] The young Camus and his family had much to contend with. His illiterate, partially deaf and mute mother was an impoverished war widow who worked as a cleaner. But she was much more than a victim of economic hardship. Along with her two children and a brother, she was forced to live with her mother, a feared authority figure who is evoked graphically both in *L'Envers et l'Endroit* and in Camus's last work, the unfinished *Le Premier Homme*, where the autobiographical is again readily detectable.

Camus's account of this strained cohabitation features in the first essay of the collection, 'L'Ironie' ('Irony'). The piece sketches three brief scenarios involving older figures: the first focusses on the isolated, illiterate old woman for whom the younger generation have no time; in the second, an elderly man narrates adventures of his life to three young men who remain unimpressed: 'un vieil homme qui va mourir est inutile, même gênant et insidieux' (*Ess*, 18) ('an old man who is going to die is useless, he is even an insidious embarrassment') (*BB*, 18);[4] the third scenario reconstructs the domestic setting experienced by the young Camus, still at school, his brother who works in an insurance office, his mother and uncle, and the feared maternal grandmother. In her bullying manner, the matriarchal figure narcissistically challenges the schoolboy to declare which of the two women in the household he prefers. Obliged to choose her, the boy can only feel 'un grand élan d'amour pour cette mère qui se taisait toujours' (*Ess*, 20–1) ('a great upsurge of love for his ever silent mother' (*BB*, 21)). When the grandmother develops a liver infection, she shows no desire to be discreet in a way that might protect the children, preferring instead to vomit noisily into the rubbish container in the kitchen before resuming the work that she deems, boastfully, to be crucial to the family's survival. Camus concludes the essay with a brief coda where, with the ironic detachment announced by the essay title, the lives and deaths of the three elderly figures are drawn together as three case-studies, 'trois destins semblables et pourtant différents' (*Ess*, 22) ('three destinies which are different and yet alike' (*BB*, 22)). Irony is also at work in the way in which the two boys view the grandmother's sickness. Well used to her theatrical displays of self-worth (her showy industriousness and her self-righteousness), they cannot conceive that what turns out to be her terminal illness is anything other than yet one more sadistic performance in a life of psychological manipulation, or in Camus's damning formulation: 'la dernière et la plus monstrueuse des simulations de cette femme' (*Ess*, 22) ('the last and most monstrous of this woman's performances' (*BB*, 22)).

Significantly, when the awareness of her death dawns on the younger grandson, he experiences no real loss and his show of grieving at the graveside is merely prompted by the outbursts of those around him.

The raw emotions which Camus's protagonist evokes in respect of the grandmother are counterpointed in the second essay in the collection, 'Entre oui et non' ('Between Yes and No') where the unassuming figure of the mother – again reflecting faithfully Camus's autobiographical experience – takes centre stage. The essay is structured around a disturbance of memory, working between a present moment in the narrator's early adulthood as he sits in a Moorish cafe on the edge of the Arab part of the city and recollection of childhood memories of life with his mother: 'Je pense à un enfant qui vécut dans un quartier pauvre. Ce quartier, cette maison! Il n'y avait qu'un étage et les escaliers n'étaient pas éclairés' (*Ess*, 24) ('I think of a child living in a poor district. That district, that house! There were only two floors, and the staircases were unlit' (*BB*, 24)). Registering the 'voix du quartier pauvre' ('voices of the poor district') was Camus's goal and indeed he had already used this formulation as the title for an early version of the material that was to feed into *L'Envers et l'Endroit*.[5]

Camus juxtaposes what negates life and what redeems it in his evocation of Belcourt, the district in Algiers where he grew up. As working-class families sit on the street outside their homes for recreation on summer evenings, the boy protagonist drinks in the beauty of the pure night sky, a beauty which assumes its full appeal, Camus argues, in the eyes of those not distracted by material comfort. Yet the signs of squalor are unavoidable: 'Il y avait derrière l'enfant un couloir puant et sa petite chaise, crevée, s'enfonçait un peu sous lui' (*Ess*, 24–5) ('Behind the child lay a stinking corridor and his little chair, splitting across the bottom, sank slightly beneath his weight' (*BB*, 24)). The uninviting interior provides the setting for an arresting portrait of the mother, a description which, notwithstanding the use of the third person to denote both mother and son, draws on autobiographical experience. Herself the daughter of a dominating mother, she had briefly experienced liberation through marriage. But once a war widow, she is forced by economic circumstances to return to the maternal home, earning a wage which she hands over to the matriarch. The taciturn mother's self-effacing role allows the grandmother to assume responsibility for the boys' education, which she oversees in a way that is punitive in both physical and psychological terms. The self-effacement brings its own complications for the children. Thus, on those occasions when the younger boy returns home to find only his mother there, he is drawn up short by this image of a vulnerable, pathetic and yet also forbidding figure:

Autour d'elle, la nuit s'épaissit dans laquelle ce mutisme est d'une irrémédiable désolation. Si l'enfant entre à ce moment, il distingue la maigre silhouette aux épaules osseuses et s'arrête: il a peur. Il commence à sentir beaucoup de choses. A peine s'est-il aperçu de sa propre existence. Mais il a mal à pleurer devant ce silence animal. Il a pitié de sa mère, est-ce l'aimer? Elle ne l'a jamais caressé puisqu'elle ne saurait pas. Il reste alors de longues minutes à la regarder. A se sentir étranger, il prend conscience de sa peine. Elle ne l'entend pas, car elle est sourde. Tout à l'heure, la vieille rentrera, la vie renaîtra: la lumière ronde de la lampe à pétrole, la toile cirée, les cris, les gros mots. Mais maintenant, ce silence marque un temps d'arrêt, un instant démesuré . . . l'enfant croit sentir, dans l'élan qui l'habite, de l'amour pour sa mère. Et il le faut bien parce qu'après tout c'est sa mère. (*Ess*, 25–6)

Around her, night thickens and then her silence is a grief without repair. If the child comes in at this moment, he sees the thin shape with its bony shoulders and stops: he is afraid. He is beginning to feel a lot of things. He is scarcely aware of his own existence, but this animal silence makes him cry with pain. He feels sorry for his mother, but is this loving her? She has never hugged or kissed him for she wouldn't know how. Then he will stand a long time watching her. Because he feels that he is separate from her, he becomes conscious of her suffering. She can't hear him, for she is deaf. In a few moments, the old woman will come back, life will start up again: the round light cast by the paraffin lamp, the oil-cloth on the table, the shouts, the swear-words. But in the meantime this silence marks a pause, an immensely long moment . . . the child thinks that the upsurge of feeling in him is love for his mother. And this must be so, because after all she is his mother. (*BB*, 25–6)

I have quoted at length from this autobiographical account to give prominence to Camus's pained, deeply ambivalent portrait of the mother. Crucially, the narrator is hesitant about equating the son's pity with love. Indeed in the concluding lines of the quotation, the strained interaction between the pair excludes any possibility of affirmative, conventional role models (the nurturing mother, the loving son). The twenty-two-year-old Camus who authors this intimate portrait can draw only negative conclusions from the failing relationship: 'Sa mère toujours aura ces silences. Lui croîtra en douleur' (*Ess*, 26) ('His mother will always have these silences. He will grow in pain' (*BB*, 26)). The scene ends with the mother, startled by her son's returning home, sending him off to attend to his homework. With resigned detachment, the narrator concludes that graduating to adulthood in no way compensates for the profound lack (of emotional communication and sustenance) that marked his childhood. Duty and societal expectation thus become alienating; or as Camus puts it anecdotally, doing one's homework and later accepting adulthood lead only to old age and, by implication, to the alienating non-resolution of the emotional conflicts thrown up by childhood.

In Camus's fictional works, the mother figure constitutes a point of continuing fascination: in *L'Etranger*, her death and Meursault's socially eccentric response to it are fundamental to the ensuing drama of his incrimination; in the play *Le Malentendu*, the relationship between mother (and daughter) and son becomes a homicidal one; in *La Peste*, Dr Rieux's mother is portrayed as an idealised, nurturing figure who helps her son through the emotional and physical strains of the plague. (By contrast, his friend Tarrou, whose words are cited in the epigraph to this chapter, exemplifies the position of the adult child psychologically scarred by a parent figure, in his case the father who, as judge, has the power to condemn people to death.)[6] In *Le Premier Homme*, where the autobiographical seam resurfaces, the search for the figure of the father headlined in the title of Part I of the novel does not exclude an analogous search for the mother. Significantly, however, by the time of writing this last text, Camus's conception of the mother has mutated and she emerges as a suffering, Christ-like figure (*PH*, 283, 295; *FM*, 232, 239). But by choosing, in 'Entre oui et non', to italicise the line '*L'indifférence de cette mère étrange!*' (*Ess*, 26) ('*The indifference of this strange mother!*' (*BB*, 26)), Camus already casts the parent figure as a source of enduring preoccupation and enigma in his writing.

In the same essay, the emotional negativity clouding the portrait of the mother finds more direct expression in the narrator's account of the domestic drama he experiences as an adult living alone in the suburbs with a dog, two cats and their kittens. One by one, the kittens die, their mother unable to feed them. The climax comes when the narrator returns home to find the sole surviving kitten half-eaten by its mother. These images of failed nurture and parental violence from the animal world allow Camus to explore emotional intensity at one remove, importantly, from the set-up with the mother. The latter remains nevertheless a figure of unresolved contradiction. Much later, in an autobiographical reference in the appendices to *Le Premier Homme*, Camus alludes to the sequence of adult relationships panning out from the strained, intimate connection with the mother: 'Maman. La vérité est que, malgré tout mon amour, je n'avais pas pu vivre au niveau de cette patience aveugle, sans phrases, sans projets. Je n'avais pu vivre de sa vie ignorante. Et j'avais couru le monde, édifié, créé, brûlé les êtres. Mes jours avaient été remplis à déborder – mais rien ne m'avait rempli le cœur comme . . .' (*PH*, 304) ('*Maman*. The truth is that, in spite of all my love, I had not been able to live that life of blind patience, without words, without plans. I could not live her life of ignorance. And I had travelled far and wide, had built, had created, had loved people and abandoned them. My days had been full to overflowing – but nothing had filled my heart like . . .' (*FM*, 244).[7] The ellipsis delivers the emotionally complex tribute to the mother.

In his preface to the second edition of *L'Envers et l'Endroit* published in 1958, more than twenty years after the first, Camus expresses an artistic reticence about publicising the raw emotions contained in these essays. He writes of a personal recklessness that needs to be checked and goes on to vaunt the merits of an artistic re-channelling of powerful affect: 'Je connais mon désordre, la violence de certains instincts, l'abandon sans grâce où je peux me jeter. Pour être édifié, l'œuvre d'art doit se servir d'abord de ces forces obscures de l'âme. Mais non sans les canaliser, les entourer de digues . . . Mes digues, aujourd'hui encore, sont peut-être trop hautes' (*Ess*, 12) ('I know my disorder, the violence of certain instincts, the graceless abandon into which I can cast myself. To be constructed, the work of art must first of all use these dark forces of the soul. But not without canalising them, surrounding them with dikes . . . Perhaps my dikes are still too high today' (*BB*, 12)).

Camus's lines convey a very palpable sense of work in progress, as well as a nostalgic desire to retrieve affective experience sidelined in the quest for artistic containment. He expresses the urgent aspiration to establish the balance between 'ce que je suis et ce que je dis' (*Ess*, 12) ('what I am and what I say' (*BB*, 13), a balance that he dreams of securing in a promised future work that was in fact never to materialise – Camus died less than two years after the publication of the second edition of *L'Envers et l'Endroit*.

In the conclusion to his preface, Camus sets as a key, longer-term career goal the creation of a language and a set of myths that will enable him to rewrite *L'Envers et l'Endroit*. He proffers the deeply held, obscure conviction that, should he fail to do so, he will have failed more generally as a writer. Fundamental to this project is the figure of the mother. As he continues to negotiate with the ambivalence of emotions in play, he insists on the central place in his work of 'l'admirable silence d'une mère et l'effort d'un homme pour retrouver une justice ou un amour qui équilibre ce silence' (*Ess*, 13) ('the admirable silence of a mother and the effort of a man to rediscover a justice or a love which matches this silence' (*BB*, 13)). The silence, once so forbidding as we saw in 'Entre oui et non', has become an object of reverence for the mature, arguably more circumspect Camus. Even in that early essay, true to the movements of affirmation and negation signalled by its title, the young adult son and his mother go on to converse warmly about the father, whose death in the First World War is to play a prominent role in *Le Premier Homme*. Nevertheless, to a degree Camus erases fundamental psychological conflict through the construction of a tidy role-play, as the following sequence illustrates: 'C'est vrai, il ne lui a jamais parlé. Mais quel besoin, en vérité? A se taire, la situation s'éclaircit. Il est son fils, elle est sa mère' (*Ess*, 29) ('It's true, he has never talked very much to her. But did he ever really need to? When you keep quiet, the situation becomes clear. He is her son, she is his mother' (*BB*, 29)). The syntactic simplicity lays claim to familial normality through the tidy designation of roles, thereby masking the central problem of emotional absence.

In the concluding lines of the same essay, Camus appears to digress, protesting about society's manipulation of language. Singling out the case of the man condemned to death, Camus dismisses talk of the criminal paying his debt to society and turns attention instead to the reality of beheading that a community's justice delivers. The alarm that Camus voices anticipates Meursault's studious horror of the mechanics of the guillotine as voiced towards the end of *L'Etranger* (*TRN*, 1204; *O*, 107–8). By configuring the portrait of the mother and the reflection on capital punishment, 'Entre oui et non' activates two of the key stimuli that will energise Meursault in *L'Etranger*.

If a disturbance of memory is the trigger for recall of dysfunctional family life in 'Entre oui et non', dislocation of a different kind provides the narrative driver in the two travel essays in the collection, 'La Mort dans l'âme' ('Death in the Soul') and 'Amour de vivre' ('Love of Life'). Camus travelled to Czechoslovakia in the summer of 1936 and spent an unhappy few days alone in Prague. 'La Mort dans l'âme' foregrounds the protagonist's sense of cultural alienation when confronted with an everyday world that is unfamiliar (its language, food and people). (We might note in passing that the play *Le Malentendu* is also set in what is presented as a land-locked Central Europe, far from the Mediterranean.) The uprootedness triggers a deep sense of estrangement. Yet travel brings its own paradoxical reward in spite of the straitened circumstances in which the narrator makes his trip to Prague. As he writes in his hotel room: 'Et quel autre profit vouloir tirer du voyage? Me voici sans parure. Ville dont je ne sais pas lire les enseignes, caractères étranges où rien de familier ne s'accroche, sans amis à qui parler, sans divertissement enfin' (*Ess*, 33–4) ('And what other profit can we seek to draw from travel? Here I am stripped bare, in a town where the notices are written in strange, incomprehensible hieroglyphics, where I have no friends to talk to, in short where I have no distractions' (*BB*, 33–4)). This is the human person stripped of any familiar backdrop, the absent 'decor' anticipating the situation of Camus's hero Sisyphus, for whom the disjunction between self and an irrational universe, between the urge to live and the brute fact of human mortality is a cause of deep alienation. 'Comme une faim de l'âme' (*Ess*, 34) ('as if my soul were hungry' (*BB*, 34)) is how Camus's narrator expresses this sense of existential unease. The young protagonist's predicament intensifies when he learns that in a neighbouring room in the hotel, a male resident may have lain dead for some time. Camus thus uses melodrama to connect back to the 'death of the soul' of the essay title.

The subsequent journey from Prague to Italy provides the narrator with the opportunity to reconnect with life, as he initially presents it. Italy is hailed as a land after his own heart and the quality of its light, its people and varied foods provide all the supports necessary 'pour qui ne sait plus être seul' (*Ess*, 37) ('for the person who can no longer be alone' (*BB*, 37)). But ultimately Camus refuses to settle for any simple juxtaposition between the morbid atmosphere of the drab Prague hotel and the luminous skies, the youthful bodies and the lush flora of the Mediterranean. For the beauty of Italy brings him closer to his own mortality, to 'l'odeur de mort et d'inhumanité' (*Ess*, 39) ('this odour of death and inhumanity' (*BB*, 38)). Camus's young narrator anticipates the plight of the hero of *Le Mythe de Sisyphe* when he sees as fundamental 'la confrontation de mon désespoir profond et de l'indifférence secrète d'un des plus beaux paysages du monde' (*Ess*, 39) ('the confrontation between my deep despair and the secret indifference of one of the most beautiful landscapes in the world' (*BB*, 39)). This divorce between human mortality and the permanence and indifference of the natural world fuels the author's assertion of an absurd human condition.

Camus's mother's family came originally from Mahón on the Balearic island of Menorca and he was a lifelong Hispanophile. The essay 'Amour de vivre' was inspired by a trip to Palma de Mallorca in 1935 with his first wife, Simone Hié whom he had married the previous year (they were to separate in 1936, Camus marrying his second wife, Francine Faure, in 1940). Travel, Camus reflects, has existential consequences:

> Car ce qui fait le prix du voyage, c'est la peur. Il brise en nous une sorte de décor intérieur. Il n'est plus possible de tricher – de se masquer derrière des heures de bureau et de chantier (ces heures contre lesquelles nous protestons si fort et qui nous défendent si sûrement contre la souffrance d'être seul) . . . Le voyage nous ôte ce refuge. Loin des nôtres, de notre langue, arrachés à tous nos appuis, privés de nos masques . . . nous sommes tout entiers à la surface de nous-mêmes.
>
> (*Ess*, 42–3)

> For what gives value to travel is fear. It breaks down a kind of inner decor in us. We can't cheat any more – hide ourselves away behind the hours in the office or at the plant (these hours against which we protest so strongly and which protect us so surely against the suffering of being alone) . . . Travel takes this refuge from us. Far from our own people, our own language, wrenched away from all support, deprived of our masks . . . we are completely on the surface of ourselves.
>
> (*BB*, 41)

Thus, whether it be the spectacle of an obese young woman performing an erotic dance to a packed male audience in a Palma cafe or a trip to the city's deserted cloister of San Francisco where the narrator watches a woman drawing water at a well, Camus sees, in these ostensibly contrasting locations and experiences, human activity that is fundamentally impermanent and thus, for him, deeply miraculous.

In Camus's characteristically tidy formulation, the break from habit can awaken both a love for life and a despair with living. Non-routine can be perceptually enhancing. Yet Camus also writes of 'la part obscure', the darker side of life, and the choice of *L'Envers et l'Endroit* as a title for the essay collection connects with this. 'L'envers' denotes, among other things, the reverse side, the 'wrong side' of a cloth or fabric, the side we do not usually see or are not meant to see; 'l'endroit' of a garment would mean the right way round, the part to be shown. As an adolescent, Camus experienced serious illness, suffering from tuberculosis which was to recur in adult life. His family lived in considerable poverty (some see his almost dandy-like appearance as a young adult as a reaction against this). His writing offers evidence of psychological scars. Talk of life's precariousness, therefore, of its other, 'wrong' side, was certainly not some abstract notion. Hence the focus in *L'Envers et l'Endroit* on life's transience, its abortive relationships, its pathology, its penury.

Death forms a leitmotif in the collection, nowhere more eccentrically than in the final short piece which bears the overall title of the collection. Here the solitary old woman invests in a burial vault and has everything prepared to receive her body when the time comes, right down to the gilt letters indicating her name. The cemetery, situated on the edge of town, becomes her regular Sunday-afternoon destination. When she is close to death, her daughter is already dressing her in her burial clothes. The young male narrator, by contrast, watches the play of light in the weak January sun. Alert to the ephemeral nature of his perceptions, he advises his reader to seize the day, counselling that to waste one's time (and spurn the miracle of perception) is sinful (*Ess*, 48; *BB*, 46). Striving to retrieve these fleeting experiences, the narrator implicitly rejects religious notions of a redemptive after-life, arguing instead that 'tout mon royaume est de ce monde' (*Ess*, 49) ('my whole kingdom is of this world' (*BB*, 47)). Consciousness of a fleeting present is the great prize for the narrator then, even if the instant itself slips through one's fingers, in Camus's analogy, like drops of mercury. But between the image of the elderly woman prematurely occupying her final resting-place and the appetite for sentient living expressed by the young narrator, the latter does not want to choose: 'Le grand courage', he concludes, 'c'est encore de tenir les yeux ouverts sur la lumière comme sur la mort' (*Ess*, 49) ('Great courage still consists of gazing steadfastly at the light as on death' (*BB*, 47)).

Camus's early essays, then, composed when he was just into his twenties, contain important scenarios and tensions which anticipate his later work. The family nexus, which he represents autobiographically, generates unresolved, often violent conflicts which the later work will return to, either directly or obliquely: a physically absent father (a victim of the First World War); an emotionally absent mother; a grandparental hegemony that induces fear; and the frail child siblings who inherit these handicaps. Even the compensatory beauty of Mediterranean nature which, in the two travel narratives, provides release from an oppressive domestic environment cannot mask the human frailty of the enraptured young narrator who beholds it.

Camus deploys a form of rhetorical shorthand in these early pieces, writing of the inseparability of a love for life and the despair of living, the *amour de vivre* and *désespoir de vivre*. The reconciliation of these seemingly polar opposites is manifest in the overall title of the collection, where the fabric of life becomes reversed and unfamiliar. The technique of defamiliarisation was to become a hallmark of Camus's work, as the opening scenarios and paragraphs of *Le Mythe de Sisyphe*, *L'Etranger*, *La Peste* and *La Chute* all confirm.

Yet two decades on, he concedes in his preface to the second edition of *L'Envers et l'Endroit* that the essays sometimes display an immature, high-flown language. The line in which Camus twins the love of life and the despair with living is one that he specifically singles out for its youthful bombast (*Ess*, 11; *BB*, 11). Yet the self-criticism quickly subsides as he reflects that what was to follow in his life (long after the essays were published in 1937) did indeed bring him to despair: 'je n'avais pas encore traversé les temps du vrai désespoir. Ces temps sont venus et ils ont pu tout détruire en moi, sauf justement l'appétit désordonné de vivre' (*Ess*, 11) ('I had not yet known the years of real despair. These years have come, and have managed to destroy everything in me, except, in fact, this uncontrolled appetite for life' (*BB*, 11)). Camus is not specific about the causes of anguish but his very public row with Sartre in the early 1950s (see chapter 9) and the intellectual and emotional isolation as a high-profile French Algerian that went with it must surely have been part of that dejection. Certainly Camus's message of self-defence can be read as an oblique response to his detractors, who ironically typecast him as the figure of the just man. His tactic was, in part, to plead guilty. He argues that while never claiming to be 'just' himself, he had asserted that an individual should indeed strive to be just, however imperfectly. Yet in a disarming move, he asks: can the person unable to enshrine justice in his life preach justice to others? His final, self-protective manoeuvre in the preface is to step outside the ethical debate, to affirm that *L'Envers et l'Endroit* embodies his own tribe – 'les miens, mes maîtres, ma lignée' (*Ess*, 11) ('my people, my masters, my race' (*BB*, 12)) – and opens up a pathway that runs through everything he has written. If the connection with family ran deep in Camus, the raw exposure given to kith and kin in *L'Envers et l'Endroit* signals a complex and often reluctant autobiographer.

NOTES

1. These are the words of Tarrou in *The Plague*.
2. Roger Quilliot estimates that Camus had completed his preface to the second edition by 1954 (*Ess*, 1180).
3. See Peter Dunwoodie, *'L'Envers et l'Endroit' and 'L'Exil et le Royaume'* (London, Grant & Cutler, 1985), p. 9.
4. The translation of *L'Envers et l'Endroit*, *Betwixt and Between*, is contained in *Albert Camus: Lyrical and Critical*, trans. Philip Thody (London, Hamish Hamilton, 1967).
5. See Roger Quilliot's editorial note, *Ess*, 1175. For Camus's earlier treatment of this material in *Voix du quartier pauvre* (1934), see *Le Premier Camus*, suivi de *Ecrits de jeunesse d'Albert Camus* (Cahiers Albert Camus 2), ed. Paul Viallaneix (Paris, Gallimard, 1973); for the English translation, see *YW*, 242–59. Two fragments from *Voix du quartier pauvre* are also reproduced in *Ess*, 1209–13.
6. For Tarrou's pained account of parental influence, see the unnumbered chapter 6 of Part IV of *La Peste*. See also chapter 12 below.
7. On the question of Camus's multiple intimate relationships, see O. Todd, *Albert Camus, une vie* (Paris, Gallimard, 1996), p. 740.

PART II

Themes, preoccupations and genres

4

DAVID CARROLL

Rethinking the Absurd:
Le Mythe de Sisyphe

Pour toujours, je serai étranger à moi-même.
(*Le Mythe de Sisyphe*, *Ess*, 111)

For ever I shall be a stranger to myself.
(*MS*, 18)

After fifteen years I have progressed beyond several of the positions which are
set down here; but I have remained faithful, it seems to me, to the exigency
which promoted them. This book is in a certain sense the most personal of
those I have published in America.
(*MS*, vi)[1]

History and resistance

Le Mythe de Sisyphe may be the most historically dated of Albert Camus's
major texts, the work most clearly marked by the conditions under which
it was written and thus the one that might appear to have aged the least
well and have the least to say to modern-day readers. The essay was written
during what Camus in his 1955 preface to its American translation calls 'the
French and European disaster' (*MS*, v), and it is difficult not to relate its sense
of tragic hopelessness to France's ignominious defeat at the hands of Nazi
Germany, the Occupation and Vichy collaboration. The text that Camus
also calls 'the most personal of those (he has) published in America' (*MS*, vi)
could also be read as a reflection of his own struggle with tuberculosis during
this period, since he was so seriously ill he expressed doubts at times that
he would survive. But perhaps even more than these historical and personal
factors *Le Mythe* may be dated by the concept of the Absurd itself to which
Camus's name is still linked today, even though he admitted as early as 1955
that he had already 'progressed beyond' (*MS*, vi) its propositions. The post-
war generation in general quickly moved beyond the Absurd as well, which
is why its interest today could be considered largely historical.

But rather than reconsider what is dated in Camus's notion of the Absurd,
the present reading focuses on what Camus calls the 'exigency' underlying the
propositions he quickly abandoned after the war and to which he claims, at

least until 1955, he still remained faithful (*MS*, vi). I shall argue that this same 'exigency' informs Camus's writings long after he abandoned the concept of the Absurd itself, in fact throughout his much too short life. Rather than a Nietzschean 'will to power', the exigency is closer to what I would call a 'will to resist', even or especially when resistance appears hopeless or turns out in fact to be completely fruitless – a will to resist that is not simply a product of history but also a resistance to history.

Le Mythe appeared only months after *L'Etranger*. The fact that the first two of Camus's texts to appear outside of Algeria were published in occupied Paris indicates that the young Albert Camus, like almost all of France's established writers, agreed to submit his manuscripts to German censorship and have them published under the conditions imposed by the Nazi occupiers of France. To publish under such conditions did not in itself, however, reflect either pro-Nazi or collaborationist sentiments, since almost all of the French writers who were on the anti-fascist Left and who would eventually join the Resistance continued to publish throughout the war. And a short time after having agreed to eliminate a chapter on Kafka in order to publish his essay, Camus himself joined the Resistance and published the Kafka section clandestinely. If he owed his first successes to a publication system controlled by Nazi censors, he also risked his life editing and writing for the clandestine Resistance newspaper *Combat* during the last years of the war. If *La Peste*, written in large part during the last years of the war and published in 1947, describes the conditions for and limits of *collective* resistance to political oppression, *Le Mythe* could be considered to describe the preconditions for and limits of *individual* resistance to the human condition itself.

To be or not to be? – the Absurd and the question of being

No one who reads *Le Mythe* can ever forget how it begins. Not with the question of the general meaning or purpose of life, not with an investigation into the nature of the individual subject and his/her freedom, not with a discussion of the formative role and purported ends of history – nor with any other abstract, philosophical questions of this type. It begins rather with the more immediate, practical question of suicide, whether life is worth living in the first place: 'Il n'y a qu'un problème philosophique vraiment sérieux: c'est le suicide. Juger que la vie vaut ou ne vaut pas la peine d'être vécue, c'est répondre à la question fondamentale de la philosophie. Le reste . . . vient ensuite. Ce sont des jeux' (*Ess*, 99) ('There is but one truly serious philosophical problem, and that is suicide. Judging whether life is or is not worth living amounts to answering the fundamental question of philosophy.

All the rest . . . comes afterwards. These are games' (*MS*, 3)). What is thus most serious in philosophy, its very condition, is life itself – whatever life is and whatever it ultimately means. All the rest is secondary, frivolous, nothing more than a game – or much worse, dogmatism, the work of 'the gods'.

Even if suicide is posited as the most fundamental *philosophical* problem, given the deeply emotional nature not just of the possible responses to the question of whether one should take one's own life but of even raising the question in the first place, philosophy necessarily comes up short when it deals with it. Philosophy can respond to the 'one truly serious philosophical problem' only partially and inadequately, since affect will inevitably play a role in any response and philosophy's domain is reason, not emotion:

> C'est l'équilibre de l'évidence et du lyrisme qui peut seul nous permettre d'accéder en même temps à l'émotion et à la clarté. Dans un sujet à la fois si humble et si chargé de pathétique, la dialectique savante et classique doit donc céder la place, on le conçoit, à une attitude d'esprit plus modeste qui procède à la fois du bon sens et de la sympathie. (*Ess*, 99–100)

> Solely the balance between evidence and lyricism can allow us to achieve simultaneously emotion and lucidity. In a subject at once so humble and so heavy with emotion, the learned and classical dialectic must yield, one can see, to a more modest attitude of mind deriving at one and the same time from common sense and sympathy. (*MS*, 4, translation modified)

The 'one truly serious philosophical problem' is thus located at the limits of or even outside philosophy itself; it is both too humble and too emotional a problem for philosophy to deal with on its own. Absurd reasoning thus demands that philosophy do more than philosophise when dealing with this fundamental question of life or death.

Estrangement

In his generally laudatory essay on *The Stranger* and *The Myth*, written just months after their appearance, Jean-Paul Sartre agrees with the general consensus that *L'Etranger* is 'le meilleur livre depuis l'armistice' ('the best book since the armistice').[2] But Sartre is more severe in his assessment of the philosophical merits of *Le Mythe*, and assuming the role of a rigorous professor of philosophy he criticises Camus not just for his philosophical deficiencies but also for showing off: 'M. Camus met quelque coquetterie à citer des textes de Jaspers, de Heidegger, de Kierkegaard, qu'il ne semble pas toujours bien comprendre' ('M. Camus shows off a bit by quoting passages from Jaspers, Heidegger, and Kierkegaard, whom, by the way, he does not always seem to have quite understood').[3] On strictly philosophical grounds, *Le Mythe* would seem to have little value for Sartre, and in his mind Camus's essay would undoubtedly have been more successful if he had not quoted philosophical texts at all.

But *Le Mythe* is less concerned with philosophy as such or what great philosophers have said about the ultimate meaning of life than with an experience that would seem to have at best extremely limited philosophical import: the momentary *feeling* ordinary people sometimes have that life suddenly no longer makes sense. 'Le sentiment de l'absurdité au détour de n'importe quelle rue peut frapper à la face de n'importe quel homme. Tel quel, dans sa nudité désolante, dans sa lumière sans rayonnement, il est insaisissable. Mais cette difficulté même mérite réflexion' (*Ess*, 105) ('At any street corner, the feeling of absurdity can strike any man in the face. As it is, in its distressing nudity, in its light without effulgence, it is elusive. But that very difficulty deserves reflection' (*MS*, 10–11)). This loss of certainty is the moment when 'les décors s'écroulent' (*Ess*, 106) ('the stage sets collapse' (*MS*, 12)) and daily routines and habits break down; in the life of people who have never previously questioned life, it is when 'le "pourquoi" s'élève' (*Ess*, 107) ('the "why" arises' (*MS*, 13)). The combination of the undeniable, unsettling force of the experience and its elusiveness is taken by Camus as an indication that something important is at stake in this 'why'.

Even though Camus explicitly compares the contradictory emotions felt at such moments to aesthetic sentiments and the question of the beautiful, they are closer in fact to the undetermined, conflicted feelings described by Kant in his analysis not of the beautiful but of the sublime: 'indéterminées, à la fois aussi confuses et aussi "certaines", aussi lointaines et aussi "présentes" que celles que nous donne le beau' (*Ess*, 105) ('indeterminate, simultaneously as confused and as "certain", as remote and as "present" as those furnished us by beauty' (*MS*, 10, translation modified)). Such feelings are remote because their source is a fortuitous occurrence outside the control of the individual, and yet at the same time they are deeply present within the self because of their unsettling emotional intensity. Which means that the self can find solace or escape from them neither in the world nor in itself.

What interests Camus especially in such feelings is that, 'comme les grandes œuvres, les sentiments profonds signifient toujours plus qu'ils n'ont conscience de le dire' (*Ess*, 105) ('like great works, deep feelings always signify more than they are conscious of saying' (*MS*, 10, translation modified)). What these feelings *say* and are conscious of saying may very well be an appropriate subject for philosophical investigation, but what they *signify* (or suggest) demands an extra-philosophical approach and type of analysis, one that recognises the limitations of what can be directly phrased and is open to what is conveyed indirectly by allusion or suggestion. Because the feeling of the Absurd *signifies* more and differently than what any explanation of the Absurd *says*, it is up to other forms of discourse, to literature in particular (and art or 'creation' in general), to supplement the inadequacies of philosophy. This leaves philosophical discourse the additional tasks of explaining why it cannot explain everything and of accounting for the distance that separates it from experience, affect and art.

The abrupt and unexpected loss of faith in habits, routines and fundamental assumptions and beliefs has profound and long-lasting effects: 'Dans un univers soudain privé d'illusions et de lumières, l'homme se sent un étranger. Cet exil est sans recours puisqu'il est privé des souvenirs d'une patrie perdue ou de l'espoir d'une terre promise. Ce divorce entre l'homme et sa vie, l'acteur et son décor, c'est proprement le sentiment de l'absurdité' (*Ess*, 101) ('In a universe suddenly divested of illusions and lights, man feels an alien, a stranger. His exile is without remedy, since he is deprived of the memory of a lost homeland or the hope of a promised land. This divorce between man and his life, the actor and his setting, is properly the feeling of absurdity' (*MS*, 6)). The *feeling* of radical divorce, of living in a once familiar but now suddenly radically alien homeland, of being adrift between past and future and unable to rely on either to give meaning to the present, of being a stranger to the world and to oneself, might appear to be cause for despair, especially since the exile from self, world and others is described as 'without remedy'. *Le Mythe* refutes such a deduction by making the consciousness of the absence of remedy for the discontents of existence the reason for living – and ultimately for resisting as well.

It is thus in a context of radical estrangement that the question of suicide is raised: 'L'absurde commande-t-il la mort?' (*Ess*, 103) ('Does the Absurd dictate death?' (*MS*, 9)). Camus responds that it does not, since suicide represents a flight from the Absurd condition it only appears to acknowledge and the destruction of the very tensions and contradictions at the heart of the Absurd it pretends to affirm. Absurd reasoning, as a thinking of difference, separation and divorce, strives to maintain these tensions and make them the reasons to live. Camus thus makes what might logically be taken as an 'invitation à la mort' ('invitation to death'), a 'règle de vie' (*Ess*, 146) ('a rule of life' (*MS*, 64, translation modified)). 'Il s'agit de vivre' (*Ess*, 146) ('The point is to live' (*MS*, 65)) – not in spite of but rather because of the Absurd and the radical divorce or difference at the very core of experience. Instead of the Cartesian, 'I think, therefore I am', *Le Mythe* proposes something like 'I experience the feeling of the Absurd, therefore I am' – and therefore I will continue to be.

What Camus calls 'the constant point of reference' of the essay is thus the indisputable fact of difference, separation or divorce: 'le gouffre qui sépare le désir de la conquête' ('the gulf that separates desire from conquest'), 'le décalage constant entre ce que nous imaginons savoir et ce que nous savons réellement' ('the hiatus between what we imagine we know and what we really know'), 'le divorce qui nous sépare de nos propres créations' ('the divorce separating us from our own creations'), 'le fossé (qui) ne sera jamais comblé . . . entre la certitude que j'ai de mon existence et le contenu que j'essaie de donner à cette assurance' (*Ess*, 110–11) ('the gap [that] will never be filled . . . between the certainty I have of my existence and the content I try to give to that assurance' (*MS*, 17–19)). And it is the 'gouffre' between the individual and the world that also paradoxically constitutes a fundamental link between them: 'Ce monde en lui-même n'est pas raisonnable . . . Ce qui est absurde, c'est la confrontation de cet irrationnel et de ce désir éperdu de clarté dont l'appel résonne au plus profond de l'homme. L'absurde dépend autant de l'homme que du monde. Il est pour le moment leur seul lien' (*Ess*, 113) ('This world in itself is not reasonable . . . But what is absurd is the confrontation of this irrational and the wild longing for clarity whose call echoes in the human heart. The Absurd depends as much on man as on the world. For the moment it is their only link' (*MS*, 21)). The problem *Le Mythe* raises is how to continue to live with or in the Absurd without either reducing the radical separation between 'man and world' or destroying the principal link between them, a linkage of differences.

The consciousness of the gap separating thought from experience locates thought in an alien, inhospitable context, which Camus describes as 'a desert' in which thought is purged of its 'phantoms', and reduced to a skeleton of itself, to almost nothing at all. In the section of *Le Mythe* entitled 'Le Suicide philosophique' ('Philosophical Suicide'), Camus evokes the work of a series of philosophers he labels 'existentialists' – Nietzsche, Husserl, Jaspers, Heidegger, Kierkegaard, Chestov and Scheler – but he focusses less on their philosophical arguments than on what he calls 'le climat qui leur est commun' ('the climate that is common to them'), 'cet univers indicible où règnent la contradiction, l'antinomie, l'angoisse ou l'impuissance' (*Ess*, 114–15) ('that indescribable universe where contradiction, antinomy, anguish, or impotence reigns' (*MS*, 23)). If the different existentialists' experiences are all 'nées dans le désert' (*Ess*, 117) ('born in the desert' (*MS*, 27)), Camus attacks all strategies for escaping from the limitations of their condition of birth, which is also the climate of his own thought. Rather, he insists that it is necessary to remain within the climate he nevertheless calls 'meurtrier' (*Ess*, 119) ('deadly' (*MS*, 29)), while continuing to reject the mirages of escape or salvation that such a climate also produces.

Hope itself is a mirage, for it is rooted in the desire for evasion from the conditions of the desert. But despair is equally illusory. What will remain of the Absurd in Camus's later work when the notion itself has been left behind is precisely a conviction of the importance both of lucidity concerning the limits of thought and action and the necessity for 'une confrontation et une lutte sans repos' ('a confrontation and unceasing struggle'): 'Tout ce qui détruit, escamote ou subtilise ces exigences (et en premier le consentement qui détruit le divorce) ruine l'absurde et dévalorise l'attitude qu'on peut alors proposer. L'absurde n'a de sens que dans la mesure où l'on n'y consent pas' (*Ess*, 121) ('Everything that destroys, conjures away, or exorcises these requirements (and, to begin with, consent, which overthrows divorce) ruins the Absurd and devalues the attitude that may be proposed. The Absurd has meaning only in so far as it is not agreed to' (*MS*, 31)). Affirmed but not agreed to, resisted but not denied, engaged in the hopeless but at the same time not desperate tasks of living, thinking and acting, meaning and value emerge precisely out of their absence and in the very nihilistic desert that both negates them and makes them possible. But this is so only if the conditions of the desert are acknowledged for what they are. The intellectual task of 'proceed(ing) beyond nihilism' (*MS*, v) without falling prey to one of its mirages is made even more difficult, if not impossible, by the fact that the fate of a consciousness of the Absurd is to be bound to the Absurd forever.[4]

Camus's agnosticism concerning not just religion but philosophy and politics as well is thus evident in *Le Mythe*, a decade before it will take on a more directly political form in *L'Homme révolté*. If in his later major essay he will attack dialectical history, whether Hegelian or Marxist, and all forms of revolution for being teleological and messianic and believing in the promise of an end of history that would justify any means used to achieve that end, the 'existentialist philosophies' evoked in *Le Mythe* are criticised in similar terms for deifying the Absurd: 'Ils divinisent ce qui les écrase et trouvent une raison d'espérer dans ce qui les démunit. Cet espoir forcé est chez tous d'essence religieuse . . . L'absurde devient dieu (dans le sens le plus large de ce mot) et cette impuissance à comprendre, l'être qui illumine tout' (*Ess*, 122) ('They deify what crushes them and find reason to hope in what impoverishes them. That forced hope is religious in all of them . . . The Absurd becomes god (in the broadest meaning of this word) and that inability to understand becomes the being that illuminates everything' (*MS*, 32–3, translation modified)). Camus calls the existentialist attitude a form of 'suicide philosophique' (*Ess*, 128) ('philosophical suicide' (*MS*, 41)), just as he will in *L'Homme révolté* attack ideology in general and the logic that the end justifies the means in particular as justifications for murder. *Le*

Mythe de Sisyphe thus inaugurates Camus's long struggle against philosophical, religious and political ideologies that promise salvation in the future at the expense of living human beings in the present. Like Sisyphus, Camus never succeeded in his task – but that was never the point. The struggle itself was.

What's art got to do with it?

Si le monde était clair, l'art ne serait pas.   (*Ess*, 177)

If the world were clear, art would not exist.   (*MS*, 98)

In order to explain Absurd existence, Camus describes three types of 'Absurd man' – Don Juan, the actor and the conqueror – which he claims are 'illustrations' of the Absurd but not 'models' to be followed (*Ess*, 150; *MS*, 68). What the three figures have in common is like certain artists, '(ils) connaissent leurs limites (et) ne les excèdent jamais' (*Ess*, 152) ((they) know their limits (and) never go beyond them' (*MS*, 70)). This is also Camus's definition of 'genius'. But Don Juan, the actor and the conqueror are only incomplete versions of 'le plus absurde des personages qui est le créateur' (*Ess*, 170) ('the most absurd of the characters, who is the creator' (*MS*, 92, translation modified)). If the awareness of the limitations of the human condition is characteristic of those who 'think clearly', the creator (the artist-writer) is presented as the figure who 'thinks' the most clearly of all. But to think clearly in Camus's sense is to know that thought itself is limited and therefore to think in part against thought. The Absurd creator cannot fall prey to the mystification of art, however, since he/she also knows that art is limited, that it too provides no escape, no salvation. The Absurd artist creates within and against the limits of art; he/she too creates without either hope or despair.

The Absurd artist nevertheless experiences what Camus calls 'un bonheur métaphysique à soutenir l'absurdité du monde' (*Ess*, 173) ('a metaphysical joy in enduring the world's absurdity' (*MS*, 93, translation modified)). His/her joy is not in changing the world, overcoming the gap that at the same time distances him/her from and links him/her to life, and certainly not in any illusory transcendence of or escape from the human condition itself. Joy comes rather in withstanding and thus maintaining the gap or divorce constitutive of the Absurd. For if the Absurd is an irreducible given of human experience, if it is the climate in which thought takes its nourishment, then the choice cannot be between whether to affirm or deny the Absurd but rather whether to live or die of it: 'On ne nie pas la guerre. Il faut en mourir ou en vivre. Ainsi de l'absurde: il s'agit de respirer avec lui; de reconnaître ses leçons et de retrouver leur chair. A cet égard, la joie absurde par excellence, c'est la création' (*Ess*, 173) ('War cannot be denied. One must live it or die of it. So it is with the absurd: it is a question of breathing with it, of recognising its lessons and rediscovering their flesh. In this regard the absurd joy par excellence is creation' (*MS*, 93)). The artist-creator is not only the most completely lucid of the Absurd types; he/she is also the most joyful, even if 'absurd joy' is itself a divided feeling, affirmative and negative at the same time, joyous in a Nietzschean sense and yet 'sans lendemain' (*Ess*, 189) ('ephemeral' (*MS*, 113)). Absurd 'man' is above all an artist – but an artist who never fulfils the ultimate project of art: to produce a finished work.

The artist achieves an even greater lucidity (and joy) than the other Absurd figures because his/her consciousness (and joy) is (are) double: 'Dans cet univers l'œuvre est alors la chance unique de maintenir sa conscience et d'en fixer les aventures. Créer, c'est vivre deux fois' (*Ess*, 173) ('In this universe the work of art is then the sole chance of maintaining his/her consciousness and of fixing its adventures. To create is to live doubly' (*MS*, 94, translation modified)). The consciousness of the artist-creator is thus at the same time both same and other, his/hers and not his/hers. The creator's consciousness is not, however, self-reflexive in the Hegelian sense, a consciousness in and for itself that has triumphed over the immediacy of experience and raised itself to a higher level. The 'absurd consciousness' of the creator is no less gratuitous and limited than existence and the human condition themselves. In art there is no escape or refuge from the Absurd, since the work of art is 'elle-même un phénomène absurde' (*Ess*, 174) ('itself an absurd phenomenon' (*MS*, 95)). As the simultaneous affirmation of and resistance to the Absurd, Absurd art is the most fully absurd of all Absurd phenomena, the one most fully engaged with its irresolvable tensions and contradictions and with the least illusions about its own ultimate effects.

An Absurd theory of the novel

Camus's discussion of what could be called the aesthetics of the Absurd culminates with a discussion of the novel, which he considers both the most philosophical and the most Absurd of all literary genres – the most Absurd because the most philosophical. Open to and tempted by ideas, novelists could be considered to be failed philosophers of sorts, but their 'failure' to think ideas turns out actually to be their strength. As Camus metaphorically puts it, novelists write 'en images plutôt qu'en raisonnements' ('in images rather than reasoned arguments'): 'Mais justement le choix qu'ils ont fait d'écrire en images plutôt qu'en raisonnements est révélateur d'une certaine pensée qui leur est commune, persuadée de l'inutilité de tout principe d'explication et convaincue du message enseignant de l'apparence sensible... Le roman dont il est question est l'instrument de cette connaissance à la fois relative et inépuisable' (*Ess*, 178–9) ('The choice they have made to write in images rather than in reasoned arguments is revelatory of a certain thought that is common to them all, convinced of the uselessness of any principle of explanation and sure of the educative message of perceptible appearance . . . The novel in question is the instrument of that simultaneously relative and inexhaustible knowledge' (*MS*, 101, translation modified)). 'To write in images' is to have more confidence in experience than in thought, more certainty in the relativity of description than in the pretensions of logical analysis and systematic explanation. It is to refuse to say more than experience allows one to say.

Camus uses identical language in a review he wrote in *Alger républicain* (20 October 1938) of Sartre's *La Nausée* (*Nausea*): 'Un roman n'est jamais qu'une philosophie mise en images. Et dans un bon roman, toute la philosophie est passée dans les images. Mais il suffit qu'elle déborde les personnages et les actions, qu'elle apparaisse comme une étiquette sur l'œuvre, pour que l'intrigue perde son authenticité et le roman sa vie' (*Ess*, 1417) ('A novel is never anything but a philosophy put into images. And in a good novel the entire philosophy has passed into the images. But the philosophy need only spill over into the characters and action for it to stick out like a label, the plot loses its authenticity, and the novel its life').[5] While anticipating a bright future for this first-time novelist, Camus nonetheless criticises the novel for what he claims is 'ce déséquilibre si sensible entre la pensée de l'œuvre et les images où elle se joue' (*Ess*, 1418) ('the noticeable lack of balance between the ideas in the work and the images that express them').[6] In other words, Sartre, by remaining too philosophical, did not succeed in putting his entire thought into images. Thus long before their serious political differences surfaced, Sartre and Camus disagreed over the relationship that should exist between philosophy and literature. For Camus, Sartre was too philosophical a novelist; for Sartre, Camus was too literary a philosopher.

The opposite of the philosophical novel for Camus is 'le roman à thèse' ('the thesis-novel'), which Camus calls 'la plus haïssable de toutes' (*Ess*, 191) ('the most hateful of all' (*MS*, 115–16)). It is the product of 'philosophes honteux' ('philosophers ashamed of themselves') who want to illustrate ideas or prove arguments, not of 'penseurs lucides' ('lucid thinkers') who know the limits of all ideas and thus what they do not know and cannot say. The latter write not to demonstrate truth but to resist the tyranny of established or imposed ideas; they are the post-Nietzschean literary precursors of 'l'homme révolté' ('the rebel').

The aesthetics of the Absurd, if such a term makes sense, is thus rooted in the diversity and inexhaustibility of experience and not the unity and finality of ideas: 'Toute pensée qui renonce à l'unité exalte la diversité. Et la diversité est le lieu de l'art' (*Ess*, 191) ('All thought that abandons unity glorifies diversity. And diversity is the home of art' (*MS*, 116)). Given its emphasis on diversity rather than sameness, on little narratives rather than grand or meta-narratives, on fragmented, incomplete, open works rather than unified, finalised forms, and finally its insistence on the relative, the corporal and the individual rather than the universal, the spiritual and the collective, *Le Mythe de Sisyphe* could be considered to lay the aesthetic-philosophical groundwork for the more explicitly political resistance to totalitarianism which will characterise Camus's war journalism and post-war essays. For what the Absurd artist can never accept is the universal applicability of the Idea itself – any Idea, whether religious, philosophical, aesthetic or political, whether it be that of God, Being, or 'Man', on the one hand, or of a people, race, class or History itself, on the other.

'Il faut imaginer Sisyphe heureux'[7]

The concluding line of the short section of *Le Mythe* that recounts the story of Sisyphus is as striking and unforgettable as the opening pages of the essay devoted to suicide. And yet Sisyphus's happiness remains a perplexing issue given the fruitlessness of his task and the total lack of hope for any change in his condition. If the worst punishment invented by the gods, as Camus claims, is that of 'le travail inutile et sans espoir' (*Ess*, 195) ('futile and hopeless labor' (*MS*, 119)) – in other words, what from the perspective of the Absurd could be considered the human condition itself – how is it possible to imagine Sisyphus happy with his miserable fate? And how could we ever be happy if our own condition and fate resemble his? And who are these gods who condemn Sisyphus (who condemn us) to such a state? And what if there are no gods and in a godless world our fate nevertheless does not change? Or if we reject those who present themselves as gods – or as superhuman humans – and who defeat us in war, dominate and politically oppress us and appear to have determined our fate once and for all, so that no act of resistance would appear to have any chance of success? What does it mean to be happy in such circumstances? And why would Camus end his essay with such an affirmation of joy?

The specific crime for which Sisyphus is punished is for disobeying the gods who allowed him to return to earth after his initial condemnation to hell. In Camus's version of the myth, Sisyphus's revolt against the gods is rooted in his refusal to give up the simple joys and pleasures of earthly existence:

'quand il eut de nouveau revu le visage de ce monde, goûté l'eau et le soleil, les pierres chaudes et la mer, il ne voulut plus retourner dans l'ombre infernale' (*Ess*, 195) ('But when he had seen again the face of this world, enjoyed water and sun, warm stones and the sea, he no longer wanted to go back to the infernal darkness' (*MS*, 120)). Sisyphus's crime in the eyes of the gods is thus the terrible crime of enjoying life and scorning the all-powerful gods who have condemned him to an after-life of misery: 'son mépris des dieux, sa haine de la mort et sa passion pour la vie' (*Ess*, 196) ('his scorn for the gods, his hatred of death, and his passion for life' (*MS*, 120)). For his defiance, he receives as punishment 'ce supplice indicible où tout l'être s'emploie à ne rien achever. C'est le prix qu'il faut payer pour les passions de cette terre' (*Ess*, 196) ('that unspeakable torture in which his being exerts itself to accomplish nothing. This is the price that must be paid for the passions of this earth' (*MS*, 120, translation modified)). Camus's version of Sisyphus is not an epic 'twilight of the gods', however, but rather a little narrative of everyday human resistance. Sisyphus refuses to accept the power of the gods and their control over his life, but he is also lucid about and thus accepts, as he resists, the limits of the condition they impose on him, which in any case he cannot change. And in understanding that everything is not possible and continuing his meaningless task with this knowledge, he is happy, even if or perhaps because his work is useless and he 'accomplish(es) nothing'. The 'nothing' he accomplishes each time he pushes his rock up to the very top of the hill is in fact the 'something' of art. Perhaps even the 'something' of a politics of revolt. His work may never in fact be finished and will always have to be redone, he will never remain at the summit of accomplishment for more than an instant before he must begin again, but it is the best he can hope for, and for Camus this is more than enough.

In a recent study *Le Mythe* has been called a post-Marxist work: 'To Marxism's claims, Camus's absurdism replied that none of our labors can solve the tragedy of death or give sense to the world. There is no direct mention of Marxism or Communism in *The Myth of Sisyphus*, but the critique is everywhere implied . . . (The text) was therefore . . . post-Marxist rather than pre-Marxist.'[8] And perhaps nowhere is this characterisation more appropriate than in the section of *Le Mythe* devoted to Sisyphus, especially if 'post-Marxist' is meant to be distinguished from anti-Marxist, which Camus's post-war political essays become. Sisyphus's lucidity may be equal to that of the Absurd artist, but the physical effort necessary to accomplish his task resembles more closely the labour of the worker. If 'Sisyphe est le héros absurde . . . autant par ses passions que par son tourment' (*Ess*, 196) ('Sisyphus is the absurd hero . . . as much through his passions as through his torture' (*MS*, 120)), his condition is that of the worker in modern society, whose 'destin n'est pas moins absurde' (*Ess*, 196) ('fate is no less absurd' (*MS*, 121)). Sisyphus is the 'prolétaire des dieux, impuissant et révolté, (il) connaît toute l'étendue de sa misérable condition . . . La clairvoyance qui devait faire son tourment consomme du même coup sa victoire. Il n'est pas de destin qui ne se surmonte par le mépris' (*Ess*, 196) ('proletarian of the gods, powerless and rebellious, [he] knows the whole extent of his wretched condition . . . The lucidity that was to constitute his torture at the same time crowns his victory. There is no fate that cannot be surmounted by scorn' (*MS*, 121)). Sisyphus's fate is sealed, his situation without hope, tragic. But the worker is also described by Camus as a tragic figure, but only 'aux rares moments où il devient conscient' (*Ess*, 196) ('at rare moments when he becomes conscious' (*MS*, 121)). *Le Mythe* says nothing more as to where such a proletarian consciousness could lead in the case of the worker, however, especially if he were to join with others in active protest and then resistance. Sisyphus, however, is lucid and thus tragic at all times, but especially each time he walks back down the hill to begin his task anew. His resistance to the gods and his condition is thus more psychological than active, more a will to resistance than resistance itself. And in Camus's story his resistance is solitary, that of an (the) individual not a class or collectivity. It is only a starting point – a possible origin for another form of history (or histories) different from the dialectical history of the class struggle and with an end that is unknown and unknowable.

The consciousness of Sisyphus, at the same time proletarian and artist, is presented in *Le Mythe* as both an aesthetic and political value in itself, even though the conditions of his enslavement are not changed either by his unceasing labour or his lucidity. Camus makes Sisyphus's lucidity about his condition and his scorn for his tormentors indications of his 'victory' over both, but his victory is individual and psychological, not collective and historical. Sisyphus's happiness is a sublime joy, a feeling of pleasure in or as pain, but no sense is given in the essay that he is anticipating joining with others who share his scorn for the gods and want to do more than push rocks repeatedly up hills. 1942, the year of *Le Mythe*'s publication, was also the year that ideas of collective resistance finally began to be put into practice in France on a larger scale than before. Sisyphus's joy in what could be called 'passive resistance' could thus be considered a step, no matter how small, on the way to active resistance; his will to resist the precondition for actual resistance. This same will or exigency can be found in Camus's later work as well – in both his political and literary texts.

What could be worse than Sisyphus's fate, one might still be inclined to ask? And yet Camus encourages us to ask at the same time what fate would in fact be better? As the precondition for other, more active forms of resistance and as an expression of scorn for the gods who control Sisyphus's fate but who have not succeeded in destroying his consciousness, his will or his attachment to life, that is, his freedom, it is perhaps not that difficult to imagine Sisyphus happy after all. Camus will soon abandon Sisyphus and the Absurd, but he will not abandon his conviction that all gods and all political and religious Ideas and ideologies should be resisted. He will never give up his conviction that the greatest value of all – before politics, before history, before justice – is human life itself, no matter how limited, oppressive or tragic the human condition and any particular political situation actually is. In spite of tuberculosis, in spite of the defeat of France, in spite of the Occupation and Vichy collaboration, in spite of philosophical nihilism – *faut-il imaginer Camus heureux?*

NOTES

1. Preface to the first American edition of *The Myth of Sisyphus*, reproduced in the English edition cited on p. vi.
2. Jean-Paul Sartre, 'Explication de *L'Etranger*', in *Situations I* (Paris, Gallimard, 1947) (originally published February 1943), p. 99; 'Camus's "The Outsider" ', in Jean-Paul Sartre, *Literary and Philosophical Essays*, trans. Annette Michelson (New York, Criterion Books, 1955), p. 24, translation modified.
3. *Situations I*, pp. 101–2; *Literary and Philosophical Essays*, p. 26.
4. I would argue that the most interesting and suggestive reading of *Le Mythe de Sisyphe* is still that of Maurice Blanchot, 'Le Mythe de Sisyphe', *Faux Pas* (Paris, Gallimard, 1943).
5. 'On Jean-Paul Sartre's *La Nausée*', in Albert Camus, *Lyrical and Critical Essays*, trans. Ellen Conroy Kennedy (New York, Vintage Books, 1967), p. 199, translation modified.
6. *Ibid.*, p. 201.
7. *Ess*, 198; 'One must imagine Sisyphus happy' (*MS*, 123).
8. Roland Aronson, *Camus and Sartre* (Chicago and London, University of Chicago Press, 2004), p. 73.

5

CHRISTINE MARGERRISON

Camus and the theatre

Although Camus's essays and prose fiction had a profound impact on the post-war generation in France and elsewhere, this is less true of his theatrical works, which had mixed success during the author's lifetime. His second play, *Le Malentendu*, in which the returning, unidentified adult son is murdered by his mother and sister, had a difficult reception in 1944. *Caligula*, Camus's earliest play, was more successful in 1945, seeming to chime with audiences who had undergone the horrors of Nazi occupation, and it ran for almost a year. *L'Etat de siège*, a collaboration with Jean-Louis Barrault, closed after only seventeen performances in 1948 and has rarely been staged since, but *Les Justes* was well-received in 1949, running for over 400 performances. Although Camus wrote no more plays, he continued his lifelong involvement with the theatre, producing six adaptations which he helped to stage, and thinking not only of writing a play on Don Juan, but of reworking *Le Malentendu* and *L'Etat de siège*. His theatrical works are still produced throughout the world and since the turn of the millennium *Les Justes*, *Caligula* and *Le Malentendu* have been on the London stage. Yet such productions are rare and although articles on single plays have been published and new editions produced, the few book-length studies of the theatre date mainly from the 1960s and 1970s.[1]

The contrast between the reception of Camus's other writings and his plays is even more marked when one considers his enduring passion for the theatre. In particular, he stressed his pleasure in working with others, a form of collaboration he associated with his time at *Combat*, or earlier when he was involved in amateur theatre in Algeria with the Théâtre du Travail in 1936, and the Théâtre de l'Equipe, which he founded in 1937 and for which he began to write *Caligula* with a view to acting the leading role. It is particularly ironic that the only area of his creative production involving direct engagement with others was also the least successful, for reasons which seem partly related to the interactive or dialogical nature of the theatre itself, which requires engagement with others on a number of levels besides those entailed in putting on a play. Some of the greatest strengths of the fictional writings become weaknesses on the stage; whereas Camus's fictional first-person narratives are a source of fascination, the sometimes long theatrical monologues caused complaints of didacticism and inaction. Moreover, Camus seemed unable to put himself in the place of his spectators and anticipate their reactions, or visualise the effect his scenes might have. The major challenge Camus faced as a playwright (one that he consistently rejected, seeing it as a resort to 'psychology') lay in putting himself in the place of others to bring opposing views to life.

Although aware of the audience's importance, including them in the collaborative enterprise when speaking in the *Equipe*'s manifesto of the 'complicité de l'acteur et du spectateur' (*TRN*, 1692) ('complicity of the actor and spectator') in consenting to the same illusion, Camus seems not to have envisaged the measure of audience autonomy this theatrical pact entailed in practice. In 1940 he wrote that the theatre was subject to a universal suffrage and must receive the agreement of all (*Ess*, 1405), but these remarks were made before Camus's own plays were put to that 'vote'. By this standard he judged that, as *Le Malentendu* had been rejected by the majority of audiences, it was 'in plain terms, a failure'.[2] This reaction is to Camus's credit, and he tried to modify *Le Malentendu* accordingly, but such audience responses provoked an increasingly difficult relationship with his public and the critics. In this sense, Camus's enthusiasm for collective activity in the theatre was marred only by others' capacity for independent judgements.

Paradoxically, on the one hand, like sport (with which he often compared it), Camus valued the theatre's collective and egalitarian nature. On the other hand, he also called it his monastery (*TRN*, 1715), a means of escaping others. Increasingly, it became a haven from the burdens of fame and fellow intellectuals in whose company he felt unease (*TRN*, 1723). Camus's comments recall his attitude in his youthful writings towards art itself, which he saw as an escape from sordid reality into a more perfect world, a view reflected some twenty years later in *L'Homme révolté*, where the creation of a closed universe enables the artist to 'refai[re] le monde à son compte' (*Ess*, 659) ('reconstruct the world to his plan' (*R*, 221)). One might add that like sport or the monastic life, this self-enclosed theatrical universe, with pre-determined rules of behaviour, is more predictable, more easily circumscribed than wider society. Moreover, in the theatre others are playing a role defined and to some degree controlled by the artist himself, without the threatening impenetrability they posed the young author in his youthful writings and earliest essays.[3]

Camus's general emphasis on egalitarianism and interdependence in the theatre contrasts with his views on the artist's position. From his readings in the early 1930s, in particular Nietzsche's *The Birth of Tragedy*, Camus was developing a conception of the god-like status of the artist. When in the *Equipe*'s manifesto he introduces the theatre as 'un art de chair qui donne à des corps vibrants le soin de traduire ses leçons' ('an art of the flesh which gives vibrant bodies the task of translating its lessons'), satisfying also the 'besoin de construction qui est naturel à l'artiste' (*TRN*, 1692) ('need for construction that is natural to the artist') one detects echoes of Nietzsche's Apollonian artist god, the divine sculptor shaping this world, creating form from the 'flesh' of humanity. Similarly, in the section on the actor in *Le Mythe de Sisyphe* where the actor is compared to a sculptor, Camus asserts that 'La loi de cet art veut que tout soit grossi et se traduise en chair' (*Ess*, 160) ('The rule of that art requires that everything be magnified and translated into flesh' (*MS*, 76, translation amended)), while in *L'Homme révolté* he claims that the greatest sculpture seeks to capture 'le geste, la mine ou le regard vide qui résumeront tous les gestes et tous les regards du monde' (*Ess*, 660) ('the gesture, the expression, or the empty stare which will sum up all the gestures and all the stares in the world' (*R*, 222)). Spanning the course of Camus's career, such comments reveal a continuity in his view of the privileged role of the artist. They indicate, moreover, a feature of Camus's theatrical works that has been a perennial focus of criticism, the reduction of the Other to an empty vessel, a receptacle for the artist's vision. The reference to the 'empty stare' seems less a distillation of humanity than the transformation of others into soulless bodies, obliterating all that makes the individual distinctively human.

One might take issue with Camus's definition of the theatre as 'la réalisation collective de la pensée d'un seul' (*Ess*, 1405) ('the collective real-isation of the thought of a single individual'), but this may explain why he was quick to correct what he perceived as misinterpretations of his work, or to insist on what he had 'really' meant. Although most notably the case with *L'Etranger*, Camus was likewise anxious to clarify the meanings of *Caligula* and *Le Malentendu* in ways which seem didactic, retrospectively giving the plays moral connotations at odds with the original context in which they were written, as when he claimed that *Le Malentendu* contained an underly-ing optimism or that *Caligula* was an illustration of the dangers of overstep-ping the limits. If audiences of the 1940s saw connections between *Caligula* and the war, Camus rejected such associations, writing to Jean Paulhan in 1943 that it had given the play an unintended meaning.[4] Such attempted corrections may explain his continuing insistence that *Caligula* was written in 1938. As originally conceived, Caligula, in whom the young playwright saw himself, was a heroic figure whose tragedy lay precisely in his status as a superior, yet mortal individual standing above the masses in the manner of the Nietzschean artist-god or poet. However, as the research of A. James Arnold has documented, the play underwent several revisions before its 1944 publication and as he was working on the final version in the summer of 1943 Camus shifted the balance towards Caligula as a tyrant, strengthening the role of Cherea in opposing the murderous Emperor (CAC4, 168–70). The play's strongly Nietzschean dimension was toned down (perhaps because of Nietzsche's appropriation within Nazi ideology) and Camus's developing preoccupation with revolt was reinforced – although we see little evidence of the social solidarity which was to be integral to the writer's later theory of revolt, as expressed in the slogan 'Je me révolte, donc nous sommes' (*Ess*, 432) ('I *rebel* – therefore we *exist*' (*R*, 28)). These successive reworkings have left contradictory traces, for Caligula remains a heroic and even Christ-like or Dionysian figure who acquiesces in his own death, yet his character is also regarded as a penetrating study of a dictator, which was not Camus's original intention. Indeed, in Arnold's opinion this remodelling of the play made it a hybrid text; what started out as the third part of a triptych on the Absurd (with *L'Etranger* and *Le Mythe de Sisyphe*) became instead the second cousin to *L'Homme révolté* (CAC4, 171, 175). At the same time, Camus was making similar changes to *Le Malentendu*, developing the role of Jan's wife (who did not originally appear until the final act) in opposing his course of action. Maria's 'Ta méthode n'est pas la bonne' (*TRN*, 128) ('Your method isn't the right one' (*COP*, 117, translation amended)) thus echoes Caligula's 'Ma liberté n'est pas la bonne' (*TRN*, 108) ('My freedom isn't the right one' (*COP*, 103)). But if Cherea proves an ambivalent opponent because he understands Caligula, Maria is mystified by Jan's behaviour. Generally regarded as the only 'human' presence in the play (however stereotypical), she is not integrated on the same intellectual level as the other characters and her more emotional reactions seem the only ones with which an audience is likely to sympathise. Camus's retrospective claim that in an unjust world a man can save himself and others through sincerity (*TRN*, 1731) – a claim voiced by Maria alone – is even less convincing if we believe Martha's declaration that she would have killed her brother even had he identified himself (*TRN*, 168; *COP*, 146).

Conflicts between authorial intention and audience reception may be more stark in the theatre where, uniquely amongst Camus's writings, the recipient of the message is present and may openly react, threatening Camus's notion of harmonious 'complicity'. If the solitary reader may sometimes feel coerced by Camus's prose, as Colin Davis argues elsewhere in this volume, a different dynamic operates in the theatre, where unexamined assertions may provoke resistance in the audience, thus threatening the theatrical illusion. Although Camus later denied it was a philosophical play (*TRN*, 1730), this seems to me to be the case in *Caligula*, with its rather inflated claims concerning Caligula's 'philosophy' and the unrelenting 'logic' of his actions. Cherea rejects Caligula's methods yet deems his philosophy irrefutable, joining the revolt through self-interest to combat 'une grande idée' ('a great idea') which could destroy everything (*TRN*, 34; *COP*, 53). As to that philosophy, although Cherea refers directly to the Absurd we are told only that it threatens his wish to live and be happy; in order to be free he sometimes desires the death of those he loves, or women forbidden to him: 'Pour être logique, je devrais . . . tuer ou posséder' (*TRN*, 78) ('Were logic everything, I'd kill or fornicate' (*COP*, 82–3)). But 'logic' is not the issue here. Likewise, Caligula's discovery that 'Les hommes meurent et ils ne sont pas heureux' (*TRN*, 16) ('Men die; and they are not happy' (*COP*, 40)) elides empirical fact and subjective opinion, seeming to confer on each equal value as a universal truth. Yet there is no logical connection between the two, and neither can any logical consequences be derived from them, and the spectator irritated by such idiosyncratic uses of the term 'logic' may only become more alienated by its repetition.

The reception of the plays seems to have caused a rift between Camus and his audience, and at least one critic has detected an irritability in some of his prefaces, particularly in the 1958 American edition of the plays where he attempts to prescribe the criteria by which *Caligula* should be judged (*TRN*, 1730).[5] In a different illustration of what Colin Davis sees as Camus's radical exclusion of reader dissent, the author then effectively dismisses those who do not share his particular model of the 'true' theatre, recommending that they spare themselves the trouble of reading further, whilst pointedly welcoming those who remain. Abandoning the youthful ideal of harmonious 'complicity', Camus firmly prioritises the wishes of the playwright over those of the audience, warning that his preference is for the classical tradition and Greek tragedy, which deals with human destiny. Although psychology, ingenious anecdotes or piquant situations might amuse him as a spectator, they leave him, he says, indifferent as an author (*TRN*, 1733–4). In some ways, these words might be seen as an attempt to deflect criticism away from the plays themselves by relocating the problem in the minds of those who do not appreciate the classical theatre.

In his 1955 Athens lecture on 'L'Avenir de la tragédie' ('The Future of Tragedy') Camus sees the psychological as undermining the tragic genre and identifies Euripides as the playwright responsible for the decline of Greek tragedy through his concentration on individual psychology (*TRN*, 1707; *SEN*, 198). Camus claims in his lecture that the material conditions for the rebirth of tragedy are favourable, beginning with the reforms of Copeau, who returned power into the hands of playwrights (*TRN*, 1703; *SEN*, 194).[6]

Camus suggests that the two great periods of tragedy in Western history, ancient Greece and eighteenth-century Europe, each marked a transition from forms of religious thinking to individualism and rationalism, reflected in the movement from the sacred to psychological tragedy. Claiming that tragedy is born in the West each time civilisation is halfway between a society regulated by religious belief and one built around man, he suggests this stage has been reached in contemporary society, where man's faith in the power of reason is challenged by the recognition that he has limits. The idea of the 'limit' or 'balance' recurs in *L'Homme révolté* and is central in his Athens lecture to his definition of tragedy where 'les forces qui s'affrontent dans la tragédie sont également légitimes, également armées en raison' (*TRN*, 1705) ('the forces confronting each other in tragedy are equally legitimate, equally justified' (*SEN*, 196)). He suggests an equal tension between the divine order and man's rebellion against that order, illustrating this by reference to Aeschylus' *Prometheus Bound*; Prometheus is both just and unjust, but his oppressor, Zeus, also has right on his side. In melodrama, by contrast, only one side is justifiable. Thus, for Camus the constant theme of tragedy is of a balance which must be maintained and a limit which must not be transgressed; those who, through blindness or passion, destroy this balance are heading for disaster.

Considering the events of the first half of the twentieth century, Camus's conviction that he and his contemporaries lived in a tragic age was entirely understandable, but his attempts to establish a specific parallel between this and earlier periods of tragedy are problematical. Camus's perhaps anxious method is less to persuade or explain than to instil agreement through a series of assertions (a method adopted, at times, in his plays). The comment that with Racine the tragic movement concludes in the perfection of chamber music (*TRN*, 1708; *SEN*, 200) may impress, but carries no explanatory power unless the listener is familiar with its source.[7] Although problems arising from Camus's attraction to vague, overarching theories of social change (or stasis) are more pertinent to discussions of *L'Homme révolté*, this approach also seems to characterise his theatrical aims, where he prioritises the abstract 'rule' or definition over the particular, speaks of 'forces' to the detriment of dialogue or viewpoint and prefers abstraction to specificity. Despite his lifelong emotional and ideological attachment to an ideal of Greece, it is unclear whether Camus was as familiar with Greek tragedy as his references to the subject might lead some to believe.[8] Those familiar with Nietzsche's *The Birth of Tragedy* (which Camus had read by 1932) will detect clear echoes of this work in Camus's lecture, and the strong continuity in his thinking about the theatre stems partly, in my view, from his allegiance to Nietzsche: his rejection of psychology, which he redefined in 1937 as 'action' rather than introspection (*CI*, 48), coincides with the beginnings of his writing career; and his modifications to *Caligula* and *Le Malentendu* are attributable to his redefinition of tragedy as a balance between equally legitimate forces in 1943 (*CII*, 103).

Nietzsche identifies Wagner as the source for a rebirth of tragedy in the West; Camus looks to the work of contemporary French playwrights, and associated himself with this enterprise, claiming at different times that all his plays were attempts to create modern tragedy (*TRN*, 1715, 1730). As in his 1958 preface, such are the criteria by which he sought to be judged. Yet, even in terms of the equilibrium he sought to establish between equally legitimate forces in confrontation, his plays arguably fail to deliver tragic greatness: in *Caligula* all the major characters have sympathy and admiration for the Emperor, whose main opponents, the patricians, are cowardly and self-serving; in *Le Malentendu* all three main protagonists overstep the limit, and Camus's adjustments to the role of Maria fail to provide an equal balance between opposing views. The writer's attention to 'forces' in his Athens speech cannot disguise the naivety of his understanding of social forces and structures, as is illustrated by his treatment of destiny, which is reduced on the level of the everyday to the figure of the old servant who unaccountably distracts Martha and her mother from discovering Jan's identity. This hardly replicates the notorious fickleness of the Greek gods. On the metaphysical level this force is replaced by the Absurd. But for the audiences of Aeschylus the workings of the divine order were a familiar and lived reality and it is, I think, highly questionable whether an abstract and unexplained theory, whose transfer to the stage robs it of meaning, can adequately substitute for this fundamental structure of Greek society.

Despite Camus's dismissal of melodrama as a simplistic opposition between a just and an unjust force, this definition seems in fact to be applicable to his own plays, particularly *L'Etat de siège*, where good and evil are opposed: La Peste's slaughter of the townspeople is unambiguously evil, while Diego's rebellion against this can only be approved. Similarly, the ideals of the Russian anarchists of *Les Justes* are admirable and the dilemma is less whether violence is justified in the attempt to create a fair society than whether it is permissible to murder children in the process. Kaliayev's refusal to do so is uncontroversial and the nihilistic Stepan, so blinded by his emotions that he dreams of destroying all of Moscow, is less a worthy opponent than a caricature. Camus's last two plays place greater emphasis on the personal dimension and some might argue that a more equal tension between the personal and the political viewpoints is established, yet elements of caricature persist. Diego and Victoria in *L'Etat de siège* are one-dimensional characters whose role is clearly to illustrate the playwright's developing philosophy of limits. But Diego's love has ethical limits, whereas Victoria appears to have none, insisting he should put their love before all heaven and earth (*TRN*, 297), and she would willingly sacrifice the entire town in exchange for his life. Marginal figures elsewhere in Camus's work, women occupy a more central role in the theatre, where they must necessarily speak. The simplistic assumption arising from this that Camus's theatrical women voice a powerful critique of masculinity is mistaken, in my view, and only sustainable in isolation from a consideration of Camus's thought as a whole. Victoria's claims illustrate that hers is far from an equally legitimate opposing viewpoint. Without ties of affection to friends, children or family, without allegiance to any social institution, this solitary woman represents private life with a vengeance. There is no social solidarity in this personal sphere and Kaliayev and Diego, each concerned with ethical considerations, must withdraw from the all-consuming love of the couple in favour of collective political action. An extreme version of other female characters, Victoria shares the contempt of Maria, or the Grand-Duchess of *Les Justes*, for men's refusal to place love before duty and honour. Although the lack of psychological depth in *Les Justes* seems an impediment, considering the play's treatment of emotional extremes (love and hatred), the portrayal of Dora is less crude in the sense that she struggles between her commitment to the cause and her love for Kaliayev. But his death resolves this conflict with her decision to rejoin him by volunteering to die throwing the next bomb. Placing her emotions before justice, she comes to resemble Stepan – as he helpfully points out. Indeed, despite some internal evidence in the play, the very lack of psychological depth makes it unlikely that the audience would arrive independently at this conclusion without Stepan's comment. Following Camus's definition of tragedy, Dora, like Victoria or Stepan and unlike Kaliayev, is driven by passion to transgress the limit (*TRN*, 1705; *SEN*, 196). But this does not make her tragic. One critic, David Bradby, who does not hesitate to apply the term 'melodrama' to all Camus's theatre, observes that tragic characters must be torn apart by their contradictions, but (like Dora) Kaliayev also resolves these in his 'limited revolt', dying not as a tragic figure but as an exemplary rebel.[9]

As in the case of Dora's transformation, internal contradictions require psychological depth rather than external 'direction'. It is difficult, however, to feel emotional involvement with some of Camus's characters, who seem little more than mouthpieces for abstract ideas. For the sake of credibility the extraordinary events of *Le Malentendu* demand a focus on character and motive, yet the audience is asked to be satisfied with a metaphysical interpretation of a situation which is, from the outset, barely acceptable in human terms. Camus's comments on Euripides show he assigned 'psychology' a pivotal role in the decline of tragedy, although this critique could be read as masking his own inability to create an individual from the inside. His approach to the theatre overlaps with everyday life when, in an echo of his 1958 preface to the plays, he says in his preface to *L'Envers et l'Endroit* that he has learned less about others than about himself because 'ma curiosité va plus à leur destin qu'à leurs réactions et que les destins se répètent beaucoup. J'ai appris du moins qu'ils existaient' (*Ess*, 10) ('I am interested more in their destiny than in their reactions, and destinies barely differ one from another. I have at least learnt that other people do exist' (*SEN*, 23)). It is tempting to think that Camus was making a virtue of necessity with his emphasis on the universal as opposed to the particular, on form over content, on the 'empty stare' rather than human complexity, seeking refuge in universal rules rather than face the challenge of the Other. Yet, this recourse does not absolve the playwright of the need to create internal coherence in his stage characters, or to endow them with recognisably human qualities. The problem here lies not in the presence or absence of a 'psychological' dimension, but in the atrophy of the Other.

In my view, Camus declines a dialogue with his audience, denying them sufficient information to participate actively in the interpretative process. This stands in sharp contrast to the tragedies of Aeschylus, where we understand the motives of characters and empathise with their plight; above all, they have personalities and histories which lend their behaviour internal coherence. The *Oresteia* is not devoid of a human dimension and, however elevated its protagonists, they invite our involvement. Within defined parameters, Aeschylus engages his audience actively in the interpretative process, encouraging independent judgement and debate rather than the requirement passively to accept.

The unpredictable external world of others seems to have been threatening to Camus, and one cannot doubt his vulnerability, expressed in his increasingly defensive reactions to criticisms of his work. Camus's tendency to compartmentalise his life and other people, reflected in the division of his work into genres (fiction, plays and essays), appears to have been necessary to his writing practice. In each area, only he has complete knowledge and the illusion, at least, of control. In choosing to write plays, he set himself, I think, the greatest challenge, not because of his proclaimed aims but for the more practical reason that this entails bringing other people to life and being able to put oneself in the place of the Other. Not that Camus was unable to create fascinating characters; that of Meursault has fuelled debate about *L'Etranger* since its publication and the dramatic monologue delivered in *La Chute* offers a complex psychological portrait. Likewise, interest in Caligula sustains the play but, as I have noted, the young playwright passionately identified with Caligula in his everyday life; equally, for Jean Grenier, Camus's former teacher, mentor, and lifelong friend, Camus likewise saw himself as the solitary and dominating Don Juan he dreamed of putting on stage.[10] Just as Rieux and Tarrou voice aspects of the author's thoughts, Cherea also expresses Camus's opinions as articulated in *Lettres à un ami allemand*. Thus, the main characters of the plays engage in the 'dialogues' of a universe where all men (if not all women) are cast in the image of their Creator.

It is perhaps not surprising that Camus defended his two least successful plays in terms of their 'resemblance' to him, an expression that points up the coincidence between his life and theatrical involvements.[11] The entire universe was a vast theatre for Camus, wrote Roger Quilliot, his editor (*TRN*, 1689), while for Grenier Camus saw the man of the theatre as a second god.[12] In 1959 Camus said that in solitude 'l'artiste règne, mais sur le vide' ('the artist reigns, but over a vacuum'), whereas in the theatre he depends on others to achieve his aims (*TRN*, 1723). Ironically, as in 'La Mort dans l'âme', where the speaker fills his world with 'formes semblables à moi' (*Ess*, 38) ('forms in my own likeness' (*SEN*, 54)), he filled his theatrical universe with either images in his own likeness, or the 'empty stare' of bodies on a stage that was not merely a means of peopling that vacuum, but of creating, directing and controlling a microcosmic universe.

Paradoxically, it is a work that escapes the self-imposed rules of Camus's theatre, namely the prose fiction, *La Chute*, that provides us with the writer's greatest dramatic monologue. There, Clamence, the self-proclaimed actor, might be speaking for Camus himself when he says that the sports stadium, or the theatre 'que j'ai aimé avec une passion sans égale, sont les seuls endroits du monde où je me sente innocent' (*TRN*, 1520) ('which I loved with an unparalleled devotion, are the only places in the world where I feel innocent' (*F*, 65)). Here, the space of innocence is that place where truth and falsity merge, or where the artifice of the Self, openly accepted as such, acquires authenticity. Although Camus certainly did not identify with Clamence, nevertheless a parallel might be drawn between the latter's world and Camus's theatrical universe:

> Je ne pouvais donc vivre . . . qu'à la condition que, sur toute la terre, tous les êtres, ou le plus grand nombre possible, fussent tournés vers moi, éternellement vacants, privés de vie indépendante, prêts à répondre à mon appel à n'importe quel moment, voués enfin à la stérilité, jusqu'au jour où je daignerais les favoriser de ma lumière. En somme, pour que je vive heureux, il fallait que les êtres que j'élisais ne vécussent point. Ils ne devaient recevoir leur vie, de loin en loin, que de mon bon plaisir. (*TRN*, 1510)

I could live . . . only on condition that all the individuals on earth, or the greatest possible number, were turned towards me, eternally vacant, deprived of independent life, ready to respond to my call at any moment, doomed in short to sterility until the day I should deign to favour them with my light. In short, for me to live happily it was essential for the individuals I chose not to live at all. They must receive their life, sporadically, only at my bidding.

(*F*, 51, translation amended)

Like Clamence's Interlocutor, the theatre audience is as integral to the performance as the actors themselves – except that the Interlocutor and audience follow no script. As Clamence discovers when his circle of admirers becomes a tribunal (*TRN*, 1515; *F*, 58), others contain the threatening capacity for judgement. However, as the above quotation suggests, the alternative is to 'reign' over an empty and sterile world. Caligula, the 'pedagogue', has already realised this. He kills his subjects in order to teach them the meaning of life – and because he has the power to do so. Yet, Camus suggests, Caligula's error lies in his denial of others: 'On ne peut tout détruire sans se détruire soi-même' (*TRN*, 1729) ('One cannot destroy everything without destroying oneself'). Few of us have such power – or inclination – but (along with the theme of judgement) this theme recurs in Camus's work. As one of those rare spaces where such temptations might be played out, perhaps the unlimited power offered by the theatre explains what drew Camus to an arena where the world, and others, might be recreated and perfected according to the artist's 'plan'. Unfortunately for Camus, perhaps, the final judgement on whether he succeeded in this aspiration lies with his audience.

NOTES

1. Raymond Gay-Crosier, *Les Envers d'un échec: étude sur le théâtre d'Albert Camus* (Paris, Minard, 1967); Ilona Coombs, *Camus, homme de théâtre* (Paris, Nizet, 1968); E. Freeman, *The Theatre of Albert Camus: A Critical Study* (London, Methuen, 1971); Virginie Lupo, *Le Théâtre de Camus: un théâtre classique?* (Villeneuve-d'Ascq, Presses Universitaires du Septentrion, 2000).

2. *Le Figaro*, 15–16 October, 1944, cited in English by John Cruickshank in *Albert Camus and the Literature of Revolt* (New York, Oxford University Press, 1960), p. 202.

3. See my 'Struggling with the Other: Gender and Race in the Youthful Writings of Camus', in James Giles (ed.), *French Existentialism: Consciousness, Ethics and Relations with Others* (Amsterdam, Rodopi, 1999), pp. 191–211. More pertinent to the present discussion is Colin Davis's treatment of 'Violence and Ethics' in this volume (see chapter 8).

4. Coombs, *Camus, homme de théâtre*, p. 80.

5. See Fernande Bartfeld, 'Le Théâtre de Camus, lieu d'une écriture contrariée', in J. Lévi-Valensi (ed.), *Albert Camus et le théâtre* (Paris, IMEC, 1992), p. 182.

6. The director Jacques Copeau (1878–1949) was an early source of inspiration for Camus, who, when setting up the Théâtre de l'Equipe, saw Copeau's influence as providing a dominant theme (*TRN*, 1713). For Copeau, the text itself was paramount, taking precedence over staging and actors. He also stressed the active participation of audiences in the performance.

7. One possible source is Oswald Spengler, *The Decline of the West*, 2 vols. (London, Allen and Unwin, 1971), who characterises chamber music as the summit of Western art (vol. 1, p. 231). Spengler's 'morphology' of history underlies much of Camus's thinking, as here.

8. For an investigation of this subject and Camus's use of secondary sources, see Paul Archambault, *Camus' Hellenic Sources* (Chapel Hill, University of North Carolina Press, 1972).

9. David Bradby, *Modern French Drama 1940–1990* (Cambridge, Cambridge University Press, 1991), p. 50.

10. Jean Grenier, *Albert Camus: Souvenirs* (Paris, Gallimard, 1968), p. 118.

11. Camus not only claimed that *L'Etat de siège* was the play that 'resembled' him the most (*Ess*, 1732), he also said this about *Le Malentendu*. See Olivier Todd, *Albert Camus, une vie* (Paris, Gallimard, 1996), p. 476.

12. Grenier, *Souvenirs*, p. 118.

6

JEANYVES GUERIN

Camus the journalist

From an early age Camus had wanted to write yet it was not by choice that he became a journalist. His tuberculosis meant that he could not be a teacher and so he had to find some other pathway. He does not appear to have considered using his experience as an actor and producer to turn professional. He was by turns editorial secretary, reporter, leader writer and editor-in-chief. Camus did not like to claim to be an 'intellectual' or a 'philosopher'. He called himself an 'artist', a 'witness', occasionally a 'professional journalist'. He once admitted that he felt that journalism was 'une des plus belles professions que je connaisse' (*Ess*, 1565) ('one of the finest professions that I can think of'). His friend Jean Daniel added that for Camus, journalism was not an exile but a kingdom, something in which he felt at home.[1] Yet it was Camus's literary successes that were to preserve the record of his journalistic achievements. If he had not written *L'Etranger*, *La Peste* and *Caligula*, then *Actuelles* would certainly not exist as a book. Who, apart from the odd historian, would ever have heard of an obscure reporter for *Alger républicain*? The leader writer for *Combat* would have been about as well known as fellow journalists on the paper such as Marcel Gimont and Georges Altschuler. *L'Express* would not have tried to sign him up.

Alger républicain

Alger républicain was where Camus cut his teeth. From 6 October 1938 to 28 October 1939, this was the name of a little newspaper which was the mouthpiece for the ideals of the Popular Front, which had come to power in France in 1936. The paper's gestation had been a long one and its launch actually coincided with the signing of the Munich Agreement. But whereas by then in France the Popular Front was in its death throes, it appears that in Algiers they remained unaware of this. Thousands of small shareholders had to be found as owners of the paper. Essentially these shareholders came from the European middle classes. Amongst them were teachers of all kinds, businessmen and government workers who were members of unions. They included socialists, democrats, republicans and secular groups. What united them was their opposition to the fascism of Hitler, Mussolini and Franco. It was a campaigning newspaper but with no declared political affiliation. From the outset it was short of money and remained so to its dying day: its circulation fell rapidly from 20,000 to 7,000 copies. Few of its writers were professionals; most were beginners but, like Camus, they soon learned the job.

Alger républicain had no consistent editorial line: its intention was to appear republican in an ecumenical way. In the autumn of 1939, the paper produced as an offshoot, an evening publication, *Le Soir républicain*. The journalist Pascal Pia, a former Surrealist and anti-conformist who was close to Malraux, liked Camus's writing and made him its editor-in-chief. In this role, Camus carried on a guerrilla war against censorship, using tactics not unlike those of the French satirical weekly *Le Canard enchaîné*, which since its foundation in 1916 had worked to combat official propaganda. In January 1940, *Le Soir républicain* was banned (*Le Canard* itself ceased to be published between 1940 and 1944). For Camus, the adventure was over. The shareholders thought it was all his fault and he had to leave Algeria, his homeland.

A total of 150 articles are attributed to Camus. Some, for *Le Soir républicain*, were written under various pseudonyms (Alius, Démos, Irénée, Marco, Jean Mersault, Vincent Capable, Zaks etc.). At the time, Camus was an actor and producer for a theatre group that was affiliated to the Communist party. *Alger républicain* served as his school of journalism. At first he was just a rewriter of news despatches, a stringer. It was 'disappointing', he wrote to his teacher, Jean Grenier in 1938, nothing but 'les chiens écrasés et du reportage' (*Corr*, 33) ('stories about dogs being run over and bits of reporting') but he liked the fact that it left him time for his writing. Camus was a reporter, at times even a great reporter, and certainly a man who worked in the field. He was a literary critic too and amongst the novels and essays reviewed in his literary column we may note Sartre's *La Nausée* (*Nausea*) and *Le Mur* (*The Wall*), Nizan's *La Conspiration* (*The Conspiracy*), Montherlant's *L'Equinoxe de septembre* (*September Equinox*) and Bernanos's *Scandale de la vérité* (*Scandal of Truth*). He only wrote about the books and authors that he liked.

Camus's work was primarily that of investigating and reporting facts. He acted as a court reporter, and used such occasions to take the lid off things. He always made the event his starting point, even if it was just some minor news item, before trying to explain its social and political implications. For example, he wrote several reports about a gas explosion in a working-class district before accusing the Mayor of Algiers of not caring about the misfortunes of his fellow citizens. 'Un maire digne de ce nom ne s'énerve ni ne se fâche. Il s'intéresse au sort de ses administrés, leur fait distinguer les vrais responsables, ne leur en veut pas de se trouver désorientés par le brusque malheur qui les frappe' (FC, 202) ('A mayor worthy of the name would not get angry or upset: he would take an interest in what happened to the people who elected him. He would show them who was really responsible and would not resent the fact that people are disturbed by the sudden misfortune that has befallen them'). At times it was as a moralist rather than as a citizen that Camus wrote editorials about what he had witnessed.

As a campaigning journalist, Camus eschewed the lyrical prose which was simultaneously the very stuff of *Noces*. Admittedly the subject did not lend itself to such treatment, not when he had to talk about the town council's budget or report on the agriculture committee. Occasionally, he would go in for mockery or polemics; he had his *bêtes noires*, such as the 'unfortunate' Mayor of Algiers, Algerian worthies and the then French President, Edouard Daladier. When the mayor came into conflict with municipal employees, Camus wrote lengthy justifications of their claims. He was quite scathing about Daladier, who had won the right to govern by decree. The sacrifices the President had called for alienated the unions and the civil servants. But did this really make him a pathfinder for fascism, as Camus asserted, or the man who dug the grave for the *Front Populaire* government? The first of a series of articles on Daladier provides facts and figures.[2] The second calls Daladier a dictator's apprentice.[3] The third, more interestingly, is a 'dialogue' in which Camus imagines what the President, who is cunning, sure of himself and paternalistic, and a humble employee might have to say to each other. The interview is broken off when, having run out of arguments, the President calls in the guards.[4] As well as Daladier, to whom historians would consider Camus had been unfair, it was professional politicians that the young journalist targeted.

Camus followed the pro-Dreyfus tradition, taking a passionate interest in a number of causes. He devoted eleven articles to the trial of Michel Hodent, an overscrupulous employee, the victim of a plot by powerful colonial interests. He then took up the case of Sheikh Okbi (a Muslim dignitary accused of having instigated the murder of a high-ranking religious official), and subsequently that of a number of locals accused of setting fire to shacks. In all three cases, Camus was attacking an administration primarily in thrall to important colonial interests. He had no hesitation about saying 'I . . .' and was discovering the power of his pen: thanks to him, both Michel Hodent and the sheikh were acquitted.

In 1958, when Camus collected together his journalistic writing on Algeria in *Actuelles III: Chroniques Algériennes (1939–1958)*, of those articles written before 1940, he kept only seven of the eleven which go to make up the series entitled *Misère de la Kabylie*. These support the view that he did not wait for the outbreak of war before taking an interest in the land of his birth. In these articles, he is not trying to write a polemical, anti-colonial political pamphlet. Neither the time, nor the place nor the supporting material lends itself to such an approach. Like André Gide when, in a different genre, he wrote *Voyage au Congo* (*Voyage to the Congo*) (1927), Camus is presenting an eyewitness report, things that he has seen and refuses to present with some kind of exotic gloss.[5] Moreover, the verb 'see' recurs constantly (*FC*, 280, 285, 286, 287, 289, etc.). Camus records: 'J'ai vu à Tizi Ouzou des enfants en loques disputer à des chiens kabyles le contenu d'une poubelle' (*FC*, 286) ('In Tizi Ouzou I saw children in rags fighting with Kabyle dogs over the contents of a rubbish bin'). The reporter confesses that he feels 'conscience-stricken' ('je me sentais une mauvaise conscience') (*FC*, 280). 'Rien ne vaut les chiffres, les faits et l'évidence des cris' (*FC*, 281) ('Nothing has greater impact than the facts and figures and the cries of suffering').

> 50% *au moins* de la population se nourrit d'herbes et de racines.　　(*FC*, 285)
>
> (At least fifty per cent of the population are living on grass and roots.)
>
> A l'école d'Azerou-Kollal, sur 110 élèves, on en compte 35 qui ne font qu'un seul repas par jour. A Maillot, on estime à 4/5e de la population le nombre des indigents.　　(*FC*, 290)
>
> (At the school in Azerou-Kollal, 35 of the 110 pupils have only one meal a day. It is estimated that four-fifths of the population of Maillot is destitute.)
>
> Tizi Ouzou a un médecin communal pour 45000 habitants.　　(*FC*, 305)
>
> (Tizi Ouzou has one local doctor for 45,000 inhabitants.)

Camus provides a wealth of statistics to demonstrate the overpopulation, the mass unemployment and the derisory wages; in short, what he sees as a slave economy (*FC*, 295). The conclusion that emerges is that 'la misère [de ce pays] est effroyable' (*FC*, 333) ('the wretchedness of this country is frightening'). An entire population is being humiliated. The fact that the road network is in a bad state, that the schools, for which the people are clamouring, and the dispensaries are so few and far between, that there is a water shortage, all this is the fault, not of the inhabitants, but of the colonial government. Kabylia has been left to rot. A few acts of charity are no substitute for a constructive social policy (*FC*, 291). In his conclusion,

Alger républicain's reporter claims that it is not an indictment that he has written. He is asking the politicians to accept their responsibilities for once. He makes a few suggestions himself for immediate measures to be taken. Camus's investigation was to have an impact far beyond the usual reader-ship of *Alger républicain*. Significantly, it immediately provoked a reassuring counter-report in the politically conservative *La Dépêche algérienne*.

It has been said that, when given responsibility for *Le Soir républicain*, Camus gave it a libertarian policy and outlook. In his view, it was not only Nazi Germany that was responsible for the war; neighbouring countries had to take a share of the responsibility because of their self-interest. In the long term, their sovereignty had to be reduced. The state of war meant that only the governments were heard, whereas the people themselves were simply dragooned into service and required to become mere pawns in the game of international politics.

At the same time as attempting to conceive international relations in a very new way, Camus opted for a strategy of harassment and provocation. The state of war had effectively reintroduced censorship. Now it was less easy than ever to 'maintenir une opinion libre' (*FC*, 718) ('uphold freedom of thought'), to 'servir la vérité' (*FC*, 717) ('serve the cause of truth'), to preserve 'les droits de la froide raison' (*FC*, 50) ('the rights of the cold light of reason'): now 'le bourrage de crâne' (*FC*, 717) ('brainwashing') was the order of the day. Camus wrote under a variety of pseudonyms, reprinting numerous extracts from newspapers, historical documents and both clas-sics and modern texts (for example the article 'War' from the *Dictionnaire philosophique*, which was partly censored) in a column headed: 'A wartime view of . . .' The aim was to make readers think, to challenge, to point out the discourse and the truth about war. The inevitable happened: the general government suspended the publication of the newspaper.

In a letter to his mentor Jean Grenier, Camus confessed to what the *Soir républicain* shareholders had accused him of, namely of having carried on a personal campaign: 'J'en ai donc fait un journal à l'usage de ce que je croyais vrai. C'est à dire que j'y ai défendu la liberté de penser contre la censure et la guerre sans haine' (*Corr*, 38) ('So I did turn it into the voice of what I believed to be the truth. That is, I used it to defend freedom of thought against censorship and war without hatred'). *Le Soir républicain* found it difficult to reconcile the anti-fascism which was its *raison d'être* and the libertarian pacifism of its young editor-in-chief. Basically, Camus had tried to fight what he knew all along was a losing battle in support of individual and collective freedoms.[6] He was to take up arms in this battle again later but in quite different circumstances. In the meantime he had lost his job and had to move to France, where Pascal Pia recruited him as *'secdac'*, editorial secretary, on *Paris-Soir*. While he published nothing at all in this paper, he found out what a major popular newspaper was like.

Combat

The Liberation of 1944 saw the birth of numerous periodicals, with many writers turning themselves into journalists. François Mauriac considered journalism to be a perfect form of *littérature engagée*, or socially committed literature, and Camus would certainly have agreed. He had joined the active resistance in 1943 and, at the request of Pascal Pia, became editor-in-chief of the clandestine newspaper *Combat*. When liberation happened, he naturally remained in post. His role was simultaneously to run the editorial team, to engage in debate and to bring in new ideas. He also fulfilled the role of principal editorial writer. There was, however, one exception to this: coincidentally in the weeks prior to the bloody quelling of the Algerian uprising in Sétif, he dispatched himself as a reporter to Algeria and brought back a series of eight articles. Six were to be reprinted in *Chroniques algériennes*.

Initially, *Combat* had a circulation of 200,000. With its youthful, pluralist team, the paper saw itself as the voice of resistance. It was also the intellectual paper of the period 1944–7 or, to quote respectively Georges Hénein and Raymond Aron, 'the newspaper for Saint-Germain-des-Prés' and 'the most highly regarded paper in the capital's literary and political milieux'.[7] Its readership was young, made up of teachers, students and trade unionists.

The collaborationist (i.e. pro-Nazi) press had left supporters of the Resistance with feelings of shame and distaste. The press of the 1930s in particular had been notoriously corrupt. From the end of August 1944, De Gaulle was putting into effect laws governing the press. At the same time, without actually mentioning these laws, Camus was trying to set a code of practice for a reformed press. For him, because the mission of the press was to serve the public, the press had to be freed from financial ties (*Ess*, 264). 'Vigilance' and 'responsibility' must be its watchwords. An 'unflinching objectivity' must win out over empty 'rhetoric' (*Ess*, 265).

In a second article, Camus develops the idea of 'critical journalism'. He writes: 'On veut informer vite au lieu d'informer bien. La vérité n'y gagne pas' (*Ess*, 265) ('There are some who want to inform quickly rather than informing properly. It is the truth that suffers'). It is better to be the second with accurate information than the first with information that turns out to be wrong. 'On cherche à plaire plutôt qu'à éclairer' ('People try to please rather than to enlighten'), sacrificing truth in the interests of sentimentality or scandal. Camus writes that 'le goût de la vérité n'empêche pas la prise de parti' (*Ess*, 266) ('a taste for truth does not preclude taking a stance'). In order not to be partisan, 'le commentaire politique et moral de l'actualité' ('political and moral commentary on current events') needs 'distance', 'scruples'; 'une idée de la relativité' ('an understanding of moral relativity') (*ibid.*). In his only news report published in *Combat*, 'Crise en Algérie' ('Crisis in Algeria'), he put these principles into effect and studiously avoided echoing the official line, unlike Sartre in the Soviet Union and Cuba.[8]

Making the distinction between fact and opinion was, for Camus, an absolute rule. In a democracy, 'le souci d'objectivité' ('a concern for objectivity') prevents any 'parti pris' or 'solidarité systématique' ('bias' or 'systematic support') and likewise obviously, its opposite, systematic opposition. The important thing is, as Camus presents it, fidelity to one's own principles and to the promises one has made to oneself.[9] In order to speak the truth you have to speak clearly and fairly. You can protest without giving offence and rebuke without resorting to slander.

There was no question at that period of speaking in hackneyed phrases. Writing undercover had taught authors and writers both the 'weight' and the 'cost' that words could have (*Ess*, 1489). 'A des temps nouveaux, il faut, sinon des mots nouveaux, du moins des dispositions nouvelles de mots' (*Ess*, 267) ('New times need, if not new words, at least using words in new ways'), 'Un langage clair' (*Ess*, 1524) ('clear language'), 'un langage respectable' (*Ess*, 264) ('language worthy of respect'), 'des termes clairs et irréprochables' (*Ess*, 1549) ('clear and irreproachable terminology'). This amounts to a leitmotif which is typical of Camus. Elsewhere he refers to '[l']effort d'exactitude' ('the struggle to be precise') and 'la recherche de nuances' (*Ess*, 1489) ('the search for nuance').

The critical function is opposed to the ideological function. Jean Grenier had warned Camus against 'les doctrines absolues et infaillibles' (*Ess*, 282) ('doctrines that were absolutist and claimed to be infallible'). A writer of editorials raises questions; he does not bombard his readers with answers. He does not provide the light of truth; he just helps people to see clearly. In their reviews of the press, *Le Monde*, *Le Figaro* and *Franc-tireur* frequently quote his editorials but not always in friendly terms. His claims to the moral high ground provoke envy and irritation. Camus found that he had to spell out the idea that he did not consider that he had 'le privilège de la clairvoyance et la supériorité de ceux qui ne se trompent jamais' ('the privilege of being clairvoyant or the advantage of never making any mistakes') but was simply trying to 'collaborer à une œuvre commune . . . par l'exercice périodique de quelques règles de conscience' ('collaborate in a shared project . . . by applying, from time to time, a few modest rules dictated by conscience').[10]

Rejecting sensationalism, Camus urges journalists to appeal to the intelligence of their readers and not to their 'sentimentality'.

The articles on journalistic ethics written in the summer of 1944 had a great impact and seemed utopian. Nevertheless, what strikes one on rereading them is the fact that they are so very general. It is easy to see that the appeal to the spirit of criticism and to 'intellectual honesty', scrupulousness and vigilance was the better received because it followed on from four long years in which the press had been subject to orders. Camus laid down a few principles and requirements. By not being afraid to use high-sounding phrases, he was, basically, stating that politics should be bound by ethics.

Whether signed Camus, Albert Ollivier or simply anonymous, the *Combat* editorials, at least initially, were the result of collective discussion. From 1945 onwards, the editorials follow and sometimes contradict each other. Where the editorial team of *Combat* had been of one mind in 1944, it subsequently became pluralist. Pascal Pia allowed Camus to express one opinion and, the next day, Albert Ollivier or Raymond Aron to argue the opposite. Part of the editorial team, including Camus, Marcel Gimont and Georges Altschuler, continued to express socialist ideas, whilst it is obvious that another, including Pia, Ollivier and Aron, was looking more and more towards De Gaulle. Whilst rival dailies were churning out reassuring certainties, *Combat*'s wavering unsettled its readers.

In 1950, Camus brought together a carefully chosen selection of his editorials in a book which he called *Actuelles I*. 'Ce volume', he wrote, 'résume l'expérience d'un écrivain mêlé pendant quatre ans à la vie politique de son pays . . . Les pages qui suivent disent simplement que, si la lutte est difficile, les raisons de lutter, elles du moins, restent claires' (*Ess*, 251–2) ('This volume sums up the experiences of a writer who, for four years, got involved in the political life of his country . . . The pages which follow are simply meant to say that, whilst the struggle may be a difficult one, at least the reasons for struggling remain clear'). At the time when he was writing *L'Homme révolté*, he opted to reproduce those articles which were closest to being essays or dissertations and excluded the greater number which were reactions to current events and which he considered to be ephemera.

Of Camus's articles for *Combat*, posterity has retained his debate with Mauriac. Camus argues for the post-Occupation purge to be directed at the ruling class which had betrayed or failed the country; such would be the price of its renewal. Mauriac, thought to be inclined towards clemency, was afraid there might be blunders, insisting that the purge should be strictly circumscribed and that the rule of law should prevail. The disagreement of these two leading lights from radically different social and cultural backgrounds was a political one. The course of events (and General

De Gaulle) went Mauriac's way, and Camus acknowledged his elder's victory.

As an editorialist at *Combat*, Camus successfully influenced events: he helped prevent a Communist Party takeover of the national Resistance movement; on 17 May 1945, he protested successfully against delays in the repatriation of deportees from Dachau (*Ess*, 303–5), reporting 'avec joie et satisfaction' ('with joy and satisfaction') two days later that American forces had supplied the means necessary to secure this. Elsewhere, however, his influence was much less. He devoted several editorials to Franco's Spain, the great political cause of his generation.[11] Yet Franco was to remain in power for another thirty years. The eight articles published under the heading *Ni victimes ni bourreaux* (*Ess*, 329–52) in November 1946 merit particular attention. The collection is a reflection on revolt, revolution and violence (offering an alternative to Merleau-Ponty's exploration of 'progressive violence' in *Humanisme et terreur* (*Humanism and Terror*) of 1947), an appeal to take Marxism out of French socialism, a theoretical consideration of the project for reform and a plea for a new international order.[12] It includes an expression which was to become famous but whose authorship is often erroneously ascribed to Raymond Aron: 'la fin des idéologies' ('the end of ideologies'). Any 'absolute utopias' are anachronistic, useless and dangerous in a rapidly changing world (*Ess*, 338). To such ideas Camus opposes a 'pensée politique modeste, c'est-à-dire délivrée de tout messianisme, et débarrassée de la nostalgie du paradis terrestre' (*Ess*, 335) ('a modest political philosophy, that is, one free of any messianic ideas or any hankering after a heaven on earth'). *Ni victimes ni bourreaux* made his break with the radical idealist tendency official. In many ways it is a prophetic text which raises the major questions of the twenty-first century.[13]

Pia's *Combat* had a lifespan of less than three years. Camus had played an intermittent role. In June 1947 he withdrew in order to give priority to literature: *La Peste* appeared at this time to widespread acclaim. Two plays, *L'Etat de siège* and *Les Justes*, were to follow and he was also working on *L'Homme révolté*. Thus he was relying on fiction and essay writing to make his views known. Whereas Camus had stopped commenting on current affairs, Sartre had a permanent column in *Les Temps modernes* and Raymond Aron and François Mauriac each had theirs in *Le Figaro*.

L'Express

In 1955 Camus joined the staff of the then weekly and later daily *L'Express* where his column alternated with that of his old adversary, Mauriac. He was given a free hand and wrote on such subjects as the condition of the working class, anti-Arab racism and Mozart's bicentenary. For the only time in his journalistic career, he endorsed a political party, supporting Pierre Mendès France's non-Communist left-wing Front républicain in the elections of January 1956.[14] A significant proportion of his thirty-five columns relate to the Algerian War, which obsessed and tormented Camus. He felt that, in France, the press – a term he used pejoratively – was doing its job badly, that it was becoming a channel for prejudice. He considered that his close personal knowledge of Algeria meant that he had a duty to act as a historian. His intention was to educate his metropolitan French readers by patiently explaining little-known truths: first, the social and political frustration of the Arab masses, who had had quite enough of promises that were never kept; then the bitterness of the French Algerians (whom he never refers to as *pieds-noirs*) who were always assumed to be wealthy colonialists, whereas the vast majority of them were ordinary wage-earners or small businessmen. He also pointed out the political responsibilities of the metropolitan deputies and governments who, by giving way to the powerful colonialists' representatives, had reduced the Arab elite to despair.

As a columnist and chronicler of the events, he wanted to believe that it was not too late and that the worst outcome could be avoided (CAC6, 41). This is why, once he arrived at his diagnosis, he suggested approaches and put forward proposals: he was counting on the representatives of the two communities in Algeria talking to each other (CAC6, 87). In a second series of articles, he revealed his plan for a civil truce aimed at avoiding the shedding of innocent blood and preventing extremism. Yet when Camus went to Algeria in January 1956, his courageous but utopian initiative failed. The government had done nothing to support it. In February 1956, isolated and aware of his inability to influence events, he was to leave *L'Express*.

Several of Camus's *L'Express* columns continued the approach that he had taken in his *Combat* editorials, as if to show that their author had not changed. His column of 11 November 1955, for example, discusses the atomic bomb and the balance of terror.[15] It clearly alludes to the celebrated editorial which had appeared on the day following the Hiroshima bomb in August 1945 but also to the idea of an 'end to ideologies'. To pay homage to Gandhi, who is presented as the anti-Lenin, is once more to affirm nonviolence. The three columns concerned with Franco's Spain are further proof of Camus's faithfulness to his own ideas.

The three periods of journalistic activity that I have briefly presented here are quite varied. The young former Communist working in Algiers in the late 1930s plays his part in a militant enterprise – taking up causes, occasionally engaging in polemic – and clearly enjoys doing so, while also discovering how complex things can be. At *Combat*, the Resistance member holds a strategic position: he has power and influence in public life. And finally, at *L'Express*, the celebrated author lends the weight of his prestige to a newspaper where he is basically just an extra.

Camus's first wish was to be a writer, an artist. For him, journalism was initially a way of earning a living. He acquired a taste for it but did not accord it any priority. The editor of *Alger républicain* continued to run the Théâtre de l'Equipe and to work on *Caligula*. It was because he considered that *Combat* left him too little time to write *La Peste* that he began to take his distance from the newspaper in September 1945. And when he came to leave *L'Express*, it was in order to finish *La Chute*.

As for Camus's novels, they present a critical image of the press. Clamence, in *La Chute*, considers that reading 'the papers' should be seen as being on the same level as fornication. In *L'Etranger*, Meursault too reads 'the papers' and fornicates. Before his trial, a reporter cynically tells Meursault: 'Vous savez, nous avons monté un peu votre affaire. L'été, c'est la saison creuse pour les journaux. Et il n'y avait que votre histoire et celle du parricide qui vaillent quelque chose' (*TRN*, 1185) ('You know, we've blown your case up a bit. The summer's the silly season for newspapers and there was only your story and the one about the bloke who killed his father that were any good at all'). The journalists seem frivolous. Only one appears to pay any real attention. 'Et j'ai eu l'impression bizarre d'être regardé par moi-même' (*TRN*, 1186) ('I had the peculiar impression that I was being watched by myself'), the first-person narrator says. It is clear that the artist has portrayed himself in the corner of the picture.

In *La Peste*, there is a highly critical, not to say sardonic view of the press. 'The papers' (and the expression is meant to be derogatory in this novel) change from frivolous exploitation of events to embarrassed concealment of them. 'La presse, si bavarde dans l'affaire des rats, ne parlait plus de rien' (*TRN*, 1245) ('The press, which had had so much to say about the affair of the rats, now had nothing to say about anything'). The epidemic affecting the population is referred to allusively. The papers (which significantly neither Tarrou nor Rieux reads) prevaricate, refuse to name the plague and trot out the communiqués issued by the *préfecture*. The narrator of *La Peste* intends his role to be to 'prendre le ton du témoin objectif' (*TRN*, 1468) ('to adopt the tone of an objective eyewitness'). His 'task' is: 'dire "ceci est arrivé" lorsqu'il sait que ceci est, en effet, arrivé' (*TRN*, 1221) ('to say: "this is what happened" when he knows that this is indeed what happened').

In the first two parts of *La Peste*, the narrator often refers to Rambert as 'the journalist'. He has arrived from the metropolis to look into the way of life imposed on the Arabs. Rieux immediately asks him whether he is prepared to 'tell the truth' and to give an eyewitness report without holding anything back. At first he tries to think of ways to get away from a town where he feels himself to be an outsider but then he allows himself to get involved in the struggle against the disaster. 'Maintenant que j'ai vu ce que j'ai vu, je sais que je suis d'ici, que je le veuille ou non. Cette histoire nous concerne tous' (*TRN*, 1389) ('Now that I have seen what I have seen, I know that, like it or not, I do belong here. This is a matter which concerns all of us'). Camus has given Rambert several of his own personality traits: his love of football and his sense of happiness, for example.

At *Alger républicain*, Camus had been a reporter and a literary critic. At *Combat*, where he had had some power, he had insisted, 'pour éviter le mélange des genres' (*Ess*, 1926) ('so as not to confuse different genres'), on not appearing as an author. He left the paper in order to write *La Peste*. He did not even publish an extract of his novel in it, whereas Pascal Pia had obtained long extracts of *La Lutte contre l'ange* (*The Struggle with the Angel*) from Malraux. Camus's commentary on *Le Malentendu* appeared in *Le Figaro*. He played no part in any of the literary debates of the period. One even has the feeling that the arts and letters page was looked after by Pascal Pia, who had been writing in the *Nouvelle Revue Française* as far back as the 1920s and who had already published one work in this field. The paper had an impressive line-up: it had recruited the prominent critics Maurice Nadeau and Jacques Lemarchand. Although, in the euphoric atmosphere of the first few weeks, Camus had obtained reportages from Jean-Paul Sartre and Simone de Beauvoir, it was subsequently Pia who succeeded in persuading leading writers such as the novelists André Gide and Georges Bernanos, the leader of the Surrealist movement André Breton, the left-wing Catholic philosopher Emmanuel Mounier and others to make occasional contributions to *Combat*. Camus's influence on the literary pages was almost non-existent.

It has often been said that politics in France is very literary. At *Combat*, Camus tried to be very professional. His editorials are exercises in reflection, not in rhetoric. They are not adorned with biblical or classical quotations like those of Mauriac, which were written at the same period. Malraux and Bernanos, the writers whom Camus admires, are referred to indirectly. Journalistic writing and the writing of novels are two areas that Camus intended to keep separate. This does not mean that the writer completely forgets that he is an author. For example, he was careful about the endings of his articles. The final word of his *Combat* editorials is often something high-flown: justice, injustice, reason, truth. It has also long been noted that there are strong intertextual links, a process of recycling of formulæ and images between, for example, *Ni victimes ni bourreaux* and Tarrou's autobiographical revelations. Similarly, the editorial of 22 December 1944, dealing with the enforced separation of loved ones, contains a theme also to be highlighted in *La Peste*.[16]

Camus remained nostalgic about *Combat*. He wrote (1 September 1944) that the journalist is a historian of the day-to-day. Newspaper reporting had been a school of writing for the future author. When putting together small news items, he had refined his visual sense. By the end of the 1930s, he had learned how to depict characters, to reconstruct a situation, as may be seen from the eyewitness material recorded in the first volume of his *Carnets*.

In *L'Etranger* and *La Peste*, journalists are chatterboxes. There is nothing to prove it but neither can we exclude the possibility that the garrulous Clamence in *La Chute* might have been a journalist. Whether he is attacking journalists or politicians, we have seen that Camus generally uses the word 'rhetoric' in a pejorative sense. It refers to a discourse that is extravagant, insincere and inauthentic. His own is concise but elegant. With its strictly fixed form, the editorial genre fits Camus's classic talent. As he wrote in his *Carnets* in October 1938: 'La véritable œuvre d'art est celle qui dit moins' (*CI*, 127) ('The true work of art is the one that says less'). All an editorial needs, he says, is 'une idée, deux exemples, trois feuillets' ('one idea, two examples, three pages') and a news report: 'des faits, de la couleur, des rapprochements' ('facts, colour and the ability to make connections').[17]

NOTES

This is an abridged version of the author's original text in French and has been translated by Mike Routledge.

1. Jean Daniel, 'Le Combat pour *Combat*', *Camus* (Paris, Hachette, coll. Génies et réalités, 1969), p. 78.
2. 'Chez les travailleurs. La spéculation contre les lois sociales', *Alger républicain*, 12 October 1938, 231–2.
3. 'Les Travailleurs contre les décrets-lois', *Alger républicain*, 27 November 1938, 233.
4. 'Dialogue entre un président du Conseil et un employé à 1200 francs par mois', *Alger républicain*, 3 December 1938, 234–7.
5. The survey is accompanied and supported by photographs.
6. Philippe Vanney, 'Albert Camus devant la guerre', *Bulletin d'études françaises* (University of Tokyo) 19 (1988), 19–55 and 21 (1990), 1–30.
7. Georges Hénein, 'Lettre à Henri Calet, 16 avril 1948', *Grandes Largeurs* 2 (autumn/winter 1981), 66; Raymond Aron, *Mémoires* (Paris, Julliard, 1985), p. 287.
8. *Combat*, 13 to 23 May 1945.
9. 'Il paraît que *Combat* a changé d'orientation', *Combat*, 9 February 1945.
10. 'Autocritique', *CC*, 345.

11. 'Nos frères d'Espagne', *Combat*, 7 September 1944, 174–6; 'A cette même place . . .', *Combat*, 5 October 1944, 231–5; 'L'Espagne s'éloigne', *Combat*, 7–8 January 1945, 435–8. See also 'Pourquoi l'Espagne?', *CC*, 345. This article is a reply to Gabriel Marcel, who had reproached Camus for situating *L'Etat de siège* in Spain rather than in a Communist country.

12. For a discussion of 'progressive violence', see chapter 7.

13. Philippe Vanney, 'A propos d'une lecture: *Ni victimes ni bourreaux* d'Albert Camus ou la problématique révolutionnaire dans les relations internationales', *Bulletin d'études françaises* (University of Tokyo) 17 (1986), 36–67. See also Maurice Weyembergh, 'Ni victimes ni bourreaux: continuité ou rupture?', in Jeanyves Guérin (ed.), *Camus et le premier 'Combat'* (La Garenne-Colombes, Editions européennes Erasme, 1990), pp. 109–24, and in the same volume Joel Roman, 'Histoire et utopie dans *Ni victimes ni bourreaux*', pp. 125–34.

14. 'Explication de vote', *L'Express*, 30 December 1955.

15. 'Le Rideau de feu', *L'Express*, 11 November 1955, 93–7.

16. 'La France a vécu beaucoup de tragédies', *CC*, 402–5.

17. Daniel, 'Le Combat pour *Combat*', p. 91.

7

MARTIN CROWLEY

Camus and social justice

Across the range of Camus's writings, two terms repeatedly ring out as the expression of his fundamental concerns: 'man' and 'justice'. The two are profoundly linked: Camus's resolute belief in the importance of social justice, and his contributions to the global political debates of his time – including those concerning the Second World War, colonialism, the atom bomb and the Cold War – are inseparable from his affirmation of the values he attaches to the figure of the human. It is impossible to find an example of a key Camusian intervention in the cause of social justice which does not argue its case via reference to the human as its core locus of value. This chapter tries to address Camus's concern for social justice by exploring some of its moral and conceptual frameworks. I do not propose to detail Camus's various interventions as such, as these are discussed elsewhere in this volume. Rather, with reference to some of these key moments, I will attempt to draw out something of the values by which Camus is driven. And I will be using the figure of the human as the common thread by which these values are held together (or, at times, by which they are held in tension). Sometimes, this figure expresses a virile, heroic resolve; sometimes, it can be pathetically vulnerable. But for Camus, 'man' will never quite be effaced; and the point of this persistence is the call for justice it unceasingly articulates. My aim here will be to provide some sense of this irreducible value of resistance.

(A note on terminology: as is typical of thinkers of his time, Camus habitually uses 'l'homme' ('man') to refer to humanity in general, despite its effacement of the female part of humanity, an effacement which has since then quite rightly been subjected to feminist critique. (Indeed, despite this critique, 'l'homme' is still much more widely used in French thought than 'man' is in English.) This masculinist bias does more than place him in his context, however: it is also a part of his particular version of humanism, in which virility and fraternity are often key values. When delineating Camus's thought, therefore, I will use his term, 'man'; when discussing matters more generally, I will revert to less exclusive terms such as 'humanity' and 'the human'.)

Demanding justice

Camus's concern for social justice may broadly be divided into two categories. First, there is the kind of concern most readily identified with the idea of social justice as such, in which what is at stake is the equitable organisation of social structures, especially as these relate to the distribution of wealth. Secondly, Camus's commitment to the idea of justice is also articulated through his engagement with world historical events. Accordingly, I will here discuss first, the straightforward egalitarian demand for social justice in the conventional sense, as expressed in Camus's early journalism on colonial Algeria and at the time of the Liberation of France towards the end of the Second World War; and secondly, the debates concerning the notion of justice in the context of national and global politics that continue from the Liberation via *Les Justes* to *L'Homme révolté*. In each of these instances, Camus is also motivated by his sense of the fundamental injustice of the human condition (put simply: that we suffer and die in the midst of a meaningless universe). I will indicate the influence of this dimension briefly where appropriate, and will address the problems it introduces into Camus's position towards the end of my discussion of his engagement with the demands of justice on a world historical scale.

Camus's concern for social justice in the strict sense receives its most dramatic early expression in the articles on poverty in Kabylia published in *Alger républicain* from 5 to 15 June 1939, many of which Camus chose to group together in *Actuelles III* under the title *Misère de la Kabylie* (*Ess*, 903–38). The title of the first of these, 'Le Dénuement' ('Destitution'), gives a clear sense of the thrust of Camus's reports: his aim is to force recognition of the bare human suffering in question, in order then more urgently to pose the question of the political action which ought responsibly to be taken. He proceeds by a combination of factual, often statistical exposition, intense, powerfully pathetic description and conclusions expressed in a tone of controlled anger. The moral centre of this method is located in its evocation of specific instances of terrible impoverishment, such as the children who fight with local dogs over the contents of dustbins, who arrive at school naked and infested with lice, or who pass out from hunger while there (*Ess*, 907–8). Anticipating that of Philippe Othon in *La Peste*, the scandalous suffering of these children is a brute fact whose immediate reality demands restitution, here of the poverty it declares (*Ess*, 909). Camus's articles accordingly seek to go beyond the humanitarian response they also evoke. While he accepts the possible usefulness of charity in such a situation, he is bitterly critical of what he has seen of the effects of charitable intervention in Kabylia. When the starving have back taxes docked from their wages, he writes, charitable works 'constituent une exploitation intolérable du malheur' (*Ess*, 913) ('constitute an intolerable exploitation of misfortune'). Thus: 'Je ne crois pas que la charité soit un sentiment inutile. Mais je crois qu'en certains cas ses résultats le sont et qu'alors il faut lui préférer une politique sociale constructive' (*Ess*, 912) ('I do not believe that charity is a useless sentiment. But I believe that in some cases, its results are, and that in such cases we must prefer constructive social policy'). Camus's intervention constitutes a demand for social justice as such, as he denounces the exploitative economic structure which underpins the immediate crisis. Those in charge of the colonial administration preside over a 'régime d'esclavage' (*Ess*, 915) ('regime of slavery'), in which ten to twelve hours' work a day earns six to ten francs, the low wages justified by various arguments in bad faith. Since 'l'exploitation seule est la cause des bas salaires' (*Ess*, 917) ('exploitation alone is the cause of low wages'), the only solution is not charitable, but rather economic: 'Il n'y a pas d'issue à cette situation. Ce n'est pas en distribuant du grain qu'on sauvera la Kabylie de la faim, mais en résorbant le chômage et en contrôlant les salaires. Cela, on peut et on doit le faire dès demain' (*Ess*, 918) ('There is no way out of this situation. Kabylia will not be saved from famine by distributing grain, but by cutting unemployment and regulating wages. This can and must be done right away'). Destitution is a result of low wages; wages are low because unemployment produces competition in a free labour market; the answer is to increase the numbers employed by the state in major building works, and to extend professional training, allowing workers a reasonable level of income. More broadly, it will also be necessary to manage emigration throughout Kabylia, Algeria and the south of France, to regulate wages properly, and to increase the value of Kabylia's agricultural production by increasing its quantity and quality and stabilising its market price (*Ess*, 929–33). Anticipating by half a century contemporary debates concerning economic relations between the so-called First and Third Worlds, Camus insists that justice demands not intermittent charity, but structural economic reform. This position is reaffirmed in the series of articles from *Combat* in 1945 collected as *Crise en Algérie* (*Ess*, 939–59), and its moral force echoes in an important denunciation of racism and torture from 1947 (*Ess*, 321–3); but it encounters its limit in the mid 1950s, when Camus's perhaps understandable refusal to consider his own class, working-class French Algerians, as structurally complicit in the injustices of colonialism, provides a powerful factor in the historical failure of his preferred solution to the Algerian crisis.[1]

Camus presents his demands in *Misère de la Kabylie* as driven by the twin principles of good economic sense and human justice, the latter occasionally rhetorically ceding ground to the former in a subtle assertion of their combined force: 'Ce n'est pas seulement l'humanité qui est foulée aux pieds par les salaires à six francs, mais aussi la logique. Et par les bas prix des productions agricoles kabyles, on ne viole pas seulement la justice, mais aussi le bon sens' (*Ess*, 929) ('It is not only humanity which is trampled on by wages of six francs a day, but also logic. And the low price of Kabylia's agricultural production violates not only justice, but also common sense'). Are his reports somehow unpatriotic, asks Camus? (This is 1939, after all.) Fine; but what is patriotism without justice?

> Il paraît que c'est, aujourd'hui, faire acte de mauvais Français que de révéler la misère d'un pays français. Je dois dire qu'il est difficile aujourd'hui de savoir comment être un bon Français ... Mais, du moins, on peut savoir ce que c'est qu'un homme juste. Et mon préjugé, c'est que la France ne saurait être mieux représentée et défendue que par des actes de justice.　　　　(*Ess*, 936)

> (Apparently, to reveal the poverty of a part of France is, today, to be a bad Frenchman. I have to say that it is difficult, today, to know how to be a good Frenchman ... But it is at least possible to know what constitutes a just man. And I persist in thinking that France can be no better represented and defended than by acts of justice.)

And if we now move forward five years to the demands for social justice expressed in some of Camus's editorials for *Combat* around the Liberation, we discover that this combination of a language of justice and humanity with a call for meaningful economic change has survived the war years intact.

On 1 October 1944, Camus spells out his vision of social justice: an economy organised on collectivist principles, allied to a guarantee of political freedoms. 'Nous appellerons donc justice un état social où chaque individu reçoit toutes ses chances au départ, et où la majorité d'un pays n'est pas maintenue dans une condition indigne par une minorité de privilégiés' (*Ess*, 1527) ('We shall therefore call justice a social state in which each individual starts with equal opportunity, and in which the country's majority cannot be held in abject conditions by a privileged few') (*BHR*, 57). What is needed, he writes in February 1945, is the creation of a true popular democracy, with a collectivist economy, in the context of 'une fédération économique mondiale, où les matières premières, les débouchés commerciaux et la monnaie seront internationalisés' (*Ess*, 1551) ('a world economic federation, in which raw materials, commercial markets and currency will be placed on an international basis' (*BHR*, 106, modified)). And in May 1945, Camus applauds De Gaulle's plan to bring credit, along with the production of coal and electricity, under national control (*Ess*, 1556). The previous month, however, Camus had been severely critical of De Gaulle's failure in his speech of 2 April to celebrate, alongside such national talismans as Joan of Arc and Henri IV, the nation's tradition of insurrection (*Ess*, 1555). At this time, Camus sees his drive for an authentic popular democracy as a revolutionary demand, as the true project of the working class (*Ess*, 1545), and as being, in the title of a piece published in *Résistance ouvrière* in December 1944, 'Au service de l'homme' (*Ess*, 1544) ('In the service of man'), in which a properly moral politics will answer 'ce désir simple et ardent, ressenti par la majorité laborieuse du pays, de voir l'homme remis à sa place' (*Ess*, 1545) ('this simple, burning desire, felt by the country's working-class majority, to see man restored to his rightful place'). The aim cannot be human happiness, wrote Camus in October of that year: the misery of the human condition would make that a vain aspiration. 'Il s'agit seulement de ne pas ajouter aux misères profondes de notre condition une injustice qui soit purement humaine' (*Ess*, 1528) ('It is simply a matter of not adding human injustice to all the other profound miseries of our condition' (*BHR*, 58)). The metaphysical appeal here serves to motivate the economic argument: here, at least, we can minimise the unhappiness that is our lot. And it is, as ever in Camus, the metaphysical invocation of 'man' that gives the demand for social justice, expressed in proposals for economic redistribution, its moral validity.

Justified violence

For the broadly progressive reader, all of this is doubtless easy enough to accept. But Camus's preoccupations at this time include another, more difficult topic, which connects his thought to the global politics of his time, and which will dominate the public presence of this thought for the next decade. This topic is the problematic link between justice and violence. At the time of the Liberation, this is famously expressed in the polemic between Camus and François Mauriac over the justifiability of execution as part of the *épuration* (the process whereby France sought to purge itself of its collaborationist links with Nazism): within this debate, Camus rejects Mauriac's invocation of forgiveness, and argues in favour of execution as an instrument of justice. France has within it, 'comme un corps étranger' ('like a foreign body'), a minority of traitors. 'C'est leur existence même qui pose donc le problème de la justice puisqu'ils forment une part vivante de ce pays et que la question est de les détruire' (*Ess*, 1536) ('Their very existence poses the problem of justice, for they constitute a living part of this country, and we must decide whether we will destroy them' (*BHR*, 72)). In the name of 'le goût de l'homme et l'espoir de sa grandeur' ('a belief in man and the hope of achieving his greatness'), 'nous avons choisi d'assumer la justice humaine avec ses terribles imperfections, soucieux seulement de les corriger par une honnêteté désespérément maintenue' (*Ess*, 1536) ('we choose human justice with all its terrible imperfections; hoping only to make up for these by holding desperately to our honesty' (*BHR*, 72, modified)). Arguing for 'une justice prompte et limitée' ('justice . . . applied swiftly and for a limited time'), Camus claims that his language is that of 'une génération d'hommes élevés dans le spectacle de l'injustice, étrangère à Dieu, amoureuse de l'homme et résolue à le servir contre un destin si souvent déraisonnable' (*Ess*, 1537) ('a generation of men brought up with the spectacle of injustice, men who are strangers to God but lovers of humanity, men who are resolved to serve humanity despite a destiny that is so often meaningless' (*BHR*, 72)). Being 'in the service of man' means not just furthering the cause of economic justice: it also means being prepared to punish the injustice of those who have betrayed him. There is an implied continuity between the *épuration* and the final struggles of the Resistance: in both cases, violence is not desired, but is the necessary means to a just end. A couple of months earlier, on 24 August 1944, amidst the Liberation of Paris, Camus wrote that 'Le temps témoignera que les hommes de France ne voulaient pas tuer, et qu'ils sont entrés les mains pures dans une guerre qu'ils n'avaient pas choisie' ('Time will bear witness to the fact that the men of France did not want to kill and that their hands were clean when they entered a war they had not chosen'); 'Une fois de plus', he concluded, 'la justice doit s'acheter avec le sang des hommes' (*Ess*, 255) ('Once more justice must be bought with the blood of men') (*RRD*, 27). And the lesson of this is indeed that force must be embraced when necessary, and hence that forgiveness will have to give way to just retribution: 'Qui oserait parler ici de pardon? Puisque l'esprit a enfin compris qu'il ne pouvait vaincre l'épée que par l'épée . . . Ce n'est pas la haine qui parlera demain, mais la justice elle-même, fondée sur la mémoire' (*Ess*, 259) ('Who would dare speak here of forgiveness? Since the spirit finally understood that a sword is needed to conquer a sword . . . It is not hatred that will speak tomorrow, but justice itself, based firmly on memory' (*BHR*, 43)).

Three years later, Camus would come to the conclusion that he had been on the wrong side in this polemic (see *Ess*, 371–2). What is of interest here, however, is the way in which his rhetoric of 'man' and of 'justice' can serve ends which to say the least might be considered in tension. For throughout the articles written around the time of the Liberation, we can see Camus starting to wrestle with the question that would preoccupy him over the coming years, and which constituted the principal frame through which he would engage with the global politics of this period: the question of justified violence. Even as he adopts a moral economy of regrettable means and justified ends in relation to the Resistance struggle and the *épuration*, he attempts to deny this same moral economy legitimacy when it is deployed in the name of a communist *realpolitik*. Although he wants nothing to do with those who peddle anti-communism, and so aligns himself with the communists against their enemies, Camus nonetheless insists that 'nous ne sommes pas d'accord avec la philosophie du communisme ni avec sa morale pratique' (*Ess*, 273) ('we agree neither with the Communists' philosophy nor with their practical ethics' (*BHR*, 59)). They may agree on matters of social justice, but Camus's *Combat* and the communists are, he insists, separated by the fact that the communists resort to 'une philosophie de l'histoire très cohérente' (*Ess*, 273) ('a very coherent philosophy of history' (*BHR*, 60, modified)) in order to justify their political realism. On this, Camus is categorical: 'Nous l'avons dit maintes fois, nous ne croyons pas au réalisme politique' (*Ess*, 273) ('As we have said innumerable times, we do not believe in political realism' (*BHR*, 60)). ('Political realism' describes a position which, from the premise that complicity with violence is inevitable, justifies its own use of violence by invoking the necessity of the end it seeks.) This represents the crucial early appearance of Camus's rejection of the moral economy of what he sees as a Marxist political eschatology (in which, according to critics such as Camus, the claim to have identified in advance the end-goal of history serves to justify violence seen as serving that end). This rejection is of major importance in the development of Camus's thought and political activity; it would culminate most famously in the polemic over *L'Homme révolté* and the justifiability or otherwise of what was referred to as 'progressive violence' (namely, violence which achieves a kind of strategic justification by virtue of the fact that it aims to rid the world of violence).[2] 'La justice sociale peut très bien se faire sans une philosophie ingénieuse', Camus declares (*Ess*, 281) ('Social justice can be realised without brilliant philosophy' (*BHR*, 85)). The messianic doctrine of inevitable progress 's'autorise de l'amour de l'humanité pour se dispenser de servir les hommes' (*Ess*, 281) ('preaches love of humanity so as to exempt itself from serving men'), as opposed to an alternative form of socialism, which 'ne croit pas aux doctrines absolues et infaillibles, mais à l'amélioration obstinée, chaotique mais inlassable, de la condition humaine' (*Ess*, 282) ('does not believe in absolute and infallible doctrines, but rather in the tenacious efforts – perhaps chaotic but always untiring – to improve the human condition' (*BHR*, 86)). In the midst of what he also presents as his revolutionary drive, Camus reveals that he will have no truck with a revolution which knows that it is justified in advance by an inevitable end. Violence can be justified, if at all, only as an unwelcome necessity, to be adopted in full awareness of its unacceptability, and not excused by an external, supposedly infallible, historical law.

This argument will return in relation to *Les Justes* and *L'Homme révolté*, and I will come back to it shortly. First, though, it is worth briefly considering the language of 'man' through which Camus justifies his position. It is astonishing, for example, that even as he rejects an eschatological communism by declaring in November 1944, 'Nous savons avec quelle rapidité les moyens sont pris pour les fins, nous ne voulons pas de n'importe quelle justice' ('We know how quickly the means become confused with the ends; it is not just any kind of justice we seek'), he states: 'Car il s'agit de faire, en effet, le salut de l'homme . . . Il s'agit de servir la dignité de l'homme par des moyens qui restent dignes au milieu d'une histoire qui ne l'est pas' (*Ess*, 279) ('Indeed, this is a question of saving humanity . . . This is a question of serving the dignity of man by methods that remain dignified in the midst of a history that is not' (*BHR*, 76, modified)). And we have already seen that in December 1944, Camus is not averse to presenting the achievement of social justice as the historic mission of the working class 'sans cesse en marche vers la grande victoire' (*Ess*, 1545) ('ceaselessly marching towards its great victory'). The next month, however, Camus would adopt his more usual position in relation to the salvation of 'man', declaring that 'Sans avoir l'ambition déraisonnable de le sauver, nous tenons au moins à le servir' (*Ess*, 287) ('We do not have the unrealistic ambition of saving him; we try only to serve him' (*BHR*, 105)). But these two aberrant, unexpectedly messianic moments signal the struggle here for ownership of 'man' as the key term of value in these debates.

Resituating these debates about the morality of leftist political action alongside those about just retribution with which they are contemporary, it is compelling to note that Camus refuses the moral economy of desired ends and justified means in the former debate and allows it in the latter by the very same appeal to 'man' as an irreducible value. 'Si nous consentons à nous passer de Dieu et de l'espérance', writes Camus in relation to the *épuration*, 'nous ne nous passons pas si aisément de l'homme . . . nous refuserons jusqu'au dernier moment une charité divine qui frustrerait les hommes de leur justice' (*Ess*, 287) ('If we consent to do without God and hope, we cannot so easily do without man . . . we will refuse until the final moment a divine charity which frustrates the justice of men' (*BHR*, 105, modified). The final irreducible value, 'man' is tossed this way and that, here affirming a messianic faith in social justice or an eschatology ('jusqu'au dernier moment') of just retribution, here refusing precisely this moral economy in the name of good sense and historical moderation.

Camus's rejection of 'political realism' underpins his interventions in the post-war debates occasioned principally by the existence of the Soviet labour camps (marked in France notably by the voices of Koestler and Rousset, denouncing Soviet violence, and Merleau-Ponty's theorisation of 'progressive violence').[3] Prior to *L'Homme révolté*, these interventions come primarily in the essays collected as *Ni victimes ni bourreaux* (*Ess*, 329–52), and then in Camus's responses to the criticism of these essays by Emmanuel d'Astier de la Vigerie (*Ess*, 353–68). In a world dominated by the opposition between Soviet communism and American capitalism, and still marked by the injustice of colonialism, Camus attempts to find a position which would be as little as possible complicit with the violence and exploitation of each of these regimes. He is not so naive, he says, as to expect a world without violence: what he wants to achieve is a world in which violence is not given a false legitimacy by some overarching political project. 'Murder' (his synecdochic figure for political violence) is inevitable, says Camus, as the only way one can oppose the world of violence is by running the risk of violence (*Ess*, 334):

> Je ne dirai donc point qu'il faut supprimer toute violence . . . Je dis seulement qu'il faut refuser toute légitimation de la violence, que cette légitimation lui vienne d'une raison d'État absolue, ou d'une philosophie totalitaire. La violence est à la fois inévitable et injustifiable. Je crois qu'il faut lui garder son caractère exceptionnel et la resserrer dans les limites qu'on peut. (*Ess*, 355)

> (So I will not say that all violence should be abolished . . . I say merely that violence must be refused all legitimacy, whether this legitimacy be derived from an absolute *raison d'Etat* or a totalitarian philosophy. Violence is both inevitable and unjustifiable. I believe we must keep it as an exception and limit it insofar as this is possible.)

Camus here develops arguments he had used to justify the Resistance (the hands of the French are pure because they did not want the war they had to fight) and the *épuration* (the imperfections of human justice can be corrected by a desperate honesty: see *Ess*, 255 and 1536, as discussed above). Violence is acceptable only if it is known to be unacceptable and practised as such. It is absolutely unacceptable if it is raised to the level of a principle or erected into an institution. Thus, with specific reference to the Soviet camps: 'Les camps ne me paraissent avoir aucune des excuses que peuvent présenter les violences provisoires d'une insurrection' (*Ess*, 365) ('The camps seem to me to lack any of the reasons which might excuse the provisional violence of an uprising'). Convulsive violence in response to intolerable injustice is acceptable (as long as it knows it is wrong); violence justified by appeals to 'historical necessity' is not. In what is a grave problem for his position, Camus does not address the problem of a convulsive uprising inspired by an understanding of historical necessity: the two are, in his terms, incompatible.

Essentially, this problem derives from Camus's conflation of metaphysical and social injustice. (This conflation is most clearly at work in *La Peste*, in which, as Simone de Beauvoir and Roland Barthes amongst others observed, human injustice is problematically translated by a metaphysical symbol.[4]) We have seen above that the drive for social justice may be motivated by the desire to institute at least the justice that is humanly possible, against a fundamentally unjust existential condition. 'La grandeur de l'homme', for Camus, 'est dans sa décision d'être plus fort que sa condition. Et si sa condition est injuste, il n'a qu'une façon de la surmonter qui est d'être juste lui-même' (*Ess*, 258) ('Man's greatness . . . lies in his decision to be stronger than his condition. And if his condition is unjust, he has only one way of overcoming it, which is to be just himself' (*RRD*, 30)). 'La justice . . . ne va pas sans la révolte' (*Ess*, 271–2) ('There is no justice without revolt'): as Camus argues in the opening sections of *L'Homme révolté*, revolt is positive in itself inasmuch as it affirms a human value, by refusing to accept the absurdity of human existence (which Camus habitually terms 'injustice'). This is why it is necessary for reactive violence to recognise its own unacceptability: only by doing so can it continue to affirm the value of life which is at the root of any movement of revolt authentically in touch with its metaphysical implications. But the justification of any specific revolt is thus derived from its existential attitude rather than its social basis: if our condition per se is unjust, it becomes impossible to tell when violent reaction might be specifically acceptable, what might justify revolt in social terms.

Violence may also be justified for Camus if the perpetrator accepts to pay the price of its unacceptability by sacrificing his or her own life. The name which for Camus crystallises the position he is attempting to formulate is that of Kaliayev, the terrorist Russian revolutionary of 1905, whose case is discussed at length in *L'Homme révolté* and forms the basis of *Les Justes*. In the position represented for Camus by the 1905 revolutionaries, murder is compensated by suicide: 'Une vie est alors payée par une autre vie et, de ces deux holocaustes, surgit la promesse d'une valeur' (*Ess*, 575–6) ('A life is paid for by another life, and from these two sacrifices springs the promise of a value' (*R*, 138)). These figures are distinguished by the fact that 'Ils ne mettent donc aucune idée au-dessus de la vie humaine, bien qu'ils tuent pour l'idée' (*Ess*, 576) ('Therefore they do not value any idea above human life, although they kill for the sake of ideas' (*R*, 138)). And in a note, Camus concludes: 'Deux races d'hommes. L'un tue une seule fois et paie de sa vie. L'autre justifie des milliers de crimes et accepte de se payer d'honneurs' (*Ess*,

578) ('Two very different species of men. One kills only once and pays with his life. The other justifies thousands of crimes and consents to be rewarded with honours' (*R*, 141)). If it keeps its exceptional quality, murder remains attached to some kind of personal responsibility, remains uncomfortable, and so continues to affirm the value it apparently denies (see *CII*, 214). The combination of local reaction against a greater evil, convulsive revolt against metaphysical injustice, and the willingness to give one's own life, affirms a value beyond the immediate historical situation and allows violence to achieve a temporary justification, as opposed to the pseudo-justification of violence in terms of historical process.[5]

Empty justice

Camus's logic here is dubious, to be sure. Insurrectionary violence is justified per se, as long as it is convulsive enough to declare its metaphysical roots. Suicide bombing – of an appropriately guilty target – is justified per se. There is nothing in Camus's arguments that would allow us to distinguish between different instances of reactive violence, to decide whether some might be justified and others not: the only distinctions to be made are between the existential attitudes of the perpetrators, which is pretty flimsy ground for moral debate. The frame here is the problematic Camus derives from Dostoyevsky's *The Brothers Karamazov*: in the absence of absolute value, how can we find a principle that might stop us torturing each other? In the *Lettres à un ami allemand*, Camus acknowledges that this absence implies ethical relativism (and so seems to permit Nazi violence), before insisting that 'man' – indeed, his 'destiny', in another moment of aberrant eschatology – constitutes an irreducible moral limit which justifies localised violence in reaction against some greater evil (and so justifies the Resistance) (see *Ess*, 213–43, esp. 228). But claiming that 'man' provides an irreducible value which will always justify resistance to evil does not bring us much closer to understanding what kinds of resistance are justified and why. In this sense, Camus's 'justice' offers little effective purchase on actual decisions. We might contrast it with Merleau-Ponty's argument in *Humanisme et terreur* (*Humanism and Terror*) that, while the victorious are not always justified, justice without victory – without effective action – is meaningless. Camus's conception of justice can seem abstract, and to have little in common with contemporary discussions of social justice, from which the Camusian tone of desperate metaphysical extremity is pretty much absent. But this tone reflects the function of this conception of justice as Camus's honest response to the extremity of the events through which it was forged. Its problematic evaluative criteria may render Camus's justice empty, or useless; but it at least keeps open a radical demand to which any politics which is not just opportunism must somewhere respond, and highlights the difficulties which beset the necessary attempts to express this demand in determinate, pragmatic action.

By way of conclusion, we might briefly compare Camus's conception of justice with that developed by a more recent thinker, namely the philosopher Jacques Derrida (1930–2004). Usually associated with the philosophical and political critiques of the humanism of Camus's generation proposed by those who came to prominence in the 1960s, Derrida nevertheless occasionally shows fascinating points of convergence with Camus, of which the question of justice is a particularly intriguing example. Justice, for Derrida, is a radical demand to which any particular instance of judgement must seek to respond, but which it can never entirely fulfil.[6] To be true to the demands of justice is never to know that I am being just. Justice, on this reading, must strive to remain empty, while also reaching determinate decisions: injustice would precisely be the result of a justice that thought it knew the limits of its duties. The difference between Camus and Derrida is that Camus has moments when he thinks it is possible to know what justice is. But he comes to the agonised position that justice can only be honoured by a genuine awareness of and responsibility for the inevitable injustice of my attempts to be just. This sounds useless, cutely paradoxical and, at times, like a strange form of bad faith. And we are bound to ask what is the real difference between a 'progressive violence' justified by its attachment to its own abolition, and a reactive, convulsive violence justified by knowledge of its own unacceptability? For Camus, however, in a world of unavoidable violence, the latter at least has the simple advantage of being likely to do less damage. And – as for Derrida (see for example his sustained public participation in the struggle against apartheid in South Africa) – the demands of straightforward social justice are not suspended by this metaphysical perplexity. Camus's justice may well be empty, then. But to an extent, at least, this might be as welcome as it is shocking.

NOTES

1. On this, see especially *Ess*, 961–1018, and Roger Quilliot's commentary (*Ess*, 1839–47).
2. On 'progressive violence', see the crucial intervention by Maurice Merleau-Ponty: *Humanisme et terreur* (Paris, Gallimard, 1947).
3. Arthur Koestler, *Darkness at Noon* (London, Cape, 1940), and *The Yogi and the Commissar* (London, Cape, 1945); David Rousset, 'Au secours des déportés dans les camps soviétiques' (1949), *Lignes* n.s. 2 (May 2000), 143–60; and Merleau-Ponty, *Humanisme et terreur*. On these debates, see Simone de Beauvoir, *La Force des choses* (Paris, Gallimard, 1963), pp. 121–6, 216–22, and 279–80; Eric Werner, *De la violence au totalitarisme* (Paris, Calmann-Lévy, 1972); and

Maurice Weyembergh, *Albert Camus ou la mémoire des origines* (Brussels, De Boeck, 1998).

4. De Beauvoir, *La Force des choses*, p. 279; Roland Barthes, 'La Peste', in *Œuvres complètes*, ed. Eric Marty, 5 vols. (Paris, Seuil, 2002), vol. 1, pp.540–5; for a critical account of such responses, see Tony Judt, *The Burden of Responsibility* (Chicago, University of Chicago Press, 1998), p. 105.

5. On these problems, see Stephen Eric Bronner, *Camus: Portrait of a Moralist* (London, University of Minnesota Press, 1999), pp. 91–2; and Jeffrey C. Isaac, *Arendt, Camus and Modern Rebellion* (London, Yale University Press, 1992).

6. See especially Jacques Derrida, *Force de loi* (Paris, Galilée, 1994).

8

COLIN DAVIS

Violence and ethics in Camus

Act 3 scene 6 of *Caligula* stages a key encounter between Caligula and Cherea, Camus's murderous protagonist and one of his eventual assassins. Here, the two men articulate the ethical impasse at the heart of the philosophy of the Absurd. Caligula suggests that Cherea must believe in 'quelque idée supérieure' (*TRN*, 78) ('some higher principle' (*COP*, 83)); Cherea does not entirely accept this, but neither does he entirely deny it:

> Cherea: Je crois qu'il y a des actions qui sont plus belles que d'autres.
> Caligula: Je crois que toutes sont équivalentes. (*TRN*, 78–9)

> Cherea: I believe some actions are – shall I say? – more praiseworthy than others.
> Caligula: I believe that all are on an equal footing. (*COP*, 83)

Cherea uses an aesthetic term rather than a moral one to characterise his position: some actions are 'plus belles' (literally 'more beautiful') than others, not inherently better or more just. Caligula's retort that all actions are *equivalent* does not necessarily contradict Cherea's argument, since neither man asserts the existence of a higher value which would make it possible to distinguish between one action and another in strictly ethical terms. It is also significant here that neither man seriously tries to persuade the other to change his views. Each states what he *believes*, but makes no attempt to offer principles, reasons or explanations which would demonstrate the validity of his own opinion. We are presented here with the confrontation of two positions which are coherent within their own terms, but which are utterly incompatible. One man believes that some actions are preferable to others, whilst the other insists that no action has inherent value above any other. Cherea does not regard Caligula as demonstrably wrong, though he deems his position to be unacceptable. His next speech draws a kind of imperative from his views even as he refrains from moral judgement: 'tu es gênant et il faut que tu disparaisses' (*TRN*, 79) ('you're pernicious, and you've got to go' (*COP*, 47)).

This scene gives dramatic form to one of the central issues of Camus's writing: the problem of establishing values and in particular of determining the conditions under which violence might be justified. Murder appears in Camus's texts as an extreme act which causes both horror and fascination. Faced with the temptation to kill, his characters confront an urgent ethical question: what is wrong with murder? When, in *L'Etranger*, Meursault encounters a man on a beach and shoots him, he may have little justification for killing him, but neither can he think of any good reason not to. Others are perceived as vaguely threatening to the subject's well being, or else they impede the realisation of his desires or dreams. So killing, be it for the sake of political ends or only for self-interest, would seem a natural response, and one which cannot be authoritatively prohibited if the existence of universal moral values is denied. The Absurd poses a version of the same ethical quandary which, later in the twentieth century, would be central to the debate around what came to be called postmodernity: what values can there be if none can ever be legitimated in the light of some secure ultimate truth? Camus states the problem eloquently at the beginning of *L'Homme révolté*:

> Si l'on ne croit à rien, si rien n'a de sens et si nous ne pouvons affirmer aucune valeur, tout est possible et rien n'a d'importance. Point de pour ni de contre, l'assassin n'a ni tort ni raison. On peut tisonner les crématoires comme on peut aussi se dévouer à soigner les lépreux. Malice et vertu sont hasard ou caprice.
>
> (*Ess*, 415)

> If one believes in nothing, if nothing makes sense, if we can assert no value whatsoever, everything is permissible and nothing is important. There is no pro or con; the murderer is neither right nor wrong. One is free to stoke the crematory fires, or to give one's life to the care of lepers. Wickedness and virtue are just accident or whim.
>
> (*R*, 13)

Here, Camus sounds uncomfortably like Caligula. In *L'Homme révolté* more generally though, he will play the role of Cherea, conceding the existence of an ethical dilemma but endeavouring to overcome it. This dilemma is dramatised in acute form in *Caligula*. In the unresolved dialogue between Caligula and Cherea we see a tension at the root of the play. We *know* that Caligula must be wrong, that his project of making people more intensely aware of the value of living by confronting them with the ever-present threat of random, meaningless death is insane and inadmissible; but it is not so easy to produce decisive arguments to *prove* that he is wrong if we deny the validity of all established, objective, transcendental values. Moreover, in opposing him Cherea allies himself with corrupt, reactionary forces, and he ends up helping to restore precisely the self-blinded condition that Caligula wanted to abolish. The play does not condone Caligula, yet it draws its seduction and dramatic power from Caligula's exorbitant desire for the impossible.

Perhaps for Camus this seduction was too strong for comfort, because he would spend much of the rest of his career trying to resist it. The encounter between Cherea and Caligula is rewritten in the discussion between Stepan and Kaliayev in Act 2 of *Les Justes*, but here the ambiguity has been expunged. All sympathy is for the humane revolt of Kaliayev rather than Stepan's uncompromising justification of violence in the name of some distant ideal. As spectators we may feel more secure about whose side we are supposed to be on than in *Caligula*. The play offers an intellectually unthrilling yet sane justification of violence and its limits. Is it legitimate to assassinate a Grand Duke who symbolises an unjust, despotic regime? Yes. Is it legitimate to kill young children in the name of a revolutionary ideal? No. Violence can be ethical as long as its perpetrators accept that, as Dora puts it, 'Même dans la destruction, il y a un ordre, il y a des limites' (*TRN*, 338) ('Even destruction has a right and a wrong way, and there *are* limits' (*COP*, 187)). Camus has now apparently detached himself from the seduction of Caligula and positioned his text and his spectators less ambiguously on the side of Cherea's sensible restraint. As Camus insists in the course of the controversy occasioned by his *Ni victimes ni bourreaux*, he does not advocate complete non-violence. He refers to 'de terribles violences qui ne [lui] ont posé aucun problème' (*Ess*, 355) ('terrible acts of violence which posed [him] no problem') committed during the Occupation. However, he insists that no principle or ideal can justify murder; and in his sketches of a philosophy of limits in *L'Homme révolté* and 'L'Exil d'Hélène' he attempts to demonstrate that violence can have ethical uses, even if it can never be finally legitimated. Indeed, the rebel's dilemma is precisely that there can never be final legitimation. The rebel may turn to violence in order to curtail violence, but she cannot be certain of the justification or outcome of her choices. Actions are undertaken in risk and contradiction, and ultimate success is never assured.

So the question of violence is at the heart of Camus's writing and his ethical deliberations. He was constantly perplexed by the question of whether or not violence could be justified and what ends it could legitimately serve. His very public and much discussed rift with Sartre in the early 1950s served to delimit the context through which his ethics have been considered ever since, with critics siding with Camus or Sartre depending on their own inclinations. Camus's supporters have admired him for defending the value of human life over abstract principles, whereas his detractors have criticised him for intellectual inconsistency and for failing to face up to difficult historical and political choices, most notably over the Algerian War of Independence. Recently, though, there have been valuable attempts to escape from the Camus/Sartre dichotomy, and to suggest different intellectual contexts for understanding Camus's ethics; for example, his work has been discussed in conjunction with the thought of Simone de Beauvoir, Maurice Blanchot or Emmanuel Levinas.[1] Such reassessments have had the benefit of restoring some of the interest of Camus's writing, emphasising for example its acute sensitivity to alterity and its agonised awareness that failure inevitably haunts any ethical project. The aim of this chapter is not primarily to contribute to this reassessment of Camus's theoretical conception of the link between ethics and violence. Rather, I want to suggest that, for all its intellectual seriousness, the theoretical and ethical discussion of murder in Camus's essays can be understood as an anxious, defensive neutralisation of the fascination with gratuitous violence which emerges, sometimes, in his fictional texts. The philosophical question, 'Under what circumstances is violence justified?', is accompanied and endangered by a desire to destroy the Other, a desire which haunts and remains irreducible to any ethical, moralising discourse.

An illustration of this is provided by the very figure who seems to exemplify the possibility of an ethical use of violence: Kaliayev in *Les Justes*. Kaliayev believes that killing the Grand Duke is justified, but that killing the children who accompany him on the first assassination attempt is not. He thereby acknowledges the existence of a limit which restricts the legitimate use of violence. Blanchot has described Kaliayev's inability to kill the children in terms of an encounter with otherness as it is theorised by the philosopher Emmanuel Levinas.[2] In such an encounter the sight of the face reveals the Other in all its vulnerability and enjoins the subject to do no harm. This reading, however, overlooks the altogether more ambiguous terms in which Kaliayev describes the experience. Initially, the prospect of killing the Grand Duke gives him real joy: 'mon cœur s'est mis à battre de joie, je te le jure' (*TRN*, 332) ('my heart began to race, with joy . . . yes, with joy' (*COP*, 182)). When he sees the children he finds himself unable to act; but he does not at first attempt to explain this on ethical grounds. On the contrary, his response to them is only a hair's breadth from extreme violence: 'S'ils m'avaient regardé, je crois que j'aurais lancé la bombe. Pour éteindre au moins ce regard triste' (*TRN*, 332) ('If they had looked at me then I think I would have thrown the bomb, if only to shut out the sad look in their eyes' (*COP*, 182–3)). For Levinas, the encounter with the face of the Other leads to an acknowledgement of the Biblical injunction 'Thou shalt not kill'. The Other's face forbids murder 'through the original language of his defenceless eyes'.[3] In Kaliayev's account, a glimpse of the Other's vulnerable and sad face risks provoking murder. Kaliayev's reluctance to harm the children appears to be bound up with spontaneous violent impulses towards them. A few lines later Kaliayev refers to earlier experiences of anxiety about harming children: 'Autrefois, quand je conduisais la voiture, chez nous, en Ukraine, j'allais comme le vent, je n'avais peur de rien. De rien au monde, sinon de renverser un enfant. J'imaginais le choc, cette tête frêle frappant la route, à la volée . . .' (*TRN*, 333) ('In the old days, when I used to go driving on our estate in the Ukraine, I always drove like a madman, because I wasn't afraid of anything . . . except of running down a child. That was my only fear. I used to imagine the shock, the small head hitting the ground . . .' (*COP*, 183)). His fear of harming a child does not actually cause him to slow down. Indeed, his vivid, graphic imagining of the effect of an accident on a child's head might even suggest that the desire to harm unconsciously outweighs any protective instinct. So Kaliayev's recollection of his past in Ukraine, which is presumably intended to explain why he could not kill the children in the Grand Duke's carriage, might, then, suggest something quite different from an ethical choice. At the moment of action, he is paralysed *by his very desire to kill*, a desire so overwhelming that it destroys the ethical standing of the subject precisely when an ethical justification is most anxiously invoked.

This reading is at the furthest possible remove from the ethical positions explicitly adopted in *Ni victimes ni bourreaux* or *L'Homme révolté*. Camus's stated concern is to get beyond the ethical impasse of the Absurd. The fact that there are no given, universal values or principles must not be allowed to reduce all actions, as Caligula would have it, to equivalence. In *Le Mythe de Sisyphe* Camus upbraided a philosophical tradition which acknowledged the Absurd only in order to turn aside from it. But much of Camus's own writing can be read as staging the impossibility of maintaining oneself unflinchingly in the domain of the Absurd. Even Meursault's resigned submission to the mechanisms of the law in the second half of *L'Etranger* suggests a preference for a system which judges and condemns, however unjustly, over a sustained exposure to the Absurd in which no overarching authority or values can be discerned.[4] In Camus's later essays, revolt serves, if not as a genuinely transcendental value, then at least as a pseudo-transcendental value, since it enables the rebel to resist the senselessness encountered in the experience of the Absurd: 'La révolte naît du spectacle de la déraison, devant une condition injuste et incompréhensible. Mais son élan aveugle revendique l'ordre au milieu du chaos et l'unité au cœur même de ce qui fuit et disparaît' (*Ess*, 419) ('Rebellion arises from the spectacle of the irrational coupled with an unjust and incomprehensible condition. But its blind impetus clamours for order in the midst of chaos, and for unity in the very heart of the ephemeral' (*R*, 16)). Both Camus's ethics and his aesthetics now become an endeavour to correct the flaw in the world whereby the human longing for sense, order and coherence is eternally frustrated. Revolt aspires to intelligibility even if it does not yet know how to establish it; and as such it is in flat denial of the founding insight of the Absurd, according to which sense is what humankind both must and cannot have.

Writing itself becomes the creative forum where the prospect of intelligibility will be sustained. Camus's prose strains to achieve an aphoristic self-evidence which only the most ill-willed reader could possibly fail to accept. So, with breathless and (I suspect) anxious rapidity, the opening pages of *L'Homme révolté* establish the sole value which will allow us to escape from the ethical impasse of the Absurd: human life. Camus's argument is essentially very simple: if I do not kill myself, it must be because I accept that my own life is a necessary good; if I accept this for myself, then I must accept it for all others as well, so that if I reject suicide I also reject murder. In Jill Capstick's succinct summary, 'The key term of Camusian ethics is the given value of human life. Consequently, any act of authentic revolt must simultaneously reject all that violates human dignity and affirm the worth of all human beings.'[5] The solitary experience of the Absurd has now been overcome by the community and solidarity established through Camus's new *cogito*: 'Je me révolte, donc nous sommes' (*Ess*, 432) ('I *rebel* – therefore we *exist*' (*R*, 28)).

How compelling is this argument? Not very, if we are to judge by its subsequent (lack of) influence, and the harsh criticisms to which it was subjected by Jeanson and Sartre. It is, to say the least, odd that an argument that begins in the frustration of rationality through the experience of the Absurd ends by endorsing a form of universalist rationalism as it insists that I extend to all human beings the values which I assert as valid for myself. Moreover, the rhetorical overkill that permeates Camus's argumentative prose risks *distracting* rather than persuading his reader. When discussing the link between suicide and murder for example, Camus allows his reader no space for dissent:

> Comment, sans une concession remarquable au goût du confort, conserver pour soi le bénéfice exclusif d'un tel raisonnement? Dès l'instant où ce bien est reconnu comme tel, *il est celui de tous les hommes*. *On ne peut* donner une cohérence au meurtre si on la refuse au suicide. Un esprit pénétré de l'idée d'absurde admet sans doute le meurtre de fatalité; *il ne saurait* accepter le meurtre de raisonnement. Vis-à-vis de la confrontation [entre l'interrogation humaine et le silence du monde], meurtre et suicide sont une même chose, qu'*il faut* prendre ou rejeter ensemble.　　　　(*Ess*, 416; my emphasis)

How can one, without indulging one's desire for comfort, keep for oneself the exclusive benefits of this argument? The moment life is recognised as a necessary good, it becomes so for all men. One cannot find logical consistency in murder, if one denies it in suicide. A mind that is imbued with the idea of the absurd will doubtless accept murder that is fated; it could not accept murder that proceeds from reasoning. In view of that confrontation which they both render impossible, murder and suicide are the same thing; one must accept them both or reject them both. (R, 14)

The rhetorical question with which this extract begins implies that the answer is known before the question is even asked, and that no one could deny it in good faith. The rest of the passage asserts a series of certainties and impossibilities which allow no margin of doubt. There is here none of the tension and hesitation inherent in the fraught dialogue between Caligula and Cherea, with which this chapter began. The issues have now been resolved, and Cherea has decisively won the argument. We are required only to listen and to learn. However, perhaps Camus's prose, through the very markers of confidence which rule out any possibility of disagreement ('On ne peut', 'il ne saurait', 'il faut') ('One cannot', 'it could not', 'one must'), weakens his case by overstating it. The dissenting reader is rhetorically denied any valid position from which a counter-argument might be mounted, but we might end up feeling less persuaded than battered by Camus's over-confident prose; and the suspicion may arise that the person Camus is most anxious to convince is himself.

The assault on the reader here is all the more significant because it contradicts the respect required by Camus's ethical position. In principle, revolt entails openness to the Other because it gestures towards a flawless community of all humans: 'L'individu n'est donc pas, à lui seul, cette valeur qu'il veut défendre. Il faut, au moins, tous les hommes pour la composer. Dans la révolte, l'homme se dépasse en autrui et, de ce point de vue, la solidarité humaine est métaphysique' (Ess, 426) ('Therefore the individual is not, in himself, an embodiment of the values he wishes to defend. It needs at least all men to comprise them. When he rebels, a man identifies himself with other men, and, from this point of view, human solidarity is metaphysical' (R, 22–3; translation modified)). But this apparent openness to the Other and the ethical generosity it entails are also disturbingly totalising. Even all men are not enough, since Camus bizarrely insists that the value to be defended requires 'au moins, tous les hommes' ('at least all men'). What is more than everybody? I assume here that Camus is not, in what would for him be an unprecedented access of feminist self-critique, taking 'les hommes' ('men') to refer only to men, so allowing some women into the sphere of solidarity as well as all men. The apparent willingness to embrace otherness in fact leaves no room for the Other who might resist the perspective of the self. All others have to be the same; all are implicated in the values and in the solidarity for which Camus argues. None may be left out: 'Mais, qu'il manque un seul être au monde irremplaçable de la fraternité, et le voilà dépeuplé' (*Ess*, 685) ('But if one single human being is missing in the world of fraternity then this world is immediately depopulated' (*R*, 245–6)).[6] Whilst pleading for inclusiveness, the text is actually performing the radical exclusion of the dissenting reader. It argues for 'mesure' ('measure') rather than 'démesure' ('excess'), but its own arrogation of a speaking position which extinguishes all doubt and summons into its orbit all men (at least) is itself excessive. Or violent even. In calling on us to refrain from murdering the Other, Camus writes in a manner which is, in the term I have used elsewhere, altericidal (i.e. Other-killing), because it denies the Other any independent position.[7]

So the language of Camus's text contradicts its key argument, as it denies alterity at the very moment that it purports to open up the solitary subject to the community of others. Solidarity, in this light, turns out to be an exclusive pact rather than a generously inclusive notion because it is intolerant of difference. This mismatch between Camus's language and his message is all the more striking when *L'Homme révolté* insists, precisely, on the value of clarity. Revolt aims to achieve an open communication between free subjects, whereas ambiguity is associated with death: 'Chaque équivoque, chaque malentendu suscite la mort; le langage clair, le mot simple, peut seul sauver de cette mort' (*Ess*, 687) ('Every ambiguity, every misunderstanding, leads to death; clear language and simple words are the only salvation from it' (*R*, 247)). This obviously chimes with the view expressed in *La Peste* by Tarrou, according to whom 'tout le malheur des hommes venait de ce qu'ils ne tenaient pas un langage clair' (*TRN*, 1426) ('all our troubles spring from our failure to use plain, clear-cut language' (*P*, 208)). The demand for clarity is clear enough; the problem is that it does not reflect Camus's own performance as writer, particularly in his literary texts. In *La Peste*, to cite a notable example, Tarrou's desire for 'un langage clair' ('plain, clear-cut language') is frustrated by a text in which sense and interpretability are constantly at issue. In Tarrou's own notebooks, Rieux's chronicle, Grand's sentence or Paneloux's sermons, meaning is never unambiguously given. It must always be painstakingly extracted from the data of experience, and it must then be repeatedly re-worked and revised. The novel as a whole is, by common agreement, an allegory, though this designation serves to open up its potential for interpretation rather than to close it down. The epigraph from Defoe, which commends representing 'n'importe quelle chose qui existe réellement par quelque chose qui n'existe pas' (*TRN*, 1215) ('anything that really exists by that which exists not' (*P*, 3)), potentially shatters any authoritative reading of the text by implying that it *could* be about *anything*. The early consensus that it was about Evil or the Occupation simplified the novel by overlooking some of its tensions and ambiguities, and in the process noticeably failed to provide comprehensive, coherent and persuasive readings. So with passing years critics seem to be less certain of what the novel means than they were immediately after its publication.[8]

Camus's writing is at its most challenging and intriguing precisely at the moments when it disturbs the smooth surface of meaning and reveals, lurking underneath it, an enigmatic core which resists easy conceptualisation. The very titles of his early essays imply a context in which meaning is unstable: 'L'Ironie', 'Entre oui et non', 'L'Envers et l'Endroit'. From Meursault's disjointed, gap-ridden narrative in *L'Etranger* to Clamence's over-smooth monologue in *La Chute*, which comes together with the warning 'Ne vous y fiez pas' (*TRN*, 1500) ('Don't rely on it!' (*F*, 36)), Camus explores ways of disturbing intelligibility and suspending his readers' sense of interpretative assurance. We are constantly reminded that we have understood too much or too little; we may be mystified by what was essentially simple, or we may have hastily simplified what was inherently complex. On his final canvas, Jonas, the disturbed protagonist of 'Jonas ou l'artiste au travail' from *L'Exil et le Royaume*, writes 'un mot qu'on pouvait déchiffrer, mais dont on ne savait s'il fallait y lire *solitaire* ou *solidaire*' (*TRN*, 1654) ('a word that could be made out, but without any certainty as to whether it should be read *solitary* or *solidary*' (*EK*, 115)). The difference between *solitaire* and *solidaire* may be minimal, but it is also crucial. The text insists on the word's unreadability, and by extension on its own pervasive ambiguity. In the same collection, the story 'L'Hôte' plays on the two meanings of *l'hôte* as guest or host, as it poses the question of which of its characters is actually at home in Algeria in the violent years prior to independence: Daru, the white teacher, or the allegedly murderous Arab to whom he plays host for a night. Each occupies the position of both host and guest, and neither occupies either position fully. The ambiguity of the word *hôte* has come to characterise their entire relation with the land they inhabit, and it creates a gulf between them which frustrates any prospect of the seamless solidarity which remained Camus's driving fantasy.[9]

Camus insists on clarity as an antidote to violence, yet his own argumentative discourse is bullying and coercive; and he associates ambiguity with murder, whilst his texts are ridden with unresolved interpretative tangles. Either way, his readers are confronted with texts which do not achieve a placid marriage of message and medium. In *L'Homme révolté*, Camus envisages a meeting of self and Other which leads to community and solidarity. The meeting of text and reader, though, is more akin to the wary, distrustful encounter in what remains the most haunting and enigmatic passage in Camus's writing, the scene on the beach in *L'Etranger* where Meursault shoots the Arab. This is the very opposite of the Levinasian encounter which Blanchot saw in *Les Justes* when Kaliayev refuses to kill the children, and which may be achieved at least momentarily in 'L'Hôte' when Daru prepares a meal for his Arab guest/prisoner.[10] In such an encounter, the self perceives in the otherness of the Other an injunction to take responsibility for and to protect its vulnerability. In *L'Etranger*, on the other hand, the Arab's otherness is seen as an intolerable challenge to the murderous subject's well-being. Meursault describes how the Arab 'avait l'air de rire' (*TRN*, 1168) ('seemed to be laughing' (*O*, 59)). It is not even certain that he is actually laughing; but in any case he is not laughing *at* Meursault, just laughing, indifferent to Meursault and at the same time mocking his entire existence, exposing him to his own absent centre. In the altericidal fantasy lurking behind the scene, the Other possesses something that I cannot have, s/he is at home whereas I am in exile, and thus I am robbed of what might have been mine. Meursault responds with violence to this imaginary theft of being. His action is at a far remove from Camus's attempt to found community in revolt through his 'Je me révolte, donc nous sommes' ('I *rebel* – therefore we *exist*'). Rather, the implicit *cogito* here is: I kill therefore I am, I kill that which is other than me so that I can exist as myself.

This passage from *L'Etranger* depicts the stand-off between self and Other as essentially violent. Meursault kills, at least in part, because, like Caligula, he can see no good reason not to. Later protagonists, such as Rieux, Kaliayev, or Daru, endeavour to create a space in which ethical responsibility is possible, but violence continues to lurk in the background of even the most ethically optimistic texts. In the final pages of *La Peste* Cottard shoots randomly into the crowd, and is viciously beaten by the police on his capture; in 'L'Hôte' the Arab's decision to go to prison leads to a threat on Daru's life. Even Kaliayev, as I suggested earlier, may be paralysed as much by the awful force of his desire to kill as by his reluctance to harm the children. Camus's texts can be seen as repeatedly re-staging, with greater or lesser lucidity, the confrontation between Caligula and Cherea, embracing and resisting murder without ever being fully able to justify one response over the other. Indeed Cherea, like Kaliayev, can only put an end to murder by committing it himself. His reasons may be different from Caligula's, at least in as far as he can articulate them honestly, but the result is the same. The assassination of Caligula continues the sequence of murders that it is intended to terminate, so it is no wonder that Caligula's final words are 'Je suis encore vivant!' (*TRN*, 108) ('I'm still alive!' (*COP*, 104)). He may die, but the principle of senseless violence which he embodies is implemented again in the very moment of his death. Violence is, as Camus puts it in defence of his *Ni victimes ni bourreaux*, 'à la fois inévitable et injustifiable' (*Ess*, 355) ('at the same time inevitable and unjustifiable'). Camus's dogged refusal to give legitimacy to violence may be the foundation of the moral stature he has acquired amongst his admirers; but it is also, as his texts constantly remind us both through their depictions of murder and through their suspension of interpretative certainty, an irrelevance in face of the conviction that violence against the threatening Other is the subject's most fundamental form of self-assertion.

On the one hand, then, there is in Camus's writing a desire for clarity, unity, community, coherence and innocence; on the other hand, there is the knowledge that contradiction, conflict and ambiguity are components of the condition of humankind. This tension is reflected throughout Camus's writing. At moments it insists on a polemical clarity achieved with a schoolboy swagger which can be irritating or even embarrassing more than it is persuasive. But his writing can also be intriguing and disturbing, as it fractures certainties and launches its reader into areas of ethical and semantic ambiguity which allow no ready resolution. Camus sometimes sides with Cherea; but Caligula's terrible melancholy, his sense that only an escalation of violence could sweep away the nonsense of the world, also hangs over his writing. He wishes to, but can never quite, expunge the fundamental insight that before all ethics is the simple desire to kill, to acquire being by annihilating what endangers my full possession of the world. In its pervasive sabotaging of his readers', his protagonists' and perhaps its author's hermeneutic security, his writing makes a mockery of the desire for stable identities, values or concepts. At its most paradoxically intense, the best it can offer is a melancholically fraught prospect: if we are lucky we might achieve a 'culpabilité raisonnable' (*Ess*, 420) ('limited culpability' (*R*, 17)), or aspire to be 'meurtriers innocents' (*Ess*, 700) ('innocent murderers' (*R*, 260)). But we can never know for sure that we are Cherea rather than Caligula, Kaliayev rather than Meursault.

What is fascinating about Camus's writing are not the answers that his essays attempt to offer us, but the intellectual deadlocks in which his texts engage his readers. The contradictions and uncertainties are sometimes submerged beneath a polemical flourish, but sometimes they re-surface through the very rhetorical confidence which aimed to stifle them. Without its tensions, Camus's writing would be blandly, bloodlessly assertive; with them, it maintains its raw, uneasy bewilderment in face of its inability to answer its and its century's founding question: why not kill? Faced with the Other, why shouldn't I just destroy it to preserve my own being?

NOTES

1. See in particular two ground-breaking doctoral theses, which have informed the discussion throughout this chapter: Jill Capstick, 'Re-reading Camus's Ethics', unpublished doctoral thesis, University of Oxford (2003), and Elizabeth Hart, 'Levinasian Ethics and the Works of Albert Camus', unpublished doctoral thesis, State University of New York (1997). On Camus and Levinas, see also Colin Davis, *Ethical Issues in Twentieth-Century French Fiction: Killing the Other* (Basingstoke, Macmillan, 2000), and 'The Cost of Being Ethical: Fiction, Violence, and Altercide', *Common Knowledge* 9.2 (2003), 241–53.

2. See Maurice Blanchot, 'Tu peux tuer cet homme', *La Nouvelle Revue française* 3 (1954), 1059–69. I am indebted to Jill Capstick's 'Re-reading Camus's Ethics' for drawing my attention to this article.

3. Emmanuel Levinas, *Basic Philosophical Writings* (Bloomington, Indiana University Press, 1996), p. 12.

4. For a more detailed reading of this aspect of *L'Etranger*, see Davis, 'The Cost of Being Ethical'.

5. Jill Capstick, 'Mastery or Slavery: The Ethics of Revolt in Camus's "Les Muets"', *Modern and Contemporary France* 11.4 (2003), 453–4.

6. Camus is alluding here to a well-known line from Lamartine's poem 'L'Isolement': 'Un seul être vous manque, et tout est dépeuplé' ('One single being is missing, and everything is depopulated') (*Œuvres poétiques complètes*, Paris, Gallimard (Pléiade), 1963), p. 3.

7. See Davis, *Ethical Issues* and 'The Cost of Being Ethical'.

8. On problems of reading *La Peste*, see for example Edward J. Hughes, *Albert Camus: Le Premier Homme/La Peste* (Glasgow, University of Glasgow French and German Publications, 1995); John Krapp, 'Time and Ethics in Albert Camus's *The Plague*', *University of Toronto Quarterly* 68.2 (1999), 655–76; and Colin Davis, 'Interpreting *La Peste*', *Romanic Review* 85:1 (1994), 125–42.

9. For more developed ethical readings of 'L'Hôte', see Jill Beer (Capstick), '*Le Regard*: Face to Face in Albert Camus's "L'Hôte"', *French Studies* 56.2 (2002), 179–92; and Elizabeth Hart, 'Face à face: l'éthique lévinasienne dans "L'Hôte"', in Lionel Dubois (ed.), *Les Trois guerres d'Albert Camus* (Poitiers, Les Editions du Pont-Neuf, 1995), pp. 172–7.

10. See Hart, 'Face à face', pp. 176–7.

9

CHARLES FORSDICK

Camus and Sartre: the great quarrel

When, during a speech on the future of Europe delivered in Brussels in February 2005, President George Bush cited a sentence from *La Chute*, it is unlikely that he intended to stir up memories of the infamous quarrel between Camus and Sartre that had occurred over fifty years before. However, by evoking Clamence's understanding of freedom as 'a long-distance race' (*F*, 97) ('une course de fond' (*TRN*, 1544)), Bush unwittingly cited from Camus's clear and bitter parody of Sartre in which the protagonist presents himself as a 'partisan éclairé de la servitude' ('an enlightened advocate of slavery'), before claiming that he used to spread the word 'freedom' on his toast at breakfast (*TRN*, 1543; *F*, 97). Bush's neo-conservative appropriation of Camus as a critic of terrorist violence accordingly backfired, for the author aims to indict those – Sartre and his colleagues at *Les Temps modernes* included – who, he claims, babble on about freedom whilst at the same time exploiting its rhetoric as a convenient smokescreen for their own oppressive purposes. The anecdote is telling for a number of reasons: not only does it suggest the enduring, resonant legacies of the Camus–Sartre dispute; it also serves as a warning to those who ignore the ambiguities of that dispute, and attempt instead to present its principal players in reductively ideological terms.[1]

Despite the persistent presence of Camus and Sartre in French culture, it is difficult five decades on to imagine the public interest generated by the philosophical, literary and ideological debates underpinning their very personal quarrel. The 1952 exchange of articles nevertheless achieved the status of a national dispute, continuing a Gallic tradition of high profile intellectual feuds. There was wide press coverage of the acrimonious exchanges, and Francis Jeanson, in the initial article that had effectively sparked the controversy, stated accurately that the disagreement encapsulated some of the most urgent issues of his time.[2] The quarrel remains a defining element in contemporary perceptions of the two men. In addition, it has persisted as a model of oppositionality, with Camus's role instrumentalised in a variety of subsequent interpretations for seemingly abstract purposes: allowing exploration of contemporary approaches to trauma and the 'crisis in witnessing'; permitting an anti-communist and anti-totalitarian critique of the residual patterns of Cold War political thought in Mitterrand's France; or positing, through the contrasting presentation of a vindicated Camus and a demonised Sartre, the possibilities of moderation within revolutionary thought.[3] It is, however, in postcolonial debates that these processes have been most apparent, for the renewed prominence of a series of key anti-colonial intellectuals (e.g. the Martinican-born psychologist and theorist of anti-colonial struggle Frantz Fanon (1925–61) and the Tunisian novelist and essayist Albert Memmi (1920-)) has triggered a reassessment of certain French metropolitan figures in the light of postcolonial concerns, occasioning in certain cases a marked change in critical fortunes. Camus's regular denigration as nostalgic imperialist has, for instance, been matched by a progressive rehabilitation of Sartre as a leading anti-colonial thinker, and while Camus's 1950s equivocation, self-contradiction and prevarication over Algeria have attracted critical reactions from prominent commentators such as Conor Cruise O'Brien and Edward Said, Sartre's anti-colonial activity has permitted his steady reassessment.

The quarrel between Camus and Sartre is customarily situated around the publication of the former's *L'Homme révolté* (*Ess*, 407–709), relating the irreparable breakdown of their relationship to the increasingly acrimonious exchanges in *Les Temps modernes* regarding the book. Despite the undeniable impact of this episode, explored in detail in a recent study by Ronald Aronson, the aim of this chapter is to suggest that the quarrel has a much longer history, not only stretching back to embryonic incompatibilities found in criticisms the two men made of each other's work before they actually met, but also reflected in the divergent positions they adopted on the Algerian War in the aftermath of their public rupture. It is possible, the chapter argues, to see Camus and Sartre engaging in a continued if indirect dialogue over the war, which itself began over two years after relations between them had irreconcilably broken down, and ended two years after Camus's premature death in 1960.

Despite the regular conflation of Camus and Sartre under a banner of postwar existentialism, significant differences separated the two men. Indeed, they were increasingly unwilling to accept any connection in terms of intellectual schools, with Camus endeavouring – from 1945 onwards – to avoid the status of junior partner by distinguishing his own personal take on the Absurd from Sartre's more systematic existentialism. In biographical terms, the differences between Sartre (from a bourgeois family and with a prestigious Parisian education) and Camus (born to working-class parents in Mondovi and brought up in colonial Algeria) are marked; in philosophical terms these distinctions are equally clear, with Peter Royle presenting Sartre as an 'existential phenomenologist in the grand European philosophical tradition', and Camus as a 'disabused heir of the Enlightenment'.[4]

The initial contact between Camus and Sartre was indirect, for they reviewed each other's books, in 1938 and 1943 respectively, with a shared mix of admiration and reserve. Camus, a young and politically active literary critic for *Alger républicain*, found in *La Nausée* echoes of his own concern with absurdity, but distanced himself from what he saw as the novel's philosophical abstraction as well as Sartre's failure to put to any clear purpose the freedom achieved by his characters (*Ess*, 1417–19). It is unknown whether Sartre was aware of this judgement, but his review of *L'Etranger* in *Les Cahiers du Sud* five years later was a generous one, granting the text the status of a philosophical novel in a Voltairean tradition. With professorial overtones, he questions Camus's understanding of Jaspers, Heidegger and Kierkegaard, but goes on to celebrate the anti-conventional humanism of the text's absurdist hero, highlighting the success of the style adopted by the author.[5] In Sartre's view, therefore, Camus is successful as a novelist, but not as a philosopher: the triumph of style over intellectual content is an accusation that would surface in the exchanges leading to their rupture a decade later.

The pair first met at the première of Sartre's re-working of the Electra story, *Les Mouches*, in 1943, and their instant rapport led to a seemingly close friendship and fruitful collaboration. Sartre initially invited Camus to appear in his existentialist drama *Huis clos*, although the play was eventually adopted by a professional company and produced in 1944; and in the final stages of the war, Camus involved Sartre in writing for *Combat*, requesting from him a prominent article to mark the Liberation of Paris and sending him in 1945 as its correspondent to the United States (where he openly praised Camus's political commitment). As they emerged as fêted post-war celebrities, the pair planned a co-edited journal and other collaborative projects (both intellectual and political). When Sartre had earlier suggested that Camus join the editorial board of *Les Temps modernes* in 1944, however, Camus declined, and although he cited in explanation his own editorial commitments at *Combat*, it is possible to track a series of divergences of opinion during the immediate post-war years that culminate in the 1952 quarrel. Camus, for instance, wrote in August 1945 one of the only critiques in the French press of the bombing of Hiroshima, avoiding the apocalyptic overtones of Sartre's comments on the event in *Les Temps modernes* three months later; the appearance of the Hungarian novelist, philosopher, historian and essayist Arthur Koestler (1905–80) in their intellectual milieu, and his exposé of Stalinist practices, led Camus to become an opponent of Soviet communism to an extent that Sartre himself rejected; and in 1948 the pair first quarrelled publicly, in an exchange of articles over the nature of democracy in Jean Daniel's monthly publication *Caliban*.

In these *Caliban* texts, there is already a sense of the two men shaping their views in relation to each other, with the reformist Camus's moderation and respect for what he perceived as the positive aspects of bourgeois democracy accentuating the revolutionary Sartre's increasing radicalism. Indeed, whereas in the 1940s fundamental differences over important philosophical questions may have been disguised by shared vocabulary and an evident mutual respect, close examination of the decade preceding the 1952 quarrel suggests that their rupture was in many ways inevitable, even pre-programmed. It was the publication of *L'Homme révolté* in 1951 that brought these tensions to the fore. Camus's text presents revolt as a means of transforming individual resistance into collective solidarity; at the same time, it suggests that the potential of revolt had been blunted by the French Revolution, and – in line with the tendency of revolutionary movements to adopt an increasingly totalitarian direction – been transformed into violence and oppression. As a reflection on the nature of history and the role of the politically committed intellectual, the study questions whether the taking of another's life can ever be justified, and – in an important divergence from a Sartrean view of revolutionary violence – claims that the ends should be seen as sanctified, and not justified, by the means. The connections Camus creates between revolutionary history and its aftermath in Stalin's Russia are clear, and although he attempts to resurrect a French 'syndicalist' tradition, his book rapidly became the target of French communists and their fellow travellers, for whom it epitomised a naive, utopian and ultimately conservative intervention in one of the principal debates of the day.

In the political climate of the Cold War, with the collapse of any hopes of social revolution in France, Sartre (and to a lesser extent Camus) had briefly flirted with the idea of creating a third political force, the 'Rassemblement démocratique et révolutionnaire'. When this project faltered, it became clear that any middle ground was rapidly disappearing: Sartre, in his desire to take sides in a country he perceived as increasingly anti-communist, drifted towards the French Communist Party (PCF); Camus, struggling to transcend politics, found himself increasingly unwilling to align himself with any orthodoxy or common cause. It was this self-imposed solitude that meant that Camus's position in the 1950s would become one of extreme personal difficulty, a situation accentuated by his apparent refusal to clarify his views on those very phenomena – freedom, justice, violence and revolt – on which he had previously commented at length. Sartre's angry response to *L'Homme révolté* was not surprising, for (although Sartre is never mentioned directly by name) Camus's study may be read as a direct challenge to him and to his emerging views on revolution. Indeed, these oblique allusions set the tone for the subsequent dispute, in which communication was conducted either by proxy or in distinctly impersonal terms. Sartre, seemingly offended by Camus's failure to name him, refused to comment in print on the book. *L'Homme révolté* was eventually reviewed in *Les Temps modernes* by his secretary Francis Jeanson, whose 'Albert Camus, ou l'âme révoltée' ('Albert Camus, or the Rebellious Soul') is an acerbic, even violent text, accusing its subject of quietism and aloofness, abstractions reflected in what Jeanson saw as Camus's excessively elegant literary style. Central to the review was a critique of anti-historicism, an observation that not only implied that Camus had failed to understand Marx, but also that he had rejected the commitment to justice implicit in his Resistance activity.

Camus himself interpreted Jeanson's review – from its highly ironic title onwards – as a calculated act of humiliation. He responded provocatively – addressing his own text to the impersonal: 'Monsieur le Directeur' ('Dear Editor') – as if Sartre and not Jeanson had written the piece. Reminding Sartre of their friendship and of his own political activism, Camus charged existentialists with complicity with Stalinism, and accused *Les Temps modernes* of wilfully misunderstanding his central theses. In self-defence, he stated that the book did not deny history but instead engaged with those whom history blinded to present suffering (alluding here to Soviet work camps). In a damning statement, Camus claimed that the reviewer supported revolt against everything 'sauf contre le parti et l'Etat communistes' ('except the Communist Party and the communist state').[6] In fact, Sartre's radicalism never led him – or *Les Temps modernes* – to approve of the violent political extremes of the Soviet Union, and a January 1950 editorial co-authored with Merleau-Ponty had even denounced work camps. However, as a result of the vehemence of the dispute, its participants ended up representing positions they did not necessarily espouse – positions that go far beyond Sartre's existentialist interpretation of Marxism, attempting to reconcile freedom with predetermination, and Camus's left-leaning rejection of communism – in order to transform the two men, respectively, into unapologetic Stalinist and reactionary apologist for Western expansionism. Sartre's response, which appeared in the same issue as Camus's, was moreover highly personal and reflects the extent to which he had been riled. His magisterial, if occasionally snide dismissal of Camus's philosophical competence ignores the ethical ambitions of *L'Homme révolté*, and proceeds to demolish the work's author. Accusing Camus of arrogance and disengagement from struggles for justice as well as abstention from historical action, he tracks the shifts in his now former friend's thought, damningly concluding that his morality had been transformed into moralism.[7]

Jeanson concluded the quarrel with a second, lengthy article,[8] and Camus drafted a final defence of his text, only published after his death (*Ess*, 1702–16), but the obviously public side to the dispute was already over. Moreover, the controversy was eclipsed by the growing Algerian crisis, in the context of which it is now increasingly understood. Such an analysis is not simply the interpretation of contemporary concerns through a historical situation. Although tensions between Camus and Sartre manifested themselves in opposing attitudes to Marxism, their quarrel was at the same time underpinned by a growing awareness in the early 1950s of the role of anti-colonialism in post-war French culture. Jeanson's initial salvo in the dispute had, for instance, included reference to Camus's failure to account for the Madagascan revolt of 1947, US napalm attacks on Vietnam and the treatment of a Tunisian arrested by the Foreign Legion.

The widening of the debate is thus clear from the outset. Camus was piqued by the intimation that he was disengaged from questions of colonial justice, reminding Jeanson that he had been involved in them for almost two decades. In his analysis of the bad faith underpinning Jeanson's review, this focus on racism and colonialism is presented by Camus as a means of avoiding discussion of Stalinism, for him the issue central to *L'Homme révolté*. In response, Sartre saw in Camus's would-be fraternal relationship with indigenous Algerians a bourgeois paternalism replacing direct action with rhetoric (a point reiterated in Jeanson's second article, where he accurately foresees Camus's alarm at anti-colonial nationalism); he even claims that Camus's embarrassment over the Vietnamese independence struggle is generated by his confusion over the Marxist allegiances of colonial nationalism: as enslaved subjects, the Vietnamese have the right to revolt; but their communist-inspired revolution turns them, for Camus, into tyrants. Focussing on the Neo-Destour Party's challenge to French colonial rule in Tunisia in late 1951, Sartre criticises Camus's abstract comments on history, claiming that 'le problème n'est pas de connaître sa fin mais de lui en donner une' ('the problem is not to *know* its end, but to *give* it one').[9]

Camus and Sartre's friendship had been overshadowed from the outset by politics, in which it is likely that Sartre initially considered Camus his superior. For while the former had spent 1934–5 in Berlin, studying the work of the phenomenologist philosopher Edmund Husserl (1859–1938) and lacking any apparent interest in his immediate political context of the rise of Nazism, Camus was already active in the Algerian Communist Party, leading its theatre troupe (before eventually being ejected from the party in 1937 for refusing to accept the termination of its campaign for indigenous civil rights) and indicting the social conditions of colonial Algeria in *Alger républicain* (*Ess*, 903–38). During the Occupation, it was Camus who took risks as an anti-fascist editor at the Resistance daily *Combat*, while Sartre concentrated on completing *L'Etre et le Néant* (*Being and Nothingness*). By the 1950s, however, it was as if the tables had turned. Sartre, who had once admired Camus as the epitome of the committed intellectual, found himself politicised, whilst Camus withdrew increasingly from direct engagement in politics. Moreover, the publication of *L'Homme révolté* may be seen to have played a catalytic role, for it was in the year following the quarrel over the text that Sartre publicly sided with the French Communist Party – the PCF – without becoming a party member. It was, however, his break with the Party in November 1956 over its support of the Soviet invasion of Hungary that led to his increased anti-colonial radicalism. A series of key articles (subsequently published as *Situations* V) appeared over the next six years, and Sartre also provided prefaces for texts by Albert Memmi and Frantz Fanon.[10]

Although, following their dispute, Sartre's public silence on Camus was not broken until the latter's death in 1960, it was clear that the break had had a profound effect on his thinking; conversely, the dispute led to Camus's increasing public silence and his growing sense throughout the 1950s of isolation and betrayal. Moving beyond PCF positions on colonialism, Sartre emerged as a Third World activist whose public pronouncements and writings, aiming to analyse colonialism whilst arguing for decolonisation, can be interpreted as a clear retort to Camus's own silence and indecision. Nowhere is this clearer than in Sartre's 'Le colonialisme est un système' ('Colonialism is a System'), a lecture delivered at the Salle Wagram in Paris on 27 January 1956, shortly after Camus's own address in Algiers calling for a civilian truce (*Ess*, 991–9). The text may be read to contain a series of veiled references to Camus, whose neo-colonial mystification of the colonial system is indicted in Sartre's critique of socio-economic explanations and of notions of 'Franco-Muslim fraternity'. Mocking the idea of reform, Sartre underlines the systemic nature of colonialism, gesturing already towards Fanon's advocacy of violent anti-colonial struggle that Sartre himself would later espouse. Recognising that any liberal solution to the Algerian situation was impossible, Sartre's anti-colonial writings are concerned with the reassertion of the agency (or direct, independent actions) of the colonised. Despite its reliance on an apology for violence, which he would later partially attenuate, Sartre's alternative insight into the situation allowed him to see the major shifts underway, leading – as he saw it – to the decolonisation not just of Algeria but also of France itself. In Sartre's analysis, colonialism operated as a system that dehumanised both coloniser and colonised, drawing the French into a self-destructive cycle of oppression: 'il est notre honte, il se moque de nos lois ou les caricature; il nous infecte de son racisme' ('It is our shame; it mocks our laws or caricatures them. It infects us with its racism').[11]

It is on this point that he differs from Camus, whose engagement in questions of Algerian identity dated back to the 1930s, when he had developed an understanding of Mediterranean culture that celebrated Algerian space as one marked by diversity and reciprocal enrichment. However, as Peter Dunwoodie has demonstrated, this new model tended to include a Muslim presence merely strategically, and was characterised by an implicit Eurocentrism.[12] The possibility of a shared, hybrid culture is not broached, and the social divisions regulating colonial society are accordingly perpetuated. As the Algerian War progressed and Arab agency in North Africa became irrefutably apparent, this fraternal Mediterranean ideal foundered; but Camus, doggedly consistent in his approach and refusing any major change, failed or refused to acknowledge such a shift, preferring to dismiss Algerian (and wider Arab) nationalism as a Soviet-inspired plot. Camus had nevertheless been one of the first *pieds-noirs* to address the poverty of the indigenous population and advocate social change, privileging in his 1939 articles the need for education as well as social and economic (if not political) equality with the French. Moreover, in 1945, reporting on the Sétif massacres, Camus was one of the few French journalists to discuss the implications of colonial violence, although he persisted in assuming that any solution to the current situation would have to be framed in the traditions of French republican democracy: 'C'est la force infinie de la justice, et elle seule, qui doit nous aider à reconquérir l'Algérie et ses habitants' (*Ess*, 959) ('It is the infinite force of justice, and that alone, that must help us to reconquer Algeria and its inhabitants'). Despite their challenge to contemporary orthodoxies, these texts – by presenting a colonial situation in socio-economic terms and refusing to countenance an Algeria outside French control – reject the politicisation Sartre would subsequently foreground, and reveal a persistently reformist belief in the values of colonial France's 'civilising mission' and the old assimilationist ideal (forcing the colonised to adjust to and adopt the values and cultures of the coloniser) on which this was based. What Conor Cruise O'Brien and Edward Said have seen as Camus's failure to incorporate Algerians into fictional writing is accordingly matched by an ultimate refusal of Algerian subjecthood in the political works.

This is surprising, for the analyses proposed by Camus and Sartre emerge from similar initial premises. In his 1955 articles in *L'Express*, for instance, Camus presents Sétif as a reflection of colonial intransigence, which is partly responsible for a descent into violence (*Ess*, 969–98). So far, his analysis seems similar to that of Sartre; yet he continues by questioning the grounds on which the Algerians could use violence to further their cause. It is at this juncture that, advocating the peace conference whose principal aim should be a civilian truce, Camus reveals a failure to understand the implications of French defeat in 1954 at Dien Bien Phu (the final battle of the Indochinese War, that effectively ended the colonial presence of France in the region) and the inexorable movement towards the dismantling of Empire in its then present form. Even revelations about torture in Algeria, to which Sartre's response was swift and savage, failed to alter his opinions. Whereas Sartre's analysis was impersonal and reliant on the identification (and dismantling) of overarching systems, Camus resorted to an increasingly ambiguous, personal and even autobiographical tone, describing his engagement as 'la longue confrontation d'un homme et d'une situation' (*Ess*, 900) ('the long confrontation of an individual and a situation'). Willing to criticise the oppressive Soviet occupation of Hungary in October 1956 as well as the use of the guillotine in France, he failed to acknowledge parallels between this situation and the continued French presence in Algeria, and increasingly retreated into public silence.

This silence marks an end to constructive solutions once it had become apparent to Camus that his earlier assimilationist beliefs increasingly lacked viability. Angered by Sartre's repeated allusions and attacked for his continued silence, Camus finally published in 1958 the self-justificatory 'Algérie 1958', whose aim was to demonstrate that he could be faithful to the concept of universal justice which underpinned his *œuvre*, whilst at the same time remaining a member of his community of origin. Any attempt to occupy a median position was, however, undermined by a refusal to recognise the legitimacy of Arab nationalism – whose romantic prematurity was dismissed in the claim that: 'Il n'y a jamais eu . . . de nation algérienne' (*Ess*, 1012) ('There has never been an Algerian nation'). Camus seemed incapable of acknowledging the impossibility of replacing colonialism with a system of co-existence that would leave existing French authority intact. Moreover, despite his condemnation of FLN violence, his commentary appeared to preclude criticism of either the French government or the destructive actions of his own French Algerian community.

Camus's understanding of the Algerian situation had thus evolved little since the 1930s, when a social and economic critique of the colonial situation had presented the French presence as a guarantee of fairness. His analyses in the 1950s reflect a continued paternalism and failure to accept the feasibility of Algerian independence; they project an imaginary Algeria that does not so much negate historical reality as offer a utopian reconfiguration of it, dependent on a contradictory fiction of community characterised by a shared culture and the harmonious co-existence of different ethnic groups. Camus's notion of a country grounded in Mediterranean culture tended to downplay any indigenous Arab contribution, not least because any shared culture to which he alluded was predominantly French. In the 1958 'Avant-propos' to *Chroniques algériennes*, Camus honours the *pied-noir* tradition in Algeria as one of working-class patriotism (*Ess*, 897–9), seeming to approve the end of colonialism whilst failing to accept any deracination of the community into which he was born. Moreover (and surprisingly given his critical reactions to the French massacres in Madagascar in 1947; *Ess*, 321–3), he continued to ignore an impending sense of historical inevitability, 'seeing', in Emily Apter's terms, 'one nation where there were at least two, [projecting] continental holism in the face of incipient binational antagonism'.[13]

An outburst at a press conference in Stockholm in December 1957, during which Camus had been repeatedly interrupted by an Algerian student in the audience, is often cited as evidence of his abdication of universal justice in favour of the interests of the social group from which he originated: 'Je crois à la justice, mais je défendrai ma mère avant la justice' (*Ess*, 1882) ('I believe in justice, but will defend my mother before justice'). Far from being a spontaneous expression of emotion, this comment echoes earlier sentiments expressed by Camus,[14] and the sentence is customarily read as a statement of solidarity with the *pieds-noirs* or as a retreat from rational politics into affective autobiography. The *pied-noir* poet Jean Sénac immediately attacked Camus for failing to acknowledge his duty to defend both his mother and justice,[15] but the statement may also be interpreted as a criticism of those for whom abstract principles were more valuable than human interrelationships, a group into which, in Camus's eyes, Sartre would certainly have fallen. This critique of Sartre surfaces elsewhere, for instance in comments on those who are willing to 'excuser de loin l'une des violences et de condamner l'autre' (*Ess*, 895) ('to excuse from a distance one type of violence and condemn another'). Moreover, after the Stockholm event, Camus attempted to diffuse the controversy by claiming greater solidarity with the student than with 'beaucoup de Français qui parlent de l'Algérie sans la connaître' (*Ess*, 1883) ('many French people who speak of Algeria without direct knowledge'), a phrase by which he again seems to target French intellectuals such as Sartre.

Camus's inability, despite his professed commitment to a universal notion of justice, to see beyond a French colonial mindset, was analysed astutely by a largely sympathetic commentator, Albert Memmi, who dubbed him a 'colonisateur de bonne volonté' ('coloniser of good will').[16] The phrase is a useful one, for it encapsulates the contradictions of Camus's position: incapable of imagining a future for Algeria outside the frame of colonialism, he nevertheless strove to avoid the intransigent and increasingly violent conservatism of extremists in the *pied-noir* community by envisaging worthy yet ultimately implausible solutions such as the civilian truce in early 1956. Despite the fact that advocacy for this cause earned him the hostility of extremists in his own community, Camus persisted in his refusal to accept either the Algerians' right to self-determination or their inherent ability for self-government (seeing the independence struggle as part of a Nasser-inspired Arab imperialist project). Even as diplomatic answers became increasingly unfeasible, Camus proposed – as he had in the late 1930s – economic and social solutions to what was an unambiguously political situation.

Aronson sums up the tensions underpinning the colonial dimension of the quarrel: 'In the name of serving the oppressed, Sartre accepted oppression. In loving his people, Camus muted his usual denunciation of oppression. Each one was half-right, half-wrong, locked into two separate but mutually supporting systems of bad faith. No longer could either learn from the other.'[17] It is arguable nevertheless that in his fictional writings Camus faced a changing situation in a way that he could not in his essays and journalism. *Le Premier Homme* may attempt to create an uneasily nostalgic fiction of the *pied-noir* community's rootedness in Algeria, but the short stories of *L'Exil et le Royaume* seem to suggest a more ambiguous position, acknowledging the ineffectiveness or even potential complicity inherent in ambivalence or neutrality, suggesting an inevitability of history, and delineating the impossibilities of the community outlined in his non-fictional work. James Le Sueur describes Camus's seeming dislocation from the political mainstream during the Algerian War as a 'posthumous blessing' since his fears over Algeria's future (and in particular over the anti-democratic tendencies of the FLN) have become increasingly true.[18] Indeed, there is a tendency to present Francophone Algerian literature as a cultural phenomenon spanning the war of 1954–62, in which connections are to be found between colonial, anti-colonial and postcolonial writers. The Algerian novelist, historian and film-maker Assia Djebar (1936–), for instance, places Camus at the head of the three processions of the dead in *Le Blanc de l'Algérie* (*The White of Algeria*), associating him accordingly not only with three very different key figures who also died in the period immediately before independence (Frantz Fanon, Mouloud Feraoun and Jean Amrouche), but also with the victims of later assassinations during the 1990s civil war in Algeria.[19] As a *pied-noir* author, Camus's prominence here is striking if not controversial, but Djebar, presenting herself as an intellectual heir to Camus, transforms him into the leader of a multilingual gathering of writers challenging *intégrisme* (politics informed by a radical interpretation of Islam, and the imposition of a single language or identity that accompanies this) and providing an alternative vision of Algerian literature in the twentieth century. In *Camus à Oran* (*Camus in Oran*), Abdelkader Djemaï explores more closely the relationship between Camus and the place of his birth, and Aziz Chouaki, in *Les Oranges* (*The Oranges*), similarly weaves Camus back into his unruly pageant of colonial and postcolonial Algeria.

Whether these recent relocations of Camus are either evidence of post-colonial reappropriation or of a reforging of fraternity in the face of contemporary history, what they suggest is a move beyond the stalemate inherent in partisan approaches to the Camus–Sartre debate, according to which commentators tend to present themselves as Camusian or Sartrean, obliged accordingly to be condemnatory or laudatory by turn. In a text written in the aftermath of Camus's death, Sartre describes their violent disagreement as 'just another way of living together without losing sight of one another in the narrow little world that is allotted us'.[20] In his unpublished and undated response to Sartre's article in *Les Temps modernes*, Camus concedes a similar point about the two men's relationship, implying that his adversary was 'une de nos voix intérieures que nous serions tentés de faire taire et qu'il faut que nous écoutions' (*Ess*, 1716) ('one of our interior voices to which we must listen despite any temptation to silence it'). It is this sense of reciprocity or complementarity, presentable even as a dialectical interdependence, that perhaps best illuminates the clash between Camus and Sartre, as well as the continued resonances of their exchange throughout the five decades that have followed. Not only does the Camus–Sartre quarrel reveal the complexities of the decolonisation process, and the often violently opposed affective and intellectual positions this bespoke; but also it suggests the need to reconsider their explosive relationship in our current context. Despite the end of the Cold War, Camus's dispute with Sartre retains an urgency since it involves issues unresolved by decolonisation that continue to shape the present: struggles for national autonomy within structures of globalised power; the role of violence in political action; the hegemonic relationship of the northern and southern hemispheres; questions of homelessness, marginalisation, identity and self-situation, of displacement and postcolonial cohabitation.

NOTES

1. A series of accounts of the relationship between Camus and Sartre has been published: Ronald Aronson, *Camus and Sartre: The Story of a Friendship and the Quarrel that Ended It* (Chicago and London, University of Chicago Press, 2004); Germaine Brée, *Camus and Sartre: Crisis and Commitment* (London, Calder and Boyars, 1974); Leo Pollmann, *Sartre and Camus: Literature of Existence*, trans. Helen and Gregor Sebba (New York, Ungar, 1970); and Peter Royle, *The Sartre–Camus Controversy: A Literary and Philosophical Critique* (Ottawa, University of Ottawa Press, 1982). For an English translation of the principal texts in the dispute, see David A. Sprintzen and Adrian van den Hoven (eds.), *Sartre and Camus: A Historic Confrontation* (Amherst, Humanity Books, 2004).

2. Francis Jeanson, 'Albert Camus, ou l'âme révoltée', *Les Temps modernes* 79 (1952), 2070.

3. See Shoshana Felman, *Testimony: Crises of Witnessing in Literature, Psychoanalysis and History* (New York, Routledge, 1992), pp. 172–8; Claudie and Jacques Broyelle, *Les Illusions retrouvées: Sartre a toujours raison contre Camus* (Paris, Grasset, 1982); and Susan Dunn, 'From Burke to Camus: Reconceiving the Revolution', *Salmagundi* 84 (1989), 214–29.

4. Royle, *The Sartre–Camus Controversy*, p. 87.

5. See Jean-Paul Sartre, 'Explication de *L'Etranger*', in *Situations 1* (Paris, Gallimard, 1947), pp. 92–112.

6. See Albert Camus, 'Lettre au directeur des *Temps Modernes*', *Les Temps modernes* 82 (1952), 331.

7. See Jean-Paul Sartre, 'Réponse à Albert Camus', *Les Temps modernes* 82 (1952), 334–53.

8. See Francis Jeanson, 'Pour tout vous dire', *Les Temps modernes* 82 (1952), 354–83.

9. Sartre, 'Réponse à Albert Camus', 352, emphasis in the original.

10. See Jean-Paul Sartre, *Situations v* (Paris, Gallimard, 1964).

11. *Ibid.*, p. 48; *Colonialism and Neocolonialism*, trans. Azzedine Haddour, Steve Brewer and Terry McWilliams (London, Routledge, 2001), p. 47.

12. Peter Dunwoodie, *Writing French Algeria* (Oxford, Clarendon Press, 1998), pp. 188–9.

13. Emily Apter, 'Out of Character: Camus's French Algerian Subjects', in *Continental Drift: From National Characters to Virtual Subjects* (Chicago and London, University of Chicago Press, 1999), pp. 65–6.

14. Mark Orme, '*Retour aux sources*: Crisis and Reappraisal in Albert Camus's Final Pronouncements on Justice', *Modern and Contemporary France* 11.4 (2003), 466–7.

15. See James D. Le Sueur, 'The Unbearable Solitude of Being: the Question of Albert Camus', in *Uncivil War: Intellectuals and Identity Politics during the Decolonisation of Algeria* (Philadelphia, University of Pennsylvania Press, 2001), p. 114.

16. See Albert Memmi, 'Camus ou le colonisateur de bonne volonté', *La Nef*, December 1957, 95–6.

17. Aronson, *Camus and Sartre*, p. 225.

18. See Le Sueur, 'The Unbearable Solitude of Being', p. 87.

19. Written in the context of the violent civil war that divided Algeria throughout the 1990s, *Le Blanc de l'Algérie* (Paris, Albin Michel, 1995) is the author's attempt to write an alternative narrative of her country that presents its past (and by extension its present) according to a re-configured set of memories. On the complex, contradictory meanings of Djebar's title, see Elizabeth Fallaize, 'In Search of a Liturgy: Assia Djebar's *Le Blanc de l'Algérie*', *French Studies* 59.1 (2005), 60–1.

20. Cited in Bernard Murchland, 'Camus and Sartre: the Anatomy of a Quarrel', in Michel-Antoine Burnier (ed.), *Choice of Action: The French Existentialists on the Political Front Line*, trans. Bernard Murchland (New York, Random House, 1968), pp. 175–94 (p. 175).

10

DANIELLE MARX-SCOURAS

Portraits of women, visions of Algeria

Although countless books have been written on Albert Camus, critical mono-graphs devoted to portraits of women in his works are extremely limited in number. To date, only two books have appeared on the subject: Anthony Rizzuto's *Camus: Love and Sexuality* and Geraldine Montgomery's *Noces pour femme seule: le féminin et le sacré dans l'œuvre d'Albert Camus* (*Nuptials for Woman Alone: the Feminine and the Sacred in the Work of Albert Camus*). Nevertheless, a number of articles have been devoted to the femi-nine, and especially the maternal, in Camus's fiction and theatre. With the posthumous publication of *Le Premier Homme* in March 1994, consider-able attention has once again focussed on the mother figure in his work, associated, more than ever, with Camus's beloved homeland, Algeria.

The mother figure is central to Camus's work, even when she is more absent than present, as in *L'Etranger*. In fact, a number of absent women haunt Camus's fiction: Rieux's wife in *La Peste* and the woman on the bridge in *La Chute*, to cite but two examples. As for supposedly secondary char-acters like Marie and even more so the Arab nurse in *L'Etranger*, they are anything but minor figures. Camus himself remarked in 1959 that the charac-ters dearest to him were, along with Céleste, the café-owner in *L'Etranger*, Marie and, from *Les Justes*, Dora (*Ess*, 1922). With respect to the nurse, whom very few critics have considered, Patrick McCarthy devotes an elo-quent albeit brief essay to this woman – watching over the French-Algerian dead – who, in her association with Meursault's mother, already foreshad-ows the psychoanalytical and political dimension that will characterise the second part of the novel.[1] Although women are rarely the protagonists in Camus's works, they, nonetheless, play key roles in refining his philosophical and political thought. Nevertheless, while they occupy centre stage in such theatrical works as *Le Malentendu* and *Les Justes*, their presence is much more emblematic in the prose fiction. Their absence-presence has often been interpreted in terms of the Arab-Other, a key subject of postcolonial studies.

The precarious status of women is thus viewed in relation to that of the indigenous, Algerian population.[2]

Clearly, the three women in *Le Malentendu* and Dora in *Les Justes*, pivotally associated as they are with the fundamental notions of desire and violence, are central to Camusian thought. Furthermore, that a short story is entitled 'La Femme adultère' is no small matter. This is, in fact, the only Camusian fictional text to have a woman as its leading protagonist.

Both *Les Justes* and 'La Femme adultère' illuminate, in a highly personalised manner, Camus's conflicting positions with respect to the ideological climate of the post-war and Cold War years. These texts shed important light on the Camus of the later part of his career, the twentieth-century icon who managed to become, in the course of a few years, one of the most criticised, ridiculed and hated French intellectuals. This is the Camus who refused to surrender to the absolutist politics of the Cold War era, a refusal brought to the intellectual fore by the publication of *L'Homme révolté* in 1951 and the ensuing polemic that pitted Camus against other French intellectuals. Before he could recover from this polemic, Camus had to deal with the Algerian crisis. Even though many French intellectuals turned to Third Worldism to salvage Marxism in the wake of Soviet repression in Hungary in 1956, Camus was not obliged to take this route for he had not been afraid to deal with the burning questions of totalitarianism and ideologically supported terrorism in the late 1940s and early 1950s. Furthermore, while many French intellectuals like Sartre 'discovered' Algeria after 1 November 1954, Camus had already spoken out against colonial policy in the mid and late 1930s. Unlike Sartre, he would not side uncritically with the Algerian Liberation Front. After his anti-communism, Camus thus estranged himself further in French and Algerian intellectual and political circles with his positions on Algeria. Camus's original proposal that an Algerian government be comprised of *pieds-noirs* and Arabs was seen by the Left as a continuation of colonialism and by the Right as a betrayal of *l'Algérie française*.

Comparing the political stances of Camus with those of his disciple, Jean Sénac, during the Algerian war, Hamid Nacer-Khodja claims – as many critics before him have done – that with respect to such concepts as justice and violence, Camus always places himself on a strictly moral, even sentimental level.[3] In dismissing Camus's political stances, Nacer-Khodja refers to *Les Justes* in light of the outbreak of the Algerian revolution five years later. With the advent of postcolonial theory – and to some degree, even earlier, with such precursor critics as Conor Cruise O'Brien – it has become common practice to reread Camus's works prior to 1 November 1954 in terms of this historical watershed. As a result, we tend to forget that a novel like

L'Etranger was not always read as colonial fiction. Furthermore, that an already emblematic character like Meursault could become the rebellious hero of the post-war, Vietnam and even punk eras, before becoming the bogey man of postcolonial studies, is unusual, to say the least. Neil Oxenhandler even claims that he identified with Meursault in 1945, because as a young American soldier, he had killed a German: 'we had both changed our lives by an act of violence . . . This set us apart, giving us a destiny that could never be justified'.[4]

Camus always maintained that violence was both inevitable and unjustifiable (*Ess*, 355). In order to make his case, he often centred his argument on the cost of civilian lives, particularly the unnecessary suffering of children, a trope that he borrowed from Dostoyevsky and which is also at the heart of *La Peste*. If Camus is not about to tolerate a God that allows the suffering of children, he is even less willing to accept the justification of terrorism and violence in the name of another abstract entity, such as History. 'Nous sommes au temps de la préméditation et du crime parfait' ('We are living in the era of premeditation and the perfect crime'), wrote Camus in the opening lines of *L'Homme révolté* (*Ess*, 413). In the wake of the Second World War, what fascinated Camus about the young Russian terrorists of February 1905 was the fact that for the last time in Western history the spirit of revolt encountered that of compassion (*Ess*, 573). The poet Ivan Kaliayev in *Les Justes* has often been considered a spokesperson for Camus's ideas on the exceptional character of violence and the need for limits. Nevertheless, these ideas are essentially fashioned by his companion, Dora Doulebov. Kaliayev's refusal to kill innocent children definitely raises moral questions that a hardcore revolutionary like Stepan Fedorov is not willing to accept. Stepan does not suffer from a tender heart; he believes that the revolution will triumph only when they stop worrying about the children (*TRN*, 336).

In his memoirs on the Battle of Algiers, Yacef Saadi, the Algerian militant, who plays himself in Gillo Pontecorvo's 1966 film classic, *La Bataille d'Alger*, explains the bomb mission of 30 September 1956 to Zohra Drif, Samia Lakhdari and Djamila Bouhired, and asks whether they have any objections. One of the women, 'encore prisonnière de la morale qu'on enseigne aux écoliers' ('still subject to a school children's morality'), exclaims that there are also civilians, that is, women and children, in the places they must bomb. After acknowledging that this is indeed the case, but that the French have subjected them to violence for over a century, Saadi concludes: 'Bien! Revenons maintenant aux choses sérieuses. Vous avez devant vous trois bombes. Une pour chacune d'entre vous' ('OK! Let's get back to serious matters now: in front of you are three bombs, one for each of you').[5] In *Les Justes*, Stepan too remarks that only the bomb is revolutionary (*TRN*, 311). Obviously

Saadi does not share the moral, even sentimental, concerns of these women who would go down in history as the first Algerians to plant bombs that killed civilians. Their concerns are not very different from those of Kaliayev and Dora, 'the delicate murderers', or those of Camus himself in his 'Appel pour une trêve civile' (22 January 1956), which preceded, by only months, the escalation of violence that would go down in history as the Battle of Algiers.

Les Justes predates the Algerian revolution by several years. It dramatises the concerns Camus wrote about in *Ni victimes ni bourreaux* and *L'Homme révolté*, post-war reflections on the ensuing Cold War years and their Manichean polarities. *Les Justes* is a dramatisation of historical events, which are also discussed in the section on individual terrorism, 'Terrorisme Individuel', in *L'Homme révolté*. For Camus, the 'delicate murderers' are the last men and women, in the history of revolt, to refuse no part of their condition or their drama (*Ess*, 573). In the foreword to the play, Camus explains that he preserved Kaliayev's name, out of respect and admiration 'pour des hommes et des femmes qui, dans la plus impitoyable des tâches, n'ont pas pu guérir de leur cœur' (*TRN*, 1834) ('for those men and women, who, in the most merciless of tasks, were not able to recover from their heart'). Not being able to let go of the heart is a noble enterprise in the eyes of Camus, for whom happiness was as vital as justice. In *Soleils d'hiver* (*Winter Suns*), another French Algerian, Jean Daniel, reiterates the central place of happiness in Camus's work, noting that without this extraordinary love of life, we would not be able to understand the need for conceptualising what assails this love.[6] Already in *Combat* (22 December 1944), Camus had asked what would be the point of justice if we did not have the chance to be happy (*Ess*, 299).

The quest for happiness, rooted in the corporal and not dissipated in some abstraction, possesses such feminine protagonists as Dora and Janine, the heroine of 'La Femme adultère', and allows us to understand why a play devoted to revolutionary terrorism was also meant to be a love story; or why a woman's unsatisfied yearnings in 'La Femme adultère' foreshadowed the end of French Algeria, which is also central to *Le Premier Homme*. The public and the private, the political and the personal, are never really disassociated in Camus, and allude to a different ethic, which we shall discuss shortly.

Roger Quilliot maintains that in writing *Les Justes*, Camus wanted to create a successful love scene (*TRN*, 1823). This was a rather unusual proposition for a play devoted to 'delicate murderers'. Although Camus's lyrical texts such as *Noces* are highly erotic, love scenes are not the norm in his work, and, when present, usually evoke other questions, often philosophical or political in nature.

Often considered to be one of the most impressive dramas of post-war France, *Les Justes*, the critic John Cruickshank argues, not only provided Camus with a subject that 'permitted a harmonious relationship between his ideas and his dramatic talent, but enabled these two elements to strengthen one another and combine to produce a powerful theatrical experience'.[7] In effect, historical events like the failed and the successful assassination of the Grand Duke occur offstage, whereas discussions of justice, terrorism and love take centre stage. We could easily dismiss such a theatrical strategy by claiming that Camus's theatre was essentially a theatre of ideas and, thus, it would have been difficult to stage the two assassination attempts. While certainly plausible, the staging or non-staging of certain dramatic events also underscores Camus's ideas. Eugène Kouchkine remarks that the most beautiful love scene that Camus ever wrote, which already appears in the *Carnets* in 1949, comprises the structural epicentre of the play.[8] It appears in Act III, several days after Kaliayev's aborted assassination attempt and before his second, successful one. Kaliayev seeks to distinguish himself from Stepan, who places justice above life itself. He claims that he, on the contrary, became a revolutionary because he loved life (*TRN*, 320). Although Kaliayev is interested in a revolution that will give life a chance, Dora will reveal the inherent contradiction of this idealist belief: 'Et pourtant, nous allons donner la mort' (*TRN*, 322) ('And yet we are going to administer death'). As Kaliayev continues to justify the revolutionary act in the name of life, noting that they consent to being criminals so that the innocent will inherit the earth, Dora sounds the death knell: 'Et si cela n'était pas?' (*TRN*, 322) ('What if it does not work out like that?'). Ironically, it is a young woman who questions the revolutionary ideals of this young poet, claiming she has more experience in the organisation. Geraldine Montgomery rightly notes that Dora's scepticism concerning the terrorist action comes from her profound instinct of life, which safeguards her from the too abstract reasoning of Kaliayev.[9] Dora is not more naive, idealistic or sentimental than Kaliayev; rather, she is more coherent. She does not avoid reason, but rather pushes it to its logical limits, which happen to apply to life itself here.

As Kaliayev fervently assumes his mission of assassinating the Grand Duke, Dora reminds him that he will have to look at the man he is about to kill; he will need to realise that he is indeed killing a man and not just a despot: 'Un homme est un homme. Le grand-duc a peut-être des yeux compatissants. Tu le verras se gratter l'oreille ou sourire joyeusement. Qui sait, il portera peut-être une petite coupure de rasoir. Et s'il te regarde à ce moment-là . . .' (*TRN*, 325) ('A man is a man. Perhaps the Grand Duke has gentle eyes; perhaps you'll see him smiling to himself, scratching his ear. Perhaps – who knows? – you'll see a little scar on his cheek where he

cut himself shaving. And, if he looks at you, at that moment . . .'). Dora
is not exactly shouting out revolutionary slogans here, but rather speaking
as though she were thinking of a loved one. The Algerian freedom fighter
Leïla Djabali adopts a similar perspective in her poem, 'Pour mon tortion-
naire, le Lieutenant D . . .' ('For my torturer, Lieutenant D . . .'), composed
at Barberousse prison in December 1957.[10] After describing the torture she
underwent there, she addresses her torturer, asking him whether his wife
stirred his coffee that morning; whether his mother thought he looked well;
and whether he caressed his children's hair. In juxtaposing the exceptional
(revolution) or the parenthetical (torture) with normal, everyday life, Djabali
reminds us that torturers and executioners are also ordinary people, capable
of love and compassion. By appealing to the human in Lieutenant D, Djabali
sets a discourse of compassion and tenderness against a reality of cruelty and
violence. She does not seek to dismiss the horrors associated with war acts.
Her oppositional discourse is no less effective than one founded on hatred.
Furthermore, Camus's Dora is not all that different from the protagonists
of Arab women writing on war, such as Evelyne Accad, Assia Djebar or
Yamina Mechakra, who affirm life over death. Something very different
occurs when life is put back into the arena of war, and revolution, for that
matter. When Act 1 ends with Kaliayev's remark that he will kill with joy,
an oxymoron if there were ever one, we are left wondering as to whether
he has not already fulfilled what both he and Dora ultimately fear: they will
then end up 'spitting in the face of beauty' (*TRN*, 322).

Dora is the only revolutionary woman in Camus's work. Although Camus
wrote sympathetically in *L'Homme révolté* about Kaliayev and Voinarovsky,
terrorists who refused to kill children and women, he also alluded to the
young girl Vera Zassulich, who in 1878 gave rise to Russian terrorism, by
shooting down General Trepov, the governor of Saint Petersburg (*Ess*, 571).
The essential contradiction that Dora embodies as both a woman (technically
a civilian) and a revolutionary relates, in fact, to the tension between love
and justice, which marks Camus's 'second cycle' (the one of *La Peste*, *Les
Justes* and *L'Homme révolté*). Michael Walzer argues that Camus 'attempted
different formulations, always maintaining an antinomy that he might better
have avoided by stating simply that a justice without room for love would be
itself unjust. I think that is what he believed; it is what his critics commonly
deny.'[11]

If Dora and Kaliayev's relationship is hampered by the revolutionary cause,
the contradictions of the latter are also unravelled by the very existence of
their amorous relationship. Kaliayev was unable to kill because of the presence of the Grand Duke's young niece and nephew in the carriage. Maurice
Blanchot maintains: 'Les enfants, la femme, leur innocence ne sont rien

d'autre que le visage du grand-duc, ce visage nu que Dora avait par avance fait voir à Kaliayev'[12] ('The children, the woman, their innocence are nothing other than the face of the Grand Duke, that bare face that Dora had shown Kaliayev previously'). It is Dora who has called attention to that key moment when Kaliayev must acknowledge the human being of flesh and blood before him, who could very well be his alter ego. Recognising limits means recognising the precarious threshold that separates life from death. Stepan, on the other hand, has little tolerance for such trifling human matters. For him, there are no limits if one truly believes in the revolution. In fact, his so-called love for the Russian people is constructed upon a logic implying endless killing. When Dora refuses to accept such a philosophy in the name of love, Stepan replies, 'Tu es une femme et tu as une idée malheureuse de l'amour' (*TRN*, 336) ('You are a woman and you have an unfortunate idea of love').

This 'unfortunate' love, which makes Dora a woman, is at the heart of Act 3. Dora wants Kaliayev to admit that he is capable of loving her in a concrete, selfish, even unjust way: 'il faut bien une fois au moins laisser parler son cœur. J'attends que tu m'appelles, moi, Dora, que tu m'appelles par-dessus ce monde empoisonné d'injustice . . .' (*TRN*, 353). ('One has to pour out one's heart, at least once. I'm waiting for you to call me, Dora, to choose me over this world poisoned by injustice . . .'). Dora wants Kaliayev to come to terms with the fact that 'L'amour est injustice, mais la justice ne suffit pas' (*CII*, 318) ('Love is injustice, but justice is not enough') (*NII*, 250). Love places limits on revolt. When in the final act, Dora asks if she is still a woman (*TRN*, 392), considering that she has volunteered to set off the second bomb, Stepan is quick to remark that she is like him now. However, this is far from being the case. Dora has not become an actual bomb carrier, and consequently a candidate for execution, because of lofty ideals – like Stepan, who loves humanity in the abstract – but because she loves Kaliayev and wishes to be reunited in death. The last line of the play belongs to Dora: 'Yanek! Une nuit froide, et la même corde! Tout sera plus facile maintenant' (*TRN*, 393) ('Yanek! A cold night . . . and the same rope. Everything will be easier now').

According to Cruickshank, 'this is her solution now that she cannot have Kaliayev's love, just as it was his solution to the conflict between his conscience and his political actions'.[13] Obviously, revolutionaries would question her motives and Camus's final statement on individual terrorism. For Dora will finally acknowledge that it is much easier to die from one's inner conflicts than to live with them (*TRN*, 385). Montgomery argues that Dora cannot go any further in love. In desiring to be hanged by the same rope as that of her lover, Dora also dies for the revolution. Ultimately, however, it is her love for Kaliayev that allows her to become an actual bomb carrier and not just a bomb maker. Montgomery perceptively notes that without this love she could have remained 'a woman', for she would not have set off the bomb. Although the revolution may have jeopardised her femininity, to the point of even claiming her lover, Dora – in asking whether she is a woman now that she has agreed to be a bomb carrier and in consequently asking for the right to die in the name of her negated femininity – becomes once again a lover, and thus a woman, in death.[14]

In the final analysis, Dora is the only one acting in the name of love. A number of critics would argue that she is no longer a revolutionary, but a mere woman; or, worse, that there is no place for women in Camus's philosophy of revolt. Such is the opinion of the critic Jeffrey Isaac, who claims that there is not a single female rebel or hero in Camus's work. This is because women stand for 'stability, nurturance, happiness, the private – for comfort and safety. The characters of Cæsonia in *Caligula*, Victoria in *State of Siege*, and Dora in *The Just Assassins* refuse the rebellious logic of their male partners, admonishing them in the name of intimacy and simple love.'[15] Although Isaac concedes – in a footnote – that Dora may be the exception, insofar as she is a political agent, and thus a co-equal of Kaliayev and the other men, he nevertheless concludes that even she 'manifests characteristically "feminine" traits and concerns'.[16] Yet it is precisely her politics of the body that allows Dora to cut through the idealistic rhetoric of both Kaliayev and Stepan. By her very body, through her intimate being, Dora unravels the contradictions that plague these revolutionaries. From the so-called private space where 'love is injustice' – since love always favours the near and the few[17] – Dora questions the so-called public space where 'justice is not enough'.

In an original study on Camusian rebellion and feminist thought, Elizabeth Ann Bartlett demonstrates that, contrary to what a number of male critics have claimed, Camus's women 'secure a rebellion that is faithful to its origins', one that is not 'disembodied'. Bartlett takes issue with Isaac when he claims that it is men with integrity who forsake their bodies and their women in the name of justice. For Bartlett, rebels who separate 'their bodies from their minds, their passions from their ideas, love from justice' forget their origins and, as a result, allow their rebellion to become something else.[18] By bringing feminist theory (one that dismantles the dichotomy in Western political thought between public and private) to bear on Camusian revolt, Bartlett is able to claim that Camus does not isolate the sphere of family and love in a non-political realm; rather, 'the values represented and nurtured therein are fundamental to rebellion'.[19] In many respects, Bartlett's perspective sheds further light on Walzer's incisive theoretical development of what was initially a curt dismissal of Camus by Simone de Beauvoir, who had remarked that the humanist in Camus had given way to the *pied-noir*. This talk about justice that masks a merely local love is viewed in a positive light by Walzer. In defending his mother over justice, Camus committed the crime of love.[20]

Of course, not everyone thought like Camus, who was too often dismissed as politically incorrect. Decades later, Algeria would give birth to fundamentalist terrorists who thought nothing of raping their sisters and slitting the throats of their mothers, of bashing the heads of babies in the name of 'justice'. In the light of the 'second' Algerian War, that is to say the civil war of the 1990s, who today would not choose one's mother over justice? How ironic that Camus has been so often condemned in the name of sentimental moralism, when, for him, the only serious moral question was murder itself (*CII*, 172).

With the publication of *Le Premier Homme* in 1994, international attention once again turned to Camus and the discovery of a 'lost world': French Algeria.[21] However, as Jean Daniel aptly noted in *Le Nouvel Observateur*, Camus's unfinished novel appeared at a time when the French in Algeria were forced to leave, once again, fearing for their lives in a war that would leave thousands of civilian casualties in its wake.[22] What a tragic twist of fate that a work kept in the closet for so many years by those close to Camus who feared that he would once again be misread with respect to Algeria, was published at the height of the second Algerian War. Furthermore, the quasi-simultaneous publication of *Réflexions sur le terrorisme* (*Reflections on Terrorism*) and Denis Salas's *La Juste Révolte* (*Just Revolt*), along with the first Folio edition of *Actuelles III (Chroniques algériennes)* in 2002 only serves to reinforce Camus's pertinence as a thinker in the wake of 9/11 and other recent manifestations of terrorism.[23]

Actuelles III was met by a glacial silence at the time of its first publication in 1958. Critics of Camus – who were legion at that time – felt that he had nothing of worth to say about Algeria, when he broke his vow of silence in publishing this collection of essays dating back to 1939. In hindsight, the most bitter illusion with respect to Algeria, shared by both Algerian and French elites, was perhaps less the Third-Worldist, Marxist slant of the revolution than the vision of a pluralist Algeria based on the co-existence and equality of her different ethnic, religious and linguistic communities. Camus shared this illusion, even if, unlike Sénac, he did not support independence. It is even articulated in *Actuelles III*. Launched by Sénac in June 1953, the literary magazine *Terrasses* advocated a pluralistic Algeria that no longer distinguished between French and Arab or Berber writers. The sole issue ever to appear contained texts by such writers as Emmanuel Roblès, Jean Daniel, Mohammed Dib, Kateb Yacine, Mouloud Feraoun and Camus. The fragile and ephemeral nature of this cultural enterprise foreshadowed what would subsequently take place on a political front.

Camus gave Sénac 'Retour à Tipasa', a stunning essay on the beloved site of his youth, where he first learned not to negate what his hands could touch and what his lips could caress, as he wrote in the much earlier piece 'Noces à Tipasa' (*Ess*, 59). It is there that he first learned to love without limits. Surrounded by barbed wire now, the Roman ruins of Tipasa to which he returns years later mark an original plenitude marred by the barbed wire of tyrannies, war, policings, the time of revolt (*Ess*, 870). Although his love for Tipasa has been mitigated by the lessons of History, Camus can still affirm, in 1952, that no matter how arduous the enterprise, he will seek never to be unfaithful to either beauty or the humiliated (*Ess*, 875). These humiliated include Camus and his beloved, those who, in 1962, would become the *rapatriés* ('repatriated') or *pieds-noirs*.

Camus's passion for Algeria was notorious. On 15 January 1943, he made the following seductive remark: 'Pour l'Algérie . . . c'est la passion sans frein et l'abandon à la volupté d'aimer. Question: Peut-on aimer un pays comme une femme?' (*CII*, 73) ('For Algeria . . . I have unbridled passion and I surrender to the pleasure of loving: Can one love a country like a woman?' (*NII*, 54)). Perhaps we could attribute a double meaning to this question in conjunction with 'La Femme adultère', where the story is told from the perspective of the female protagonist. A highly erotic undertone pervades this short story, where the representation of the female body and desire itself exist not only in opposition to the colonial paradigm associated with the institution of marriage, but also in conjunction with what the female protagonist Janine cannot attain: the Algeria of Algerians.

While literary critics – and university students for that matter – have pondered endlessly over Janine's curious intercourse with the elements atop the terrace parapet, I have always been more interested in what was taking place below: the social intercourse, or lack thereof in this Algerian hinterland, modelled on Laghouat, which Camus visited in December 1952. There is that remarkable scene – just screaming to be filmed – in the square, beginning with the moment in which Janine's husband, the *pied-noir* travelling salesman Marcel, rubs his hands, while looking affectionately at the trunk in front of them. Janine then calls out 'Look'. From the other end of the square, a proud and distinguished Arab is advancing towards them. He reminds Janine of the French officers that she has occasionally admired. Although the Arab is coming towards them, he is looking beyond them, carrying himself, with the dignity of a general: 'Oui, ils avaient tous ici cet air d'orgueil, mais celui-là, vraiment, exagérait' (*TRN*, 1568) ('Yes, all of them here had that look of pride; but this one, really, was going too far'). The square may be empty, but he walks straight towards the trunk without seeing it, and without seeing them. As the distance separating them rapidly decreases, Marcel seizes the handle of the trunk, pulling it out of the way. The Arab passes without noticing and heads toward the ramparts. Janine catches her husband's despondent look as he asserts: 'Ils se croient tout permis, maintenant' (*TRN*, 1568) ('They think they can get away with anything now'). Although Janine does not say anything, she despises the Arab's arrogance and suddenly feels unhappy.

The Arabs clearly have the upper hand here. Whoever said that Arabs – and women – were neglected characters in Camus's writing obviously failed to consider the truly disruptive space they occupy in this story. How humiliating it must be for this French Algerian male to bend down and move the infamous trunk so that the 'proud' Arab can pass! Judging by the manner in which Marcel also holds tightly to the little canvas suitcase set between his knees in the opening scene of the story, it is clear that his affection is for his material possessions, not his wife; whereas Janine's admiration is for the Arab Other, not her colonial spouse. The fact that the Arab crossing the square looks like French officers Janine has admired is not perchance either. For, in the opening scene of the story, while Marcel's attention is focussed on his suitcase, Janine feels the gaze of a French soldier and eventually blushes. Her first reaction upon noticing the gaze was to note that the man looking at her was not an Arab (*TRN*, 1561).

Unlike Marcel, who is desperately clinging to his material possessions, for his colonial identity is bound up with them, Janine is eager to be rid of her excess baggage, which is personified by her very body. She longs for a body that will take up less space, like the Algerians she observes around her: a body bound to the earth and deemed worthy of local recognition. Taking up less space means being an integral part of the land, from which Janine feels visibly detached. Ironically, though she feels conspicuous, no one is returning her gaze. Her physical discomfort ends up assuming a seductive quality. However, at best, she only can take frightened pleasure from the burnouses that brush against her as three Arab men cycle past. She races towards the fort, where, with her body leaning heavily against the parapet, she will consummate the sexual act alone.

Identity, for Camus, has always been associated with an acute sense of place, even when it is articulated in terms of non-belonging or exile. The plight of Marcel and Janine as *pieds-noirs* without bearings in the Algerian hinterland clearly reveals the connection between space and identity. Their identity is challenged by an ever-shrinking space. For Marcel, it is reduced to the space of the canvas bag and trunk to which he desperately clings; for Janine, it is interiorised in her body. Her marriage in this colonial society has made her an undesirable being. It is therefore not surprising that she will seek to consummate the sexual act beyond the walls of the conjugal room, in a landscape apparently devoid of colonial markers.

The insatiable thirst for beauty, and the sensual happiness that comes with it, which still haunts Camus in 'Retour à Tipasa' (*Ess*, 871), cannot easily be quenched in this parched interior, far from the Mediterranean coast that marks the youthful Camus of the mid 1930s. Here, in 'La Femme adultère', everything is stone. The Algerian landscape, which critics claim Camus hid behind, actually spells out a barren nature, which parallels the barrenness of one of its characters. Janine and Marcel are childless. Rizzuto fittingly remarks that 'Camus's characters, for the most part, have no biological future'.[24] Could this fictional reality be hinting at the impossible future haunting the *pieds-noirs*?

The setting for this short story is clearly not that of 'Noces à Tipasa'. In fact, the metaphor of marriage takes on oppressive, even bloody connotations in *Actuelles III*, where it is used to represent the difficult relationship between 'French' and 'Arabs' in Algeria. Conceived in 1952 and initially published in 1954 by Charlot in Algiers, 'La Femme adultère' anticipates the impossible dialogue Camus would advocate in his 'Appel pour une trêve civile' in January 1956.

An unsatisfied yearning for love, which can only be consummated in the orgasmic present of adultery with the beloved land, reveals another side of Algeria, both geographically and historically. For the Algeria of the 1950s is no longer that of the 1930s, and a new backdrop (as well as a new nation) is in order. If Assia Djebar could claim that Camus had only embraced the coast in *Noces*, whereas she, as an Algerian woman writer, had claimed the entire region, including the hinterland, what could be said then about 'La Femme adultère', which takes Camus even further south than Djebar's writings?[25] At that time, Djebar was obviously dismissing Camus's legitimacy as an Algerian writer. It would take the Algerian Civil War of the 1990s for Algerian writers and critics to give Camus back his *Algérianité*. Nevertheless Camus's identity crisis as a French-Algerian writer has not yet been resolved. In *Albert Camus. Assassinat post-mortem (Assassination Post-Mortem)* (2005), the Algerian critic Mohamed Lakhdar Maougal laments the visible absence of Camus in the 2004 Franco-Algerian encounter, 'L'Année de l'Algérie' ('The Year of Algeria'). That Algeria continues to assassinate him post-mortem is not all that surprising given that she has yet to realise her much desired democracy. However, that France did not give him a place of honour in this year of commemorations is truly disturbing.[26] Maougal proposes to give Camus back to France, at a time when France, perhaps even more so than Algeria, is prey to what the critic Hélé Béji refers to elsewhere as a cultural radicalism that cannot accommodate the Other.[27]

NOTES

1. Patrick McCarthy, 'The First Arab in *L'Etranger*', *Revue CELFAN Review* 4.3 (1985), 25–6.
2. See, for example, Louise Horowitz, 'Of Women and Arabs: Sexual and Racial Polarization in Camus', *Modern Language Studies* 17.3 (Summer 1987), 54–61.
3. Hamid Nacer-Khodja, *Albert Camus. Jean Sénac ou le fils rebelle* (Paris, EDIF, 2004), p. 64.
4. Neil Oxenhandler, *Looking for Heroes in Postwar France. Albert Camus, Max Jacob, Simone Weil* (Hanover, Dartmouth College/University Press of New England, 1996), p. 20.
5. Yacef Saadi, *La Bataille d'Alger* (Algiers, Entreprise Nationale du Livre, 1984), p. 284.
6. Jean Daniel, *Soleils d'hiver. Carnets 1998–2000* (Paris, Grasset, 2000), p. 219.
7. John Cruickshank, *Albert Camus and the Literature of Revolt* (New York, Galaxy Books/Oxford University Press, 1959/1960), p. 215.
8. Eugène Kouchkine, '*Les Justes*: le tragique de l'amour et du renoncement', in Jacqueline Lévi-Valensi and Agnès Spiquel (eds.), *Camus et le lyrisme* (Paris, Editions SEDES, 1997), p. 161.
9. Geraldine F. Montgomery, *Noces pour femme seule. Le féminin et le sacré dans l'œuvre d'Albert Camus* (Amsterdam/New York, Rodopi, 2004), p. 272.
10. Denise Barrat (ed.), *Espoir et parole* (Paris, Seghers, 1963), pp. 99–100.
11. Michael Walzer, 'Albert Camus's Algerian War', in *The Company of Critics* (New York, Basic Books, 1988), p. 138.
12. Maurice Blanchot, *L'Entretien infini* (Paris, Gallimard, 1969), p. 279.
13. Cruickshank, *Albert Camus and the Literature of Revolt*, p. 219.
14. Montgomery, *Noces pour femme seule*, pp. 283–4.
15. Jeffrey C. Isaac, *Arendt, Camus, and Modern Rebellion* (New Haven, Yale University Press, 1992), p. 233.
16. *Ibid.*, p. 307, n. 17.
17. Walzer, 'Albert Camus's Algerian War', p. 137.
18. Elizabeth Ann Bartlett, *Rebellious Feminism: Camus's Ethic of Rebellion and Feminist Thought* (New York, Palgrave/Macmillan, 2004), pp. 14–15.
19. *Ibid.*, p. 16.
20. Walzer, 'Albert Camus's Algerian War', pp. 138, 145.
21. See, for example, Tony Judt, 'The Lost World of Albert Camus', *New York Review of Books* 41.16 (6 October 1994), 3–5.
22. Jean Daniel, 'Le Suicide d'une nation', *Le Nouvel Observateur* 14–20 (April 1994), 28.
23. J. Lévi-Valensi and D. Salas (eds.), *Albert Camus: Réflexions sur le terrorisme* (Paris, Nicolas Philippe, 2002); D. Salas, *Albert Camus: La Juste Révolte* (Paris, Broché, 2002).

24. Anthony Rizzuto, *Camus. Love and Sexuality* (Gainesville, University Press of Florida, 1998), p. 4.
25. Assia Djebar, 'Afterword', in *Women of Algiers in Their Apartment* (Charlottesville, University Press of Virginia, 1992), p. 177.
26. Mohamed Lakhdar Maougal (ed.), *Albert Camus. Assassinat post-mortem (2005)*, (Algiers, Editions APIC, 2005), pp. 11–12.
27. Hélé Béji, 'Radicalisme culturel et laïcité', *Le Débat* 58 (January–February 1990), 47.

PART III

Texts and contexts

11

PETER DUNWOODIE

From *Noces* to *L'Etranger*

In February 1937 twenty-four-year old Albert Camus delivered the opening address at the launch of a new *Maison de la Culture* in Algiers. He
placed the undertaking squarely within the cultural debate going on in an
Algiers dominated by a group of well-established European artists and intellectuals known as the 'Algerianists', supporters (under the leadership of the
novelists Louis Bertrand and Robert Randau) of the reactionary politics of
Maurice Barrès and Charles Maurras in mainland France. As Camus's title
made clear, for the young people launching this new venture – a group of self-
styled 'left-wing intellectuals' (*Ess*, 1321) united through university, amateur
theatre, political activism – the issue of the day was 'La culture indigène. La
nouvelle culture méditerranéenne' ('Indigenous Culture. The New Mediterranean Culture'). To today's (postcolonial) reader, this title might suggest
an anthropological assessment of a colonised culture and its absorption
into, and contribution to, a new, perhaps hybridised, cultural construct.
The stated objective, announced with a high seriousness scarcely veiled by a
declared modesty, would seem to reinforce this perception: 'servir la culture
méditerranéenne, contribuer à l'édification, dans le cadre régional, d'une culture dont l'existence et la grandeur ne sont plus à démontrer. Nous voulons
seulement aider un pays à s'exprimer lui-même. Localement. Sans plus. La
vraie question: une nouvelle culture méditerranéenne est-elle réalisable?'[1]
('to serve Mediterranean culture, to contribute, within a regional framework, to the construction of a culture whose existence and grandeur are
widely recognised. We simply wish to help a country express itself. Locally.
That's all. The real question: is a new Mediterranean culture possible?'). To
a listener in 1937, on the other hand, both title and opening statement would
have been provocative, rather than consensual, because the positions implied
– on what was indigenous, new or 'Mediterranean', but also on the make-
up of an indigenous 'culture' – were hotly contested. As Camus's rhetoric
makes clear, his lecture was in fact a manifesto, both polemical and prospec-
tive. The self-contradictions evident therein – a 'widely recognised' culture

somehow still open to questions regarding its feasibility; a Mediterranean culture, yet the local cultural expression of a specific country – derive, no doubt, from his dual objective. This was, firstly, to declare the group's hostility to the Eurocentric, confrontational and somewhat provincial cultural identity fostered by Algerianism; and secondly, to signal allegiance to an alternative geocultural space labelled 'Mediterranean'.[2] Camus's early lyrical essays, *L'Envers et l'Endroit* (1937) and *Noces* (1939), are grounded in this engagement, and in reviewing the cultural and political context thereof in the first part of this chapter my objective is to show how the attitudes and values embodied therein help us understand the unprepossessing hero of Camus's best-known work, *L'Etranger* (1942), discussed in the second part.

It was to Louis Bertrand and the colony's French historians (Gaston Boissier and Stephan Gsell in particular) that the Europeans in Algeria owed the self-representation which, by the 1930s, had hardened into the Eurocentric colonialist doxa that the *Maison de la Culture* group opposed. At the heart of this doxa (and of the association of writers it spawned) lay the notion of 'Latin Africa', the racially exclusive bedrock of a European Algerian region of *la grande France*, a province actively participating in France's national saga (though frequently at odds with its republican ideals). The material base for this ethnically biased notion lay primarily in the wealth of archaeological remains being mapped throughout Algeria at that time, like the great ruins at Cherchell and Tipasa, Thimgad and Djemila. The essence of the construct, for which these vestiges served as anchors, lay in privileging historical time and anteriority while relegating as insignificant, indeed artificial and illusory, both the present and the recent past. In the words of Louis Bertrand: 'A travers le Méditerranéen d'aujourd'hui, je reconnus le Latin de tous les temps. L'Afrique latine perçait, pour moi, le trompe-l'œil du décor islamique moderne. Elle ressuscitait dans les nécropoles païennes et les catacombes chrétiennes, les ruines des colonies et des municipes dont Rome avait jalonné son sol.'[3] ('Through today's Mediterranean man I recognised timeless Latin man. Latin Africa was thrusting through the trompe-l'œil of the modern Islamic décor. It was being reborn in the pagan necropolises and the Christian catacombs, in the ruins of the colonies and towns Rome had spread across the land.') Even where modified by later Muslim invaders in a process of adaptation, Bertrand claimed in 1921, the region remained stubbornly 'Latin'.[4] Treated as mere surface illusion peddled by a generation of orientalising Romantic prejudice, the Arab/Berber civilisation of the Maghreb was derided, then elided within an imaginary geography of 'virgin territory'. This was then claimed as the rightful inheritance of the European settler, mythologised by Bertrand as an aggressive, conquering Man of Action who reconfigured the colony's imaginary and socio-economic spaces as exclusively European, thanks to a 'Latin spirit' said to be actively forging an 'intellectual regionalism' based on the values and traditions of Athens and Rome.

This is the discourse – carrier of the selective history and colonialist cultural and economic project operative in pre-war Algeria – that Camus is seeking to counter in his *Maison de la Culture* speech of 1937. In the opening paragraph, his chosen terms, 'Mediterranean culture' and 'Mediterranean regionalism', mask the shift that he is proposing, remapping a cultural space inherited from Greece, and thereby relativising the impact of Rome: 'Toute l'erreur vient de ce qu'on confond Méditerranée et Latinité et qu'on place à Rome ce qui commença dans Athènes' (*Ess*, 1321) ('The mistake is caused by merging Mediterranean and Latin, and locating in Rome what began in Athens').[5] The anteriority which was the cornerstone of the Algerianist world view is thus acknowledged, but reappropriated. It was, claimed Camus, the misunderstanding regarding cultural regionalism that his speech aimed to dissipate, and the alternative that he proposes is grounded in a systematic denunciation of the 'Roman'. It mixes the cultural, political and personal in a structured polarisation replicated in the essays he was writing at that time (*L'Envers et l'Endroit, Noces*). The 'race curieuse et forte . . . [les] hommes débraillés, [la] vie forte et colorée' ('an inquisitive, strong race, carefree men, a strong, colourful life') are said to link the various Mediterranean peoples in a single community (*Ess*, 1322), a living reality, and separate them from Rome and the Romans who constructed only an abstract and conventional Mediterranean (*Ess*, 1323). The Mediterranean, Camus counters, 'est ailleurs. Elle est la négation même de Rome et du génie latin' (*Ess*, 1324) ('lies elsewhere. It constitutes a negation of Rome and the Latin spirit').[6] This resounding rejection of the Algerianist line (and its influential right-wing French metropolitan equivalent) is accompanied by an equally forceful denunciation of Mussolini and Hitler, purveyors of a 'Latin order' driven by a warlike spirit and a soulless violence (*Ess*, 1324), on lies, pomp and a stifling self-restraint totally foreign to the *joie de vivre* of the peoples of the Mediterranean basin (*Ess*, 1322).

The claim to an immediate, direct, personal contact with the vitality of the region is typical of the ambiguities formulated in Camus's lecture. Beyond the opposition to the 'Romanisation' of Algerian/Mediterranean history, and the ready-made and essentialist counter-assertions regarding a vitality supposedly specific to the lucky inhabitants of the Mediterranean region (but not to 'Romans'), it is unclear *where* Camus locates the Mediterranean in the early texts. It is on these, nevertheless, that critics have repeatedly based the claim to his 'mediterraneity' and his status as an Algerian writer. Elements of a response are discernible in the assertiveness, if not the coherence, of the 1937 lecture:

> Bassin international traversé par tous les courants, la Méditerranée est de tous les pays le seul peut-être qui rejoigne les grandes pensées orientales. Car elle n'est pas classique et ordonnée, elle est diffuse et turbulente. Ce goût triomphant de la vie, ce sens de l'écrasement et de l'ennui, les places désertes à midi en Espagne, la sieste, voilà la vraie Méditerranée et c'est de l'Orient qu'elle se rapproche. Non de l'Occident latin. (*Ess*, 1324–5)

> (An international basin criss-crossed by numerous currents, the Mediterranean is perhaps the only country to have links with major eastern doctrines. For it is diffuse and turbulent, not classical and ordered. The all-embracing taste for life, the sense of *ennui* and of being crushed, Spain's deserted midday squares, the siesta, these are the real Mediterranean. It is closer to the Orient than to the Latin West.)

The essays of *Noces*, written in 1937–8, might be expected to illustrate this encounter. What their lyricism actually reveals, however, is a Eurocentric experience mixing the vitality and sensuality of the author, an overt reappropriation of the icons of 'Algerianity' (the Roman ruins of Tipasa and Djemila in particular) and the rejection of the ethos (of labour and possession) embodied in the colony's settlers. Camus's lyricism articulates the intensity of subjective experience, the profusion, indeed excess which greet the individual willing to abandon him/herself to 'Nature'. It thus privileges the present, immediacy, spontaneity. And if its poignancy can be heightened by awareness of the ephemerality of the experience and the inevitable return of a feeling of loss and separation (key feature of *L'Envers et l'Endroit*), it resolutely excludes the nostalgia of the Romantics, the facile exoticism of orientalising travel-writers and the historicity foregrounded by Louis Bertrand. Only a historian can seek a history lesson among ruins, Camus protests in an unused passage for 'Noces à Tipasa', in 1937–8. In fact, he concludes, what they teach is both more immediate and more spiritual: their function is not to anchor the individual in time (an Algerianist strategy designed to legitimise the occupation of space), but to be a privileged, almost sacred, space, a space outside temporality (*Ess*, 1350). It is here that the individual can, unexpectedly, fleetingly, experience the fusion that Camus evokes in 'Le Vent à Djémila': 'Sans arrêt, il sifflait avec force à travers les ruines . . . Je me sentais claquer au vent comme une mâture. Creusé par le milieu . . . ma peau se desséchait jusqu'à ne plus être la mienne; j'étais poli par le vent, usé jusqu'à l'âme. J'étais un peu de cette force selon laquelle je flottais, puis beaucoup, puis elle enfin.'[7] (*Ess*, 62) ('It blew ceaselessly, and with force, among the ruins. I felt myself flapping in the wind like a sail. Hollowed out from within, my skin dried out and felt no longer mine; the wind polished me, eroded my very soul. I felt a small part of that force on which I was drifting, then very much part of it, and finally fused with it'). While such experiences are the rare cases in which Camus's writing is freed from the bounds of contemporary society (which swamp Meursault in Part II of *L'Etranger* and, in metaphorical guise, exhaust Rieux and his companions in *La Peste*), the rhetoric of *Noces* generates a heady mix of physicality (indeed sexualised contact with Nature) and mythologising reflection posing as philosophical questioning. Voicing the anguished yet satiated self-consciousness of being-in-the-world, total absorption in the here-and-now, it fashions a twentieth-century hedonism riven by the awareness that 'le monde finit toujours par vaincre l'histoire. Ce grand cri de pierre que Djémila jette entre les montagnes, le ciel et le silence, j'en sais bien la poésie: lucidité, indifférence, les vrais signes du désespoir ou de la beauté' (*Ess*, 65–6) ('in the end, the world always defeats history. The cry from Djemila's stones, echoing around the mountains, the sky and the silence, has a deep poetic resonance for me: lucidity, indifference, the true signs of despair or beauty'). What characterises these exceptional experiences of Camus's narrator, though rarely his characters, is a suspended moment, occasionally one of stasis, in which consciousness of the self slips imperceptibly into absorption in immediate surroundings, via the heightened receptiveness of the senses, sexualised as *le grand libertinage* (*Ess*, 56).[8] Immersed in the immediacy of a 'natural' world, a space in which the timelessness of old stones is paired with the eruptive growth of the flowers and grasses that overrun them, Camus's narrator lives an intensely private experience. This counters the Algerianists' privileging of the topos of action, the creative destruction driving settler society, on the one hand; and on the other, it articulates what was to become a lasting feature of Camus's thought, namely the cultural divide between Mediterranean hedonism and northern Europe's thin-blooded rationalists, accused of being estranged from both nature and what Louis Bertrand called the *villes solaires* (sun-drenched cities), so prominent in Camus's own writing.[9]

The cultural, intertextual input into the Mediterranean construct elaborated in *Noces*, although essential, can be raised only very briefly here. It was fashionable in the 1930s, and can be traced for instance in the work of the poet Paul Valéry (including his 1936 Algiers lecture, 'Impressions de Méditerranéen' ('A Mediterranean's Impressions')) and, especially, in the work of the philosopher and essayist Jean Grenier, Camus's teacher.[10] The mediation through art unsettles the once-popular critical argument that Camus's Mediterranean imaginary resulted solely from the immediacy and intensity of existential experience. It serves as a reminder that this imaginary was constructed in part through a reworking of values rendered urgent, locally, by the unrelentingly polarised nature of colonial relations in Algeria and, globally, by the spread of fascism – especially the Italian version whose youthful, physical vitality and cult of the body (shorn of Mussolini's ponderous Romanisation and grandiloquent theatricality) had been greeted enthusiastically in France by writers like Drieu la Rochelle.[11]

This alternative, Mediterranean humanism was also actively promoted in Algeria from the 1920s, especially by Gabriel Audisio, a friend and writer only a few years older than Camus but greatly admired by Algeria's young hopefuls in the 1930s, not least as an author published by Gallimard in Paris.[12] In a series of locally influential texts Audisio roundly rejected the racially exclusive self-glorification of the 1930–1 celebrations marking the centenary of French colonial rule in Algeria, and turned to a paradigmatic Mediterranean text, the *Odyssey*, and a mythical figure, Ulysses, in order to promote a lively, indeed boisterous, alternative form of mediterraneity, as Camus claimed.[13] The sea, the sun, physicality, adventure and, above all, movement constituted the essence of this vision, a joyous evocation of youthfulness and unbridled appetite. It was expressed through a vocabulary and an imagery which privilege work and freedom, not in the petty-bourgeois, grasping embodiment popularised by the colony's Algerianist novel, but in picaresque stories of seafarers who share with their mythical Greek ancestor the *joie de vivre*, vitality and camaraderie of ports, ships, travel: 'à toute heure, le plaisir du départ' ('at any moment, the pleasures of departure').[14] The Mediterranean for Audisio was thus a space of pleasure, indeed excess, of youthful exuberance, diversity, healthy animality and the cult of satiety. His texts promoted an expansive, non-conflictual mediterraneity, a space of freedom (*le large* or open sea) in which work merges with seafaring, erasing frontiers and deviating from the Muslim–European confrontation hardening in Algeria (and left largely unchanged by the brief period in government in France of the *Front Populaire* in 1936). Camus's mediterraneity shared much of this, but it evoked more easily circumscribed spaces, whether in coastal Algeria or southern European towns like Florence or Fiesole. This distinction is important insofar as it helps us recognise that in Algeria the experiences mapped in the lyrical essays of *Noces*, like the solipsistic tête-à-tête with the natural world evoked later in *L'Etranger*, could be deemed to exist only in the preserved margins of, and in an artificially suspended time within, the colonial system:

Non, ce n'était pas moi qui comptais, ni le monde, mais seulement l'accord et le silence qui de lui à moi faisait naître l'amour. Amour que je n'avais pas la faiblesse de revendiquer pour moi seul, conscient et orgueilleux de le partager avec toute une race, née du soleil et de la mer . . . et [qui], debout sur les plages, adresse son sourire complice au sourire éclatant de ses ciels.

('Noces à Tipasa', *Ess*, 60)

(No, I was not what counted, nor the world, but simply the harmony and silence that awakened love between us. It was a love which I was not naive enough to claim as my own; I was conscious and proud to be sharing it with an entire race, born of the sun and sea, standing upright on the shore, and whose complicitous smile was turned to the bright smile of its skies.)

Camus's coastal imaginary produced a mythologising evocation of a 'race' firmly and intensely grounded in leisure time and pleasure.[15] The appeal to European fantasies on Edenic spaces and to the desire to dissociate the self from its historical responsibilities via an intense relationship with Nature, was clearly driving this construct.[16] The unsaid on which it was based, however, is the existence of reserved, protected spaces – marked on Algeria's beaches (and, no doubt, its archaeological sites) by signs which read: 'Interdit aux mendiants, aux chiens et aux Arabes' ('No beggars, dogs or Arabs').[17] As a central signifier, the 'Mediterranean' allows an undefined expansion of such fantasised spaces, thus sidestepping the issue that *L'Etranger* will later confront, namely the fact that the pleasure-laden spaces invented by the European are also always spaces traversed by, and claimed by, the *indigène* (as the native inhabitants were called).

If we now look back to Camus's 1937 Algiers lecture, we can see that while intellectual acknowledgement, and a congenial hybridisation, of East–West, Muslim–Christian, are lauded, the evidence called upon to ground the claim remains strictly Eurocentric: the linguistic unity of Romance languages; the Guilds and Orders of medieval and feudal Europe; a civilisation able to absorb foreign ideas and doctrines (*Ess*, 1325). As Jean Sarocchi remarks tartly in a special issue of the periodical *Perspectives* devoted to Camus and the Mediterranean, the claims made in that lecture-manifesto are 'un guêpier d'erreurs et d'inexactitudes' ('a hornets' nest of errors and imprecision'), and Camus's mediterraneity a problematic dream marred by ethnocentricity.[18] In the same issue, one should add, other critics wholeheartedly adhere to Camus's position, on the contrary, eulogising 'une mythologie du réel, fondée sur un véritable mythe de la Méditerranée' ('a mythology of the real, grounded in a veritable Mediterranean myth'),[19] and 'un lieu symbolique, source de vérité, de "vraies richesses"' ('a symbolic space, source of truth and "true riches"').[20]

Camus's Mediterranean, one has to conclude with Sarocchi, is clearly not that of geographers, cultural historians, economists or politicians. His lyrical essays of the period reveal that it is a privileged, imaginary geography, indeed arguably a 'personal myth' founded, imaginatively, on a number of essential, defining values: abundance, excess, spontaneity, generosity and sensuality, the Dionysian.[21] The most lucid summary of that Eurocentric paradigm is provided by Camus himself in 1938, the year after the opening of the *Maison de la Culture* and during which he was finalising the texts of *Noces*. In an introduction to a new periodical, *Rivages*, launched as an alternative to the colony's dominant, Algerianist publications, he wrote:

> A l'heure où le goût des doctrines voudrait nous séparer du monde, il n'est pas mauvais que des hommes jeunes, sur une terre jeune, proclament leur attachement à ces quelques biens périssables et essentiels qui donnent un sens à notre vie: mer, soleil et femmes dans la lumière. Ils sont le bien de la culture vivante, le reste étant la civilisation morte que nous répudions. (*Ess*, 1330–1)

> (At a time when the taste for doctrines is striving to cut us off from the world, it is good that young men, in a young land, proclaim how attached they are to those few perishable and essential things that give life a meaning: sea, sun, and women in the light. These things belong to living culture, and the rest is a dead civilisation that we reject.)

Whereas customarily, economics, labour and commerce constitute the values shaping colonial space, the easy hedonism of the figures in the quotation is central to the impact of *Noces*, no doubt, as the evocation of a carefree space located not at the margins of colonial life (as might have been expected when projecting a utopia), but at the centre of a conscious remapping of colonial space. Camus goes beyond that hedonistic alternative and uses *Noces* to promote an asceticism which generates its own alternative, stark lyricism. Moreover, to the colonial theme of rootedness through labour and ownership, and the perception of space solely in terms of profitable transformation, Camus opposes a state of permanent 'déracinement' ('uprootedness') via the evocation of a harsh mineral world. In this world the individual has no place; yet like a mirage, it is tantalisingly offered, as the 1952 short story 'La Femme adultère' makes clear: 'Au-dessus du désert, le silence était vaste comme l'espace . . . Là-bas, plus au sud encore, à cet endroit où le ciel et la terre se rejoignaient dans une ligne pure, là-bas, lui semblait-il soudain, quelque chose l'attendait qu'elle avait ignoré jusqu'à ce jour et qui pourtant n'avait cessé de lui manquer' (*TRN*, 1569–70) ('Above the desert, the silence was as vast as the space . . . In the distance, still farther south, at the point where sky and earth met in a pure line, it suddenly seemed to her that, there, something awaited her, something of which until that moment she had been unaware although it had always been lacking'). But this fantasy, that she could join the desert nomads in a supposedly privileged space, was openly contradicted in a section of Camus's 1939 essay 'Le Minotaure', entitled

'Le Désert à Oran' ('The Desert at Oran'), whose opening lines effect a poignant, nostalgia-laden foreclosure: 'Il n'y a plus de déserts. Il n'y a plus d'îles' (*Ess*, 813) ('There are no more deserts, no more islands'). Once again, it is clearly not physical geography that is at issue here. The loss is that of an imaginary geography – of elemental, primordial space – because 'le désert lui-même a pris un sens, on l'a surchargé de poésie' ('the desert itself has acquired meaning, it is now overladen with poetry') (*Ess*, 814). The consciousness and/or the quest of European protagonists like Janine ('La Femme adultère') and Daru ('L'Hôte'), or the narrator who confronts the urban desert in 'Le Minotaure', are thus haunted by the awareness that they do not 'belong' in the world they so ardently seek to embrace. In a tense, disjointed sentence that replicates the heroine's heightened excitement and inner tension, Janine comes to realise that 'ce royaume, de tout temps, lui avait été promis et que jamais, pourtant, il ne serait le sien, plus jamais, sinon à ce fugitif instant, peut-être' (*TRN*, 1570) ('this realm had been eternally promised to her, and never, however, would it be hers, never again, except in this fleeting moment, perhaps'). And in the case of Daru, Camus grants him a burdensome conclusion: 'dans ce désert, personne, ni lui ni son hôte n'étaient rien. Et pourtant, hors de ce désert, ni l'un ni l'autre, Daru le savait, n'auraient pu vivre vraiment' (*TRN*, 1617) ('in this desert nobody, neither he nor his guest, meant anything. And yet, outside this desert neither of them could live really'). Camus's characters, one might conclude, are constructed as either outsider characters, like Janine, typified by the malaise of the threshold always about to be crossed; or insider characters, like Daru, threatened by the excommunication that challenges their sense of belonging. Both constructs, however, constitute responses to an existential drive for rootedness which, as a more openly personal text like *L'Envers et l'Endroit* highlights, can be overcome only by divesting the self of such illusions and consciously adopting the spirit of *detachment* fostered by the Absurd:

> Ce qui me frappait alors ce n'était pas un monde fait à la mesure de l'homme – mais qui se refermait sur l'homme. Non, si le langage de ces pays s'accordait à ce qui résonnait profondément en moi, ce n'est pas parce qu'il répondait à mes questions, mais parce qu'il les rendait inutiles. Ce n'était pas des actions de grâces qui pouvaient me monter aux lèvres, mais ce Nada qui n'a pu naître que devant des paysages écrasés de soleil. Il n'y a pas d'amour de vivre sans désespoir de vivre. (*Ess*, 44)

> (What struck me then was not a world made to measure for man – but one which closed in on man. No, if the language of these countries harmonised with what sounded deeply within me, it was not because it answered my questions,

but because it rendered them superfluous. It was not a prayer of thanks that came to my lips, but the Nada that could only have originated in a country crushed by the sun. There can be no love of life without despair at life.)

Noces went unnoticed in mainland France. *L'Etranger*, on the other hand, published in Paris in 1942, was an immediate success, thanks largely to an 'Explication de *L'Etranger*' published by Jean-Paul Sartre in the Resistance periodical *Les Cahiers du Sud* of February 1943.[22] For some it was a brilliant updating of the French novel's concern with moral issues; for others a defence of individualism; while yet others read in it an antidote to the guilt, greyness and self-flagellation imposed on a defeated population in Vichy France. Sartre's article, and the publication in December 1942 of Camus's *Mythe de Sisyphe*, swept the novel up in the rising enthusiasm for the 'Absurd', an interpretation reinforced by the stark, unrelenting evocation of existential angst driving the plays that Camus completed at that time, *Caligula* and *Le Malentendu*. For all of these readings, the spatial setting of the novel (the colonial arena), recognised as central by today's reader, remained largely undiscussed, no doubt because Algiers and the surrounding countryside were merely familiar elements of a sunny French coastal *département*,[23] and the lives described were banal, working-class, indeed resolutely unremarkable. As for the hero's crime, the text itself reflects ironically on the fact that the killing of an Arab is devoid of interest and might make the pages of the metropolitan press only because their correspondent was filling in time while awaiting the trial of a parricide (*TRN*, 1185–6). Today, on the contrary, we cannot escape the institutionalised violence of that colonial situation, and when the hero pumps five bullets into the inert body of an anonymous Arab found occupying the cool space that he had been seeking, it is the challenge to the beach's protected status that Meursault confronts, and the stasis lyrically evoked in *Noces* that he disrupts: 'l'équilibre du jour, le silence exceptionnel d'une plage où j'avais été heureux' (*TRN*, 1168) ('the harmony of the day, the exceptional silence of a beach where I'd been happy').

When, in 1959, Robert Champigny launched a reading of *L'Etranger* freed from the philosophising interpretation prevalent since Jean-Paul Sartre's 'Explication', he convincingly portrayed the protagonist as a 'pagan hero'. He was, no doubt, responding to the 'saveur un peu barbare' ('slightly barbarian flavour') that Gabriel Audisio privileged in his own novels and that Camus foregrounds in the first part of an early essay, 'Amour de vivre' (1936), and throughout 'L'Eté à Alger' (1937–8).[24] The eschewal of the conventionally moral in the face of natural abundance was central to the sexualised lyricism of everyday life evoked in *Noces* – 'une précipitation à vivre qui touche au gaspillage' (*Ess*, 72) ('an appetite for life that borders on wastefulness').

It was reasserted in the amicable mockery to which Camus subjects Oran in the 1939 essay 'Le Minotaure ou la halte d'Oran' (published in 1954); and it is encapsulated in a unique moment in *L'Etranger* where the opacity of the hero, steadfastly maintained via the subject's muteness and the ritualised verbosity of the legal system, is fleetingly penetrated: 'mes besoins physiques dérangeaient souvent mes sentiments' (*TRN*, 1172) ('my physical needs often got in the way of my feelings').

One of the key roles of Part I of the novel is, precisely, the illustration of the extent to which, in both lifestyle and attitude, the protagonist is indistinguishable from the spontaneous, uncomplicated, European *barbares* devoid of self-awareness (a 'peuple sans esprit'), but devoted to sensual satisfaction. These are the people who, Camus's early essays avow, populate the colony.[25] Meursault's singularity thus lies more in his reticence than in his much-discussed amoralism. Such a representation is in marked distinction to the energetic, conquering heroes of the Algerianist novel who are portrayed as hard-working, self-sacrificing agents engaging directly, often aggressively, in France's appropriation of Algerian land and wealth. The much-hyped passivity, laissez-aller and indifference of the shipping-office clerk Meursault ensure that he can be read as untouched by this colonial economy. His actions were thus often read by critics merely in terms of psychology (antisocial apathy) or of the philosophy of the Absurd (lucidity in the face of societal illusion). But to seek no further than this interpretation is to be complicitous in eliding the political, hence perpetuating the erasure which, for instance, allows for only European witnesses during the trial (thus marginalising both the victim and his sister).

To complete the picture, we need to recognise that the hero of *L'Etranger*, in both his (in)action and his perceived inarticulateness, is also the embodiment of Camus's counter-claims regarding 'Mediterranean man', foregrounded in characterisations like those referred to earlier. Every episode detailed in Part I of *L'Etranger*, located outside the world of work (a simple backdrop evoked only via summary or incongruous detail), conforms to this model. Hence, in Part II, when cogitation and memory replace physical pleasure and immediacy, the hero's position is grounded explicitly in the loss of what Camus called in his *Rivages* article the few perishable, essential things ('ces quelques biens périssables et essentiels' (*Ess*, 1330)) that give life a meaning: 'Par exemple, l'envie me prenait d'être sur une plage et de descendre vers la mer' (*TRN*, 1180) ('For example, I would have the urge to be on a beach and to go down to the water'); 'J'ai dit qu'il y avait des mois que je regardais ces murailles . . . Peut-être, il y a bien longtemps, y avais-je cherché un visage. Mais ce visage avait la couleur du soleil et la flamme du désir: c'était celui de Marie' (*TRN*, 1209) ('I said I had been looking at these walls for months. Perhaps, way back, I had looked for a face in them. But that face was the colour of the sun and the flame of desire: it was Marie's'). This awareness, acquired in prison, derives from the fact that he is now fully conscious of the inanity of regretting what is no longer accessible, since he is motivated, on the contrary, by that *appetite* Camus identified as essentially Mediterranean: 'je n'avais jamais pu regretter vraiment quelque chose. J'étais toujours pris par ce qui allait arriver, par aujourd'hui ou par demain' (*TRN*, 1197) ('I had never really been able to feel remorse for anything. I was always caught up in what was about to happen, caught up in today or tomorrow'). When desire is forestalled, as the closing paragraph shows, a ship's siren announces only 'des départs pour un monde qui maintenant [lui] était à jamais indifférent'(*TRN*, 1211) ('departures for a world to which [he] was now forever indifferent'). Camus's hero thus confronts (and learns from) the truth that the seafaring *jeunesse méditerranéenne* of his friend and colleague Audisio had been able to evade, the moment when closure is imposed on an individual 'project' (to adopt Sartre's term), lived until then as the freedom encapsulated in the central Audisian topos referred to earlier: 'à toute heure, le plaisir du départ' (*Hommes au soleil*, p. 62) ('at any moment, the pleasures of departure').

The famous a-literary language of *L'Etranger*, what Roland Barthes called a 'zero degree of writing',[26] and the apparent existential uninvolvement of its hero, mask at first reading this continuity between the novel and Camus's lyrical, highly personal, pre-war writing. Its colonial Algerian background continued to attract little comment until the 1970s, when the critic Conor Cruise O'Brien subjected *L'Etranger* to an overtly political reading. Yet O'Brien, in the opinion of a leading postcolonial critic like Edward Said, let Camus off the hook by granting him a less implicated position 'on the frontiers of Europe' and ennobling him as the 'voice of Western consciousness'.[27] If the reader is to take at face value the hero's claim that he is 'absolument comme tout le monde' (*TRN*, 1173) ('just like everyone else') – another rare insight into his make-up parsimoniously inscribed in the text – then it is no longer merely as Everyman, in the universalising reading propagated by many critics. More concretely, it is in his status as 'colonial man' that his self-confessed indistinguishability (hence, problematically, his representativity) resides. The limits of the much-discussed introspection and lucidity of Part II are thus endowed with a collective significance, signalled in two ways in the text. Firstly, in the hero's failure to understand the transformation of the mundane 'qualités d'un homme ordinaire' (*TRN*, 1196) ('the qualities of an ordinary man')[28] into 'des charges écrasantes contre un coupable' (*ibid.*) ('crushing accusations against a guilty man').[29] And secondly, in the narrative's reticence regarding the hostility born of unwanted European–Muslim proximity in Part I. In the second part of the novel, the language of assessment and reason – 'j'ai compris . . . pour la première fois . . . je peux dire que . . . le fond de sa pensée, si j'ai bien compris . . .' ('I understood . . . for the first time . . . I can say that . . . his argument, if I understood him correctly . . .') – overlies the language of physicality, need and desire – 'j'avais chaud . . . j'avais envie de dormir . . . j'avais envie de serrer son épaule par-dessus sa robe . . .' ('I felt hot . . . I felt like sleeping . . . I wanted to squeeze her shoulder through the dress'). It announces the stages at which the genial, unthinking and seemingly passive pleasure-seeker of an Algiers shipping office is forced into self-reflexive consciousness, yet maintains his stance of detachment. The manuscript of the novel shows that Camus took great pains to ensure that his protagonist is condemned not for the (seemingly incidental) killing of an Arab, but for unselfconsciously parading that attitude of self-satisfied, animal banality (a lack of so-called spirituality periodically denounced in mainland France and, indeed, by colonial intellectuals themselves when in collective self-flagellating mode). It is on this egotistical, all-consuming taste for life, emphatically foregrounded in Camus's 1937 lecture, that Meursault's closing outburst is founded, in outspoken defiance of State and Church (in)justice.[30] But there is no place in that valorised model for European–Muslim co-existence and equality, and while 'il est toujours intéressant d'entendre parler de soi' (*TRN*, 1195) ('it's always interesting to hear people talk about you'), there is clearly no interest in talking or hearing about the victim. Indeed, the protagonist himself concludes that 'on a beaucoup parlé de moi et peut-être plus de moi que de mon crime' (*ibid.*) ('a lot was said about me, and perhaps more about me than about my crime').

Camus's protagonist is characterised more by inattentiveness and confusion, partly as a result of physical discomfort, partly because he has not (yet) transcended the complacent immediacy he shares with the European community. In highlighting details in an otherwise depersonalised space in which he feels superfluous ('petit bruit continu de papier froissé, éventails de paille, costume neuf, bouton de cuivre, lèvre inférieure toujours un peu gonflée' (*TRN*, 1187, 1190, 1191)) ('a continuous low rustling sound, fans of woven straw, a new suit, a brass collar stud, the little pout of her lower lip'), the text underlines the extent to which the consciousness of the hero is focalised on the concrete, the present, the everyday. Camus's novel, seemingly in gestation by 1938, should thus be read in relation to the cultural movement he defined in *Rivages*, later (somewhat misleadingly) labelled the 'Ecole d'Alger': 'un mouvement de passion et de jeunesse [qui] est né sur nos rivages' ('a passionate and youthful movement born on our shores'), marked by 'une barbarie harmonieuse et ordonnée' ('a harmonious and ordered barbarity') (*Ess*, 1330–1).[31] The childish games played on the street with Emmanuel or in the sea with Marie, the absence of ambition and, above all, his apathy, thus signal a significant reorientation of the colonial hero, positioning Meursault outside the materialistic economy of the colony, but still within its biased race relations.

By valorising only the hedonistic 'jeunes dieux' ('young gods') and 'barbares' of this 'Mediterranean' settler community, Camus nevertheless forged an icon for post-war Europe: 'la jeunesse du monde se trouve toujours autour des mêmes rivages . . . [N]ous autres méditerranéens vivons toujours de la même lumière. Au cœur de la nuit européenne, *la pensée solaire, la civilisation au double visage*, attend son aurore' (*L'Homme révolté* (*Ess*, 703); my emphasis) ('the world's youth is always to be found on the same shores . . . [We] Mediterraneans always live by the same light. In the depth of the European night, solar thought, a double-faced civilisation, awaits the dawn').

Much critical attention has been paid to the notion of dualism in Camus's work, a dualism in which, like Audisio, he privileges lucidity, the awakening from routine, into the existential (but ahistorical) awareness discussed earlier: 'il n'y a pas d'amour de vivre sans désespoir de vivre' (*Ess*, 44) ('there can be no love of life without despair at life'), and its ethical consequence: 'Ce n'est plus d'être heureux que je souhaite, mais seulement d'être conscient' (*Ess*, 49) ('I no longer wish to be happy, merely to be conscious'). The contrasting, seemingly less spontaneous style of Part II of *L'Etranger* articulates this evolution, the 'aventure intelligente' ('intelligent adventure') of Camus's hero, leading to his consciously embracing the 'vie absurde [qu'il] avait menée' (*TRN*, 1210) ('the absurd life he had led'). The pleasures of life as a free man, the illusion that survival is possible or that others can be made to understand, the struggle between instinct and intelligence, each is sloughed off in turn until the hero comes face to face with the truth – with which he had seamlessly coincided in Part I.[32] Lucidity here, in other words, brings consciousness of the outsiderness proclaimed in the novel's title, allowing Meursault to get beyond the danger inherent in convention, in 'la vie sociale [qui] risque . . . d'en faire un pantin dépourvu d'âme' ('social life, which risks . . . turning him into a soulless puppet').[33] In the enforced immobility of incarceration, Camus's hero thus reaches the limits of lucid self-awareness and self-fulfilment (in a radical alternative to Algerianist values): 'Moi, j'avais l'air d'avoir les mains vides. Mais j'étais sûr de moi, sûr de tout . . . Oui, je n'avais que cela. Mais du moins, je tenais cette vérité autant qu'elle me tenait' (*TRN*, 1210) ('It looked as though I was empty-handed. But I was confident, about me, about everything. Yes, that was all I had. But at least I had a hold on this truth just as much as it had a hold on me').

In the opinion of the French Algerian novelists of the interwar years, the trait which best categorised their work was 'muscular' writing, the reflection of a tough, no-nonsense people who, in the words of Louis Bertrand, had learned to 'become barbarians again', and hence could only view with disdain what they had long derided as the effeminate, intellectual output of metropolitan France.[34] In marked contrast to that literary trend in the colony, in an article published in *Confluences* in 1943, Camus voiced his admiration for the 'classical' French novel (of Mme de Lafayette, Stendhal and Proust for instance) in which he saw 'une conception particulière de la force' (*TRN*, 1897) ('a very particular concept of strength'), later defined as an intense, unwavering concentration on a certain conception of man that intelligence seeks to highlight via a limited number of situations (*TRN*, 1898). In his conclusion, this conception is identified with an ideal site where the forces of destiny come up against human choice (*TRN*, 1900). In this perspective the idea of virility that he holds up as a model to contemporary readers is 'l'exercice supérieur d'une intelligence qui n'a de cesse qu'elle domine' (*TRN*, 1902) ('the higher exercise of an intelligence which strives until it overcomes'), not the animal energy deployed, often destructively, in the works of his Algerian contemporaries. In 1950, however, he noted that his own work to date did not actually conform to the model he admired since he had created only 'des êtres sans mensonge, donc non réels. Ils ne sont pas au monde. C'est pourquoi sans doute et jusqu'ici je ne suis pas un romancier au sens où on l'entend. Mais plutôt un artiste qui crée des mythes à la mesure de sa passion et de son angoisse' (*CII*, 325) ('beings who harbour no lies, hence are not real. They are not part of the world. And that, no doubt, is why to date I am not a novelist as commonly understood. Rather, an artist who creates myths to suit his passion and his anguish').

That the hero of *L'Etranger* should have become an iconic figure of the second half of the twentieth century can, no doubt, be largely attributed to myth's ability to serve as vehicle for the zeitgeist or world view of a generation. The tragic (and supposedly Mediterranean) hedonism eulogised by critics is lodged in an unlikely champion whose ambition is to get through the working week competently so that he can enjoy the resolutely banal pleasures of the weekend. To be frustrated by him, as readers often are, is to believe that there is (should be) more to life. Yet the values promoted in *L'Etranger*, and in the early essays, are resolutely grounded in the tangible and the visible, 'jouissance' ('pleasure') in a world in which transcendence is mere illusion – 'les fureurs de l'éternelle adolescence' ('the unbridled forces of eternal adolescence'), as Camus was to write later in an unused page for *L'Homme révolté* (*Ess*, 1658). Hence, perhaps, their resonance for the post-war period, attracted by the overt amorality and by the inarticulate, un-thought-through challenge to fixed positions and orthodox perspectives enacted by the protagonist. In writing *La Peste* (1947), Camus was at pains to confront the moral consequences of that stance, countering solipsism with social conscience: 'il n'y [a] pas de honte à préférer le bonheur. "Oui, dit Rambert, mais il peut y avoir de la honte à être heureux tout seul"' (*TRN*, 1389) ('there is nothing shameful about preferring happiness. "True," said Rambert, "but there can be something shameful about being the only one who is happy"').

In identifying himself as 'an artist who creates myths' rather than a conventional novelist, Camus is pointing to an alternative writing strategy, the importance of which is perhaps best revealed in a little text of 1952 on Herman Melville, whom Camus praises as a creator of myths, indeed of a single, all-consuming quest myth 'construit . . . sur le concret, non dans le matériau du rêve . . . [C]hez Melville le symbole sort de la réalité, l'image naît de la perception' (*TRN*, 1909–10) ('based . . . on what is concrete, not on the stuff of dreams . . . In Melville the symbol grows out of reality, the image springs from perception'). That this description also fits Camus's own approach becomes clear when we relate it to a 'dialogue' included in his *Carnets* of 1942, triggered by contemporary reviews of *L'Etranger*: 'Vous me prêtez l'ambition de faire réel. Le réalisme est un mot vide de sens . . . S'il fallait donner une forme à mon ambition, je parlerais au contraire de symbole' (*TRN*, 1933) ('You maintain that I strive for the real. Realism is a word devoid of meaning . . . If I had to articulate my ambition, I would, on the contrary, talk about symbols'). The advantage of symbols, one might argue, is that they constitute nodes of resistance to readings seeking closure and, on the contrary, embrace the polysemy which encourages a constantly renewed engagement with the text. It is in this spirit that the present reading is proposed, a reading which reinserts *L'Etranger* into the colonial Algerian context out of which it developed, and into the problematic *méditerranéité* evoked in *Noces*, metaphor for the reworked European–Muslim contact zone in which Camus and 'Ecole d'Alger' colleagues like Gabriel Audisio hoped a spirit of fraternity and exchange would reshape the colony's always insecure frontiers.

NOTES

1. *Jeune Méditerranée*, 1 (April 1937); in *Ess*, 1321–7.
2. For details, see P. Dunwoodie, *Writing French Algeria* (Oxford, Clarendon, 1998).
3. Louis Bertrand, Preface to *Le Sang des races* (Paris, Ollendorf, 1899), xiii.
4. Louis Lambert, in *La Revue des deux mondes* (December 1921), 488.
5. The attack by Gabriel Audisio, Camus's friend and fellow writer, was no less direct: 'Parmi les provocations de la latinité il faut ranger ce que j'appelle le préjugé favorable, à savoir que Rome a toutes les vertus, tous les mérites, a tout

inventé, qu'on lui doit tout, et que tout ce qui nous paraît bien dans le monde, c'est à Rome qu'il faut l'attribuer sans hésitation' (*Le Sel de la mer* (Paris, Gallimard, 1936), p. 96) (Among the provocations generated by the Latin idea one has to include what I call positive bias, namely the idea that Rome has every quality, every merit, invented everything; that we owe it everything; and that everything we find worthwhile in the world has to be attributed unhesitatingly to Rome).

6. This assertiveness again matches Audisio's bluntness in *Le Sel de la mer* where he insists: 'Le monde ne commence pas avec Rome, et il ne finit pas avec Rome. La Méditerranée non plus. Et la Méditerranée n'est pas Rome' (p. 101) ('The world did not start with Rome, and it doesn't end with Rome. Nor does the Mediterranean. And the Mediterranean is not Rome').

7. In his notes Camus refers to 'Le Vent à Djémila' as 'the essay on ruins' (*C1*, 47).

8. In one of the only reviews of *Noces* to appear in France (*OFALAC*, 1939), Gabriel Audisio highlighted 'a sensitivity and a spirit of meditation which give North African writing a new accent', Lottman, *Albert Camus. A Biography* (New York, Braziller, 1980), p. 194.

9. The *villes solaires* also explicitly counter the *villes d'or* ('cities of gold') frequently evoked by Bertrand; see in particular *Les Villes d'or: Algérie et Tunisie romaines* (Paris: Fayard, 1921).

10. See Jean Grenier, *Albert Camus. Souvenirs* (Paris, Gallimard, 1968). Grenier noted in particular that Camus was especially sensitive to 'la passion du soleil' ('passion for the sun'), *Inspirations méditerranéennes*, p. 30. See also Toby Garfitt's discussion of Grenier in chapter 2.

11. See, for example, *Gilles* (1939) and *Ecrits de jeunesse* (1941).

12. See Camus's student friend Max-Pol Fouchet, *Un jour, je m'en souviens . . . Mémoire parlée* (Paris, Mercure de France, 1968), p. 43.

13. Gabriel Audisio, *Hommes au soleil* (1923), *Héliotrope* (1928) and, most directly, *Jeunesse de la Méditerranée* (1935) and its second volume, *Le Sel de la mer* (1936).

14. A typical source of influence in this area for Camus would have been Gabriel Audisio. See, for example, Audisio, *Hommes au soleil* (Maupré, Le Mouton blanc, 1923), p. 62.

15. Gide, for instance, was well aware of the political significance of the displacement effected by Audisio.

16. The insistence on youth, seemingly unremarkable in texts of the 1930s which privilege beauty, vitality, and the body, furthers this escapist perspective since youth is without a past and hence without historical responsibility.

17. The selective nature of place in Camus's lyrical essays is best exemplified by contrasting it with a novel like *Fantômes au soleil* (Paris, Gallimard, 1949), written by his demythologising contemporary and friend, Jean-Pierre Clot.

18. Jean Sarocchi, 'La Méditerranée est un songe, Monsieur', *Perspectives. Revue de l'Université hébraïque de Jérusalem* 5 (1998), 109–29 (111).

19. J. Lévi-Valensi, 'Terre faite à mon âme: pour une mythologie du réel', *Perspectives* 5 (1998), 185–97 (186).

20. F. Bartfeld, 'Anti-Méditerranée et lyrisme de l'exil', *Perspectives* 5 (1998), 213–25 (213).

21. See also M. El Houssi, 'Camus ou le désir de Méditerranée', *Africa, America, Asia, Australia* 15 (1993), 29–39; N. Stéphane, 'La Mer heureuse', *Europe* 77 (October 1999), 132–44; R. Davison, 'Mythologising the Mediterranean: The

Case of Albert Camus', *Journal of Mediterranean Studies* 10. 1–2 (2000), 77–92.

22. 'L'Explication' was reprinted in *Situations I* (Paris, Gallimard, 1947), pp. 99–122. For an English translation, see 'Camus's "The Outsider"', in Jean-Paul Sartre, *Literary and Philosophical Essays*, trans. Annette Michelson (New York, Criterion Books, 1955), pp. 24–41.

23. Algeria was already a holiday destination with an English-language newspaper, and home to British and French artists' colonies.

24. R. Champigny, *Sur un héros païen* (Paris, Gallimard, 1959).

25. See *TRN*, 1186, 1188, 1195, 1196, 1197, 1199.

26. R. Barthes, *Le Degré zéro de l'écriture* (Paris, Seuil, 1953).

27. E. Said, *Culture and Imperialism* (London, Vintage, 1994), p. 209. See also C. Achour, *L'Etranger si familier* (Algiers, EnAP, 1984). Although Camus's personal political involvement in the 1930s and 1950s has been comprehensively studied, it is occasionally still subject to grossly inflated claims like that of Denis Charbit in 'Camus et l'épreuve algérienne' where he is given star status as 'one of the first, if not the first French Algerian to draw attention to colonial exploitation and oppression', *Perspectives* 5 (1998), 157–81 (160).

28. A figure the French call 'Monsieur Tout-le-monde'.

29. The issue of guilt in a colonial context, both moral and historical, is treated at length in *Le Premier Homme*.

30. See *CI*, 29–30 for the importance attributed to this passage.

31. The oxymoron shows that *barbarie* has actually been resemanticised by Camus. Audisio's position is remarkably close to Camus's: 'quand l'Afrique vous reprend, elle vous enseigne qu'il ne fallait pas lui demander d'autre style que la vie, d'autre tradition que d'*être*, d'autre race que la beauté des races mêlées' (*Le Sel de la mer*, p. 18) ('when Africa seizes you again it teaches you that one should have asked for no other style than life itself, no other tradition than *being*, no other race than the beauty of mixed races').

32. The instinct/intelligence tension is one of the 'ambivalences' Camus, Audisio and the Berber poet Jean Amrouche identified as constituents of the 'Mediterranean spirit' at a conference in Paris in 1947 – along with action/meditation, balance/violence. Camus also makes it a central pole of *L'Homme révolté*: 'La Méditerranée, où l'intelligence est sœur de la dure lumière' (*Ess*, 702–3) ('The Mediterranean, where intelligence is the sister of the hard light'). In *Ulysse ou l'intelligence* Audisio sees dualism as an essential factor, inflecting their writings through tensions such as Romanticism/Classicism, euphoria/despair, material pleasure/the call of the spiritual.

33. Camus, *L'Express*, April 1957.

34. See Louis Bertrand, 'Nietzsche et la Méditerranée', *La Revue des deux mondes* 25 (1915), 181–2. The main targets of the French Algerian novelists were Gide and Proust.

12

MARGARET E. GRAY

Layers of meaning in *La Peste*

'Deuxième série: le monde de la tragédie et l'esprit de révolte' (*CI*, 229)
('Second series: the world of tragedy and the spirit of revolt') (*NI*, 193),
wrote Camus in April 1941, and the scattered notes and sheets of what was
to become *La Peste* acquired further shape and context. Having completed
the cycle of 'the Absurd', in a France torn by war and enemy occupation,
Camus had for some time been convinced that 'Si ignoble que soit cette
guerre, il n'est pas permis d'être en dehors' (*CI*, 167) ('However vile this
war may be, no one can stand aside from it' (*NI*, 139)). Such a conviction is
at work throughout Camus's second cycle, which includes *La Peste* (1947),
the essay *L'Homme révolté* (1951) and the plays *L'Etat de siège* (1948) and
Les Justes (1949). In keeping with this cycle's exploration of tragedy and
revolt, *La Peste* chronicles the imprisonment, exile, oppression and suffering
experienced by the citizens of Oran when a plague strikes. Yet the novel also
dramatises the victory of human spirit and solidarity over that which would
threaten and dismember it: a plague, an enemy occupation, existence itself.
In alluding to such varied forms of oppression, Camus asserted, referring to
his experience of the German occupation: 'Je veux exprimer au moyen de la
peste l'étouffement dont nous avons tous souffert et l'atmosphère de menace
et d'exil dans laquelle nous avons vécu' (*CII*, 72) ('I want to express by means
of the plague the stifling air from which we all suffered and the atmosphere of
threat and exile in which we lived' (*NII*, 53)). Yet, he went on – announcing
the text's various layers of meaning and their dynamic oscillation between
event and abstraction, literal and figurative meaning, chronicle and allegory –
'Je veux du même coup étendre cette interprétation à la notion d'existence
en général' (*CII*, 72) ('I want at the same time to extend that interpretation
to the notion of existence in general' (*NII*, 53)). These strata of meaning are
also emphasised in the novel's epigraph from Defoe's *Robinson Crusoe*: 'Il est
aussi raisonnable de représenter une espèce d'emprisonnement par une autre
que de représenter n'importe quelle chose qui existe réellement par quelque
chose qui n'existe pas' (*TRN*, 1215) ('It is as reasonable to represent one

kind of imprisonment by another, as it is to represent anything that really exists by that which exists not').[1] An exhortation to read *La Peste* on various levels, it argues for the legitimacy of representing one sort of imprisonment by another – and for concluding, ultimately, with Rieux's elderly patient in the novel's closing pages, 'Mais qu'est-ce que ça veut dire, la peste? C'est la vie, et voilà tout' (*TRN*, 1472) ('But what does that mean – "plague"? Just life, no more than that' (*P*, 295)).

The 'imprisonment' with which the Defoe epigraph opens *La Peste* is thus a central experience in the novel, as is its attendant condition, solitude. Indeed, 'Tous', wrote Camus in 1942 of the characters in what was to become *La Peste*, 'sont renvoyés à leur solitude. Si bien *que la séparation devient générale* . . . Faire ainsi du thème de la séparation le grand thème du roman' (*CII*, 80) ('All are forced into solitude, *so that separation becomes the general condition* . . . Make the theme of separation the main theme of the novel' (*NII*, 60, translation modified)). We quickly notice the isolation of each of the main characters within a certain irremediable solitude. The departure of Dr Rieux's wife in the novel's opening pages only seems to emphasise the distance that inhabits the couple; putting her on the train to the mountain retreat they hope will bring a cure to her illness, Rieux promises they will make a fresh start upon her return (*TRN*, 1225; *P*, 8). The secretive Cottard perversely revels in the plague's extension of his own solitude and isolation to all citizens of Oran, while the outsider Tarrou finds in the plague an image for his own solitary moral convictions. City-clerk Grand is haunted by his failure to retain the wife he loved, and journalist Rambert yearns for his far-away mistress. Along with such feelings of solitude and separation come, necessarily, those of exile, of a loss of home and rootedness: feelings Camus himself must have known keenly in the summer of 1942 when, having returned to Oran from France in 1941 to live with his wife Francine, he again fell ill with the tuberculosis that had dogged him since his teenage years, obliging him to leave Algeria for a retreat near unoccupied St Etienne, France, in the hope of restoring his health. However, the Allied landings in North Africa just a few months later and the subsequent occupation of all of France by the German army essentially closed contact with France's North African colonies. Communication between Camus and Francine became tenuous and sporadic. 'Il y a des mois que je suis sans nouvelles de toi' ('I've been without news of you for months') wrote Camus to her soon after the Liberation of France.[2] For the Algerian-born Camus himself, then, solitude in France became inextricably experienced as exile, and we notice that one of the early titles he considered for his novel was *Les Exilés* (*The Exiles*); indeed, the title he gave the excerpt published in *Domaine français* in 1943 was 'Les Exilés dans la peste' ('The Plague and its Exiles') (*TRN*, 1959–67).

Camus's own experience of physical and emotional exile during the war is evoked in the novel through the ordeal of journalist Rambert. He becomes an exemplary victim of Oran's closed gates, for, separated from his mistress and home in Paris, his imprisonment is also an exile – and as such, typifies the emotional exile experienced by all citizens of Oran separated from loved ones. Such exile brings the sting of memories of a former life that may or may not have any link to a possible future (*TRN*, 1276; *P*, 67). Bereft of fond connection to a remembered past or a future invested with hope, Oran's citizens are stranded in an endless present: 'il n'y avait plus pour nous que des instants' (*TRN*, 1367) ('nothing was left us but a series of present moments' (*P*, 175)).

The divestiture of past and future, however, is only the beginning of the plague's progressive destruction, as even within the wastes of an eternal present, communication among citizens falters. Struggling to express his own solitary and singular anguish in carefully wrought language that nonetheless, however, fails to reach his fellows (*TRN*, 1280; *P*, 72), each prisoner of the plague discovers new extremes of solitude. For under the coercion of common speech, obliged to communicate 'sur le mode conventionnel, celui de la simple relation et du fait divers, de la chronique quotidienne' (*TRN*, 1280) ('using the current coin of language, the commonplaces of plain narrative, of anecdote and of daily event' (*P*, 72, translation modified)), Oran's citizens are forced to convey their suffering through banality and convention as the price of communication. The language with which, like Rambert, one seeks urgently to communicate the singularity of one's own experience – the differences of one's own case – is flattened to a common coin, to a neutral, conventional 'chronique'.

Intriguingly, however, the narrator – Dr Rieux, as we only discover in the final pages – here uses the precise term he gives his own account in his effort to provide an impartial rendering of collective experience. And through this overlapping use of 'chronique', we are implicitly invited to consider the cost borne by the narrator's account: the price in silencing and suppressing individual expression so as to favour Rieux's deliberately collective and historical testimony. Rieux's chronicle itself, in privileging the collective over the personal, represents a deliberate choice in favour of solidarity, the experience of the group over the experience of the individual. Yet, again, his additional use of 'chronique' to imply the flattening, the emptying, of authentic human contact under the impact of the plague, implicitly invites us to appreciate all that his own 'chronique' excludes.

Alongside the generalised flattening of communication imposed by the plague – the reduction of human contact to lame cliché – we might notice other examples of strained or failed communication in the novel. There is, for instance, the endlessly rewritten opening line of Grand's unwritten novel. His obsessive and stalled effort to launch his trotting horsewoman into her May morning is undoubtedly connected to his original failure to find the words that would have kept his wife, Jeanne, with him (*TRN*, 1286; *P*, 78). When letters are banned as potential bearers of infection, Rambert invites Rieux to make use of his own system of clandestine correspondence. Yet Rieux discovers difficulty in writing to his wife, as though he had somehow lost the language he needed (*TRN*, 1431; *P*, 250). Increasingly, the plague coerces the imprisoned citizens of Oran into silence, as without recourse to letters, they are forced to collapse all sentiment into the choppy clichés of telegrams: 'Vais bien. Pense à toi. Tendresse' (*TRN*, 1274) ('Am well. Thinking of you. Love' (*P*, 65, translation modified)).

We notice that such telegraphic density and restraint finds an analogue in Rieux's chronicle, with its own restraint, its evenness, its understatedness. In his opening lines, Rieux suggests that the events he is about to recount are a bit out of the ordinary. Such measured tones, for so extreme a catastrophe, lend further nuance to Rieux's deliberately collective chronicle, suggesting additional reasons for his choice to omit all personal experience. As we saw above, Rieux implicitly invited us to recognise the omission of this experience – and indeed, tacitly, the impoverishment of his account as a result. But we begin to have a sense that this omission is perhaps more complicated than we had realised; we wonder whether Rieux has not imposed such objective conditions upon his chronicle in an effort to avoid the danger of 'infection' by excess and sentiment. We are not surprised to notice his somewhat stiff mention, in describing a jubilant Oran at the end of the plague, of embracing couples 'qui ne craignaient pas de se donner en spectacle' (*TRN*, 1464) ('who were unafraid of making a spectacle of themselves' (*P*, 287, translation modified)).

And yet, this same no-nonsense approach becomes a weapon against the plague, as we see in Rieux's efforts to persuade the authorities to take more decisive measures. When Rieux succeeds in forcing the *Préfecture* to call a meeting at the plague's onset, all present at last agree on the need to act 'comme si la maladie était une peste' (*TRN*, 1259) ('as though the epidemic were plague' (*P*, 49)). In irritated irony, Rieux flings their own squeamish, hypothetical language back at the assembled doctors and Prefect, doubling negatives to end with a terse and terrifying possibility: 'Disons seulement que nous ne devons pas agir comme si la moitié de la ville ne risquait pas d'être tuée, car alors elle le serait' (*TRN*, 1259) ('My point is that we should not act as if there were no likelihood that half the population wouldn't be wiped out; for then it would be' (*P*, 49)). And Rieux's demands for direct-ness of language and action are ultimately adopted in the curt governmental telegram closing Part 1 of Rieux's chronicle, 'Déclarez l'état de peste. Fermez la ville' (*TRN*, 1269) ('Proclaim a state of plague Stop close the town' (*P*, 61)). Such directness, however, while initially a means of combating the plague, becomes yet another sobering symptom of its crushing effect on all communication. Human expression is reduced to the groans and cries of victims, which become, for Oran's oppressed and hardened citizens, a sort of natural or normal language (*TRN*, 1310; *P*, 107). Ultimately, human exchange is splintered into silence as Oran is reduced to 'une nécropole où la peste, la pierre et la nuit auraient fait taire enfin toute voix' (*TRN*, 1359) ('a necropolis in which plague, stone and darkness had effectively silenced every voice' (*P*, 166)).[3]

As an ultimate image of this coercion into silence, suffocation becomes a central symptom of the plague's victims. The context of Camus's own respiratory illness allows us to appreciate more keenly *La Peste*'s images of asphyxiation, as Camus saw in his own visceral, corporeal experience of suffocation an analogy to life under the German occupation. While in the United States in 1946, he writes, amidst impressions of his travels, '*Peste*: c'est un monde sans femmes et donc irrespirable' ('*Plague*: a world without women and thus unbreathable').[4] Images of asphyxiation proliferate in such a world, as symptoms of the plague (*TRN*, 1234; *P*, 17); as the hushed and desperate pleas of the living (*TRN*, 1395; *P*, 206); as the muffled footfalls in a silenced city (*TRN*, 1369; *P*, 178); as the stifling sky and air (*TRN*, 1397; *P*, 208) that seal the prison of Oran. Consequently, of course, the ability to breathe marks resistance to the plague; it is one of the first symptoms of recovery from the fever, and marks rare moments of respite, as in Rieux's fraternal, wordless swim with Tarrou – where, strangely happy, Rieux breathes at length, listening to Tarrou's own breathing (*TRN*, 1429; *P*, 246). Ultimately, dwindling fatalities indicate that 'enfin il allait être permis de respirer' (*TRN*, 1441) ('finally one was going to be allowed to breathe' (*P*, 259, translation modified)), in a densely figural as well as literal use of the image.

Yet suffocation is only one symptom endured by the plague's victims; beyond such silencing, the plague carries out a dismembering of the body, both the body physical and the body politic. Indeed, the plague's histrionic 'écartèlement', or drawing-and-quartering, of the suffering body becomes itself emblematic of a dislocated social order. Victims of the disease evoke, through their disjointed limbs, 'une attitude de pantin' (*TRN*, 1230) ('a clockwork doll' (*P*, 14)); as the disease progresses, however, the various symptoms map an 'écartèlement intérieur' (*TRN*, 1249) ('internal dismantling' (*P*, 37, translation modified)). Extending the image of dismemberment, Paneloux – who, in an initial sermon, had argued that the plague was divine retribution for loss of faith – pronounces a second sermon, this one under the impact of the death of Othon's son. In it, he emphasises the suffering of children and the need to face such 'dismemberment' of meaning as faith's ultimate challenge, a moment of truth in which one is called to 'tout croire ou tout nier' (*TRN*, 1402) ('believe everything or deny everything' (*P*, 214)). Exhorting a dwindled congregation to remain within the scandal and contradiction of such dismantled meaning, Paneloux urges fidelity to 'cet écartèlement dont la croix est le symbole' (*TRN*, 1402) ('that great symbol of all suffering, the tortured body on the cross' (*P*, 214)). Indeed, Paneloux's own contorted body, discovered half-thrown from his deathbed after a mysterious illness that may or may not have been the plague, would itself seem to remain faithful, in its very posture, to the tortured body on the cross. Ambiguously, however, we are not told whether or not he is found still to be clutching his crucifix, as he had throughout the fever (*TRN*, 1410; *P*, 223). Despite his exhortations, Paneloux thus embodies a faith that, under the impact of the suffering of innocents, becomes itself shaken, 'écartelé'; and we are not surprised to learn that in an earlier version of the episode, Paneloux lost his faith altogether.[5]

Extending the image of 'écartèlement' to the body politic, we notice the plague's dislocation of social health, signalled by the narrator's opening indication that the events he is about to recount 'n' . . . étaient pas à leur place' (*TRN*, 1219) ('were out of place' (*P*, 1)). The proper place and position of civic order is emphasised in the narrator's observation that until the closing of the city, each citizen had pursued his occupations 'à sa place ordinaire' (*TRN*, 1273) ('in his ordinary place' (*P*, 63, translation modified)). Under the plague, however, 'tout se détraquait' (*TRN*, 1324) ('everything was breaking down' (*P*, 125, translation modified)). Such social dislocation is particularly visible in the deterioration of burial decorum imposed by the escalating numbers of plague victims. So as to evade a decency it can no longer accommodate, the city decides to bury victims at night. In a climactic image of the social and corporeal dismemberment wrought by the plague, ambulances rush back and forth in burlesque haste, piled ever higher with contorted bodies to be dumped into mass graves. 'On enterra pêle-mêle, les uns sur les autres, hommes et femmes, sans souci de la décence' (*TRN*, 1362) ('this last remnant of decorum went by the board, and men and women were flung into the death-pits indiscriminately' (*P*, 169)) runs Rieux's description of the scene's macabre, dislocated puppetry.

So gruesome and histrionic a spectacle of the drawn and quartered body, both corporeal and social, recalls Camus's dramatic designation for his second cycle as that of 'tragédie'. For we have become increasingly aware of the strain between Rieux's resolutely measured, documentary account and the tragic spectacle or drama produced by the plague. Such strain is perhaps particularly visible in the description of Rieux's 'calm' reaction to his wife's death, announced by telegram: indeed, a reaction so composed that Rieux himself attempts to justify it, framing his explanation, however, with the ambiguous 'sans doute' ('no doubt'): 'Voilà pourquoi, sans doute, le docteur Rieux, au matin, reçut avec calme la nouvelle de la mort de sa femme' (*TRN*, 1459) ('That, no doubt, explains Dr Rieux's composure on receiving next morning the news of his wife's death' (*P*, 280)). In the middle of his narration, Rieux reminds us of his effort to avoid 'les effets de l'art, sauf en ce qui concerne les besoins élémentaires d'une relation à peu près cohérente' (*TRN*, 1365) ('artistic effect, except those elementary adjustments needed to present his narrative in a more or less coherent form' (*P*, 173)). Yet, given the significant dramatic value of the events he recounts, we are only too acutely aware of the rising tension between such drama and the narration's neutrality and restraint. Indeed, despite his claims, Rieux's measured account betrays, in various ways, efforts to convey the drama of all he witnessed.

Rieux's chronicle of the onset, rise, triumph, decline and disappearance of the plague is neatly divided, for instance, into five parts. Himself a playwright, author of the plays *Caligula*, *Le Malentendu* and *Les Justes*, as well as of theatrical adaptations from the Spanish, French, English and Russian, Camus was only too deliberately structuring his novel according to the five acts of classical tragedy. Moreover, such tragic undertones acquire explicit dramatic force and impact when Cottard and Tarrou attend a performance of Gluck's tragic opera, *Orphée et Eurydice*. Elegant citizens of Oran exchange greetings as they take their seats, intent not to miss their cues in unwitting performances in the auditorium itself; for, playing urbane roles of suave self-delusion in a drama more desperate, more compelling than that onstage, spectators delude themselves that 'l'habit chassait la peste' (*TRN*, 1381) ('evening dress was a sure charm against the plague' (*P*, 189, translation modified)). Yet this spectators' drama and its illusion of normalcy is exploded, brought down as suddenly and decisively as the singer playing Orphée himself; for, overcome by the plague during the third act, he collapses grotesquely, taking the stage sets with him, before the horrified spectators.

This eruption of an explicit, classical tragedy – that of Orpheus and Eurydice – within the plague's own tragic events provides a particularly visible illustration of dramatic forces at work within Rieux's narration. We might read such drama in terms of Camus's own vision for *La Peste* as a text of revolt, for, between the lines of Rieux's tautly controlled cadences, we sense his effort to convey the essential triumph of the human spirit. It is through this triumph, despite suffering and loss, that the spirit of revolt among Oran's citizens becomes clear – and we begin to understand the purpose, despite his explicit claims to the contrary, of the drama with which Rieux endows certain episodes of his narration. There is, for example, the long, detailed description of Tarrou's illness and death: a passage we read in agonising suspense, torn between what we know of the plague's deadliness, and its rare, capricious clemency. In this passage, Rieux's characteristic restraint, as he describes his powerlessness, yields to metaphor in an image of Tarrou's body disappearing from his grasp: 'Cette forme humaine qui lui avait été si proche, percée maintenant de coups d'épieu, brûlée par un mal surhumain, tordue par tous les vents haineux du ciel, s'immergeait à ses yeux dans les eaux de la peste et il ne pouvait rien contre ce naufrage' (*TRN*, 1457) ('This human form, his friend's, lacerated by the spear-thrusts of the plague, consumed by searing superhuman fires, buffeted by all the ravaging winds of heaven, was floundering under his eyes in the dark flood of the pestilence, and he could do nothing to avert the wreck' (*P*, 277)). The image of Tarrou's body sinking in the 'waters' of the plague before Rieux's eyes is all the more ironic and resonant when we recall the 'waters' of their swim, with its wordless communion, friendship and solidarity. Indeed, the sea has always offered a backdrop to their friendship; Rieux's desire to confide in Tarrou occurs as he looks through the window at the vague and distant sea (*TRN*, 1323; *P*, 123), while Tarrou similarly chooses, as the setting for confiding in Rieux, a rooftop terrace with a view of the indistinct 'palpitation' where sea and sky meet (*TRN*, 1419; *P*, 234). It is the context of this friendship implicitly embraced by the sea that lends further pathos to the 'shipwreck' of Tarrou's body. 'Il ne pouvait rien contre ce naufrage', Rieux tells us, speaking of course, as we increasingly suspect, of himself. 'Il devait rester sur le rivage, les mains vides et le cœur tordu, sans armes et sans recours, une fois de plus, contre ce désastre' (*TRN*, 1457) ('He could only stand, unavailing, on the shore, empty-handed and sick at heart, unarmed and helpless yet again under the onset of calamity' (*P*, 277)). For all the mastery and control, the restraint and discipline of Rieux's narrative, for all the healing he *is* able to accomplish, he nevertheless remains vulnerable, human and thus one of us: confronting circumstances that overwhelm and engulf him, but to which he refuses to succumb.

Rieux's narration also tends elsewhere towards the dramatic, as in the account of Rambert's ultimate decision, the very evening of his planned escape, to stay and fight the plague. When Rambert goes to see Rieux, we presume it is to inform the doctor that his escape will be carried out at midnight; but we discover only in the episode's closing line that Rambert has in fact already cancelled the plan so as to join the ranks of the sanitary teams. We have in Rambert's stunning reversal a resounding demonstration of solidarity, rendered all the more apparent precisely through the dramatic shape with which Rieux endows the episode. In answer to the question

Tarrou asks Rambert at midnight, the hour planned for his escape – as to whether Rambert has informed his would-be liberators of his decision to stay in Oran – Rambert turns his head. 'J'avais envoyé un mot, dit-il avec effort, avant d'aller vous voir' (*TRN*, 1390) ('"I'd sent them a note" – he spoke with an effort – "before coming to see you"' (*P*, 200)). Rambert's admission is the episode's closing line, which lends it yet further weight and drama. It is through subtly dramatic story-telling of this sort that Rieux emphasises the victory of human solidarity. For as Rambert explains, 'il peut y avoir de la honte à être heureux tout seul' (*TRN*, 1389) ('it may be shameful to be happy by oneself' (*P*, 199)). Rambert's dramatic choice in favour of solidarity over his own happiness emblematises Oran's response to the plague. For at Tarrou's initiative, citizens organise themselves into teams, fighting the disease as best they can, and counting among their ranks members as different as Paneloux and Judge Othon; the exhausted Grand spends evenings devoting his clerical skills to the cause. In yet another example of the solidarity with which the city responds to the plague, and to which his chronicle testifies, Rieux points to the stunning fact that throughout the epidemic, there was never a shortage of nurses and grave-diggers, despite their greater risk of infection (*TRN*, 1362; *P*, 170).

We might now distinguish two countervailing movements in *La Peste*. On the one hand, there is the effective collapse of the human carried out by the plague in its asphyxiation and dismemberment of the physical and social body, its pull 'du fond de la terre' (*TRN*, 1234) ('from the depths of the earth' (*P*, 19)) of the human into oblivion. On the other hand, there is the narration's resistance to such oblivion through the implicit dramatisation, the spectacle or staging, of this tragedy in five acts. These two movements, the movement towards effacement and the movement towards spectacle, converge in the death scene of Judge Othon's son. In a searing reprise of the dramatic scene at the Opera House in Oran, where Tarrou and Cottard were spectators to the unplanned drama of Orphée's collapse, Rieux and Tarrou now become unwilling spectators to the drawn-out drama of the child's death: 'l'agonie d'un innocent' (*TRN*, 1394) ('the death-throes of an innocent child' (*P*, 205)). The child's 'écartèlement' – or drawing and quartering, as we have seen in Rieux's recurring term for the plague's effect upon the body – is recounted in stark detail as he is shaken by the plague's typically dismembering, convulsive movements: the agitation and stiffening of his body by turns; the curling up and flinging open of limbs; the claw-like hands; the long inhuman plaint. Ultimately, the child's skeletal body assumes the pose of a 'crucifié grotesque' (*TRN*, 1394) ('a grotesque parody of crucifixion' (*P*, 205)). This dramatisation of the plague's crushing and dismembering, its drawing-and-quartering of this most innocent of beings in a sacrificial crucifixion, prompts Rieux's only outburst in the narrative, flung at Paneloux: 'Ah! Celui-là, au moins, était innocent, vous le savez bien!' (*TRN*, 1396) ('Ah! That child, anyhow, was innocent – and you know it as well as I do!' (*P*, 207)). Rieux's revolt against the plague's meaningless evil summarises and expresses our own reaction.

And such protest involves crying out, like Rieux, against oppression. The human voice persists, emerging from the plague's carnage and oppression, resisting the plague's effort to silence it. There is Rieux's own voice itself, with its testament to solidarity: 'pour ne pas être de ceux qui se taisent' (*TRN*, 1473) ('so that he should not be one of those who hold their peace' (*P*, 296)), explains Rieux of his decision to recount Oran's ordeal. Grand's immobilised narrative ultimately renews and regenerates itself in his letter to Jeanne, a letter begun further down on the manuscript's final page: a gesture towards responsibility and apology, an opening on to a possible reconciliation, after years of distance and silence: 'Ma bien chère Jeanne, c'est aujourd'hui Noël' (*TRN*, 1434) ('My dearest Jeanne, today is Christmas Day' (*P*, 253)). Sterile and stalled narration thus transforms itself, becoming apostrophe, address, direct action – its tortured starts and stops, its hesitation and immobility yielding at last to the promise of movement. Yet, convinced he is dying of the plague, Grand demands that the manuscript be burned; equally convinced that Grand is lost, Rieux complies, throwing the manuscript into the fire. But Grand improbably recovers, and the dashed promise of change, bearing its possibility of a new beginning with Jeanne, is restored: 'Ah! Docteur . . . j'ai eu tort. Mais je recommencerai. Je me souviens de tout, vous verrez' (*TRN*, 1435) ('Yes, doctor . . . I was over-hasty. But I'll make another start. You'll see, I can remember every word' (*P*, 254)).

Similarly, Tarrou's voice would seem to be lost to the plague, suffocated, cruelly, as one of its last victims; yet Rieux, like Grand, 'remember[s] every word' (*P*, 254), and quotes Tarrou at length within his chronicle. The different discourse brought to Rieux's account through Tarrou's confession offers a perspective unavailable to Rieux's resolutely historical depiction of a collective event. For Tarrou's voice offers a moral and metaphorical view of the plague that counterbalances not only Paneloux's initial lacerating claim for the plague as divine retribution, but Rieux's own account as a strictly historical chronicle of 'curious events' (*P*, 1). Originally, Rieux's insertion of Tarrou's notebooks within his own account appeared potentially to offer a rival chronicle, though Rieux appears careful to consign Tarrou's notes to 'secondary' importance, suggesting that they offer 'une foule de détails secondaires qui ont cependant leur importance' (*TRN*, 1236) ('a host of secondary details which yet have their importance' (*P*, 22, translation modified)). Such care to relegate Tarrou's notebooks to secondary status is significantly absent, however, from Rieux's subsequent account of Tarrou's confession. Tarrou's monologue, moreover – initiated by Tarrou with his question to Rieux, 'Voulez-vous que cette heure soit celle de l'amitié?' (*TRN*, 1419) ('Would you like this to be a moment of friendship?' (*P*, 235, translation modified)) – would not seem immediately pertinent to Rieux's resolutely collective chronicle. Quoted at such length that it appears entirely to overtake Rieux's own account, usurping it for a rival purpose, Tarrou's confession instead opens up for the reader a dimension Rieux had explicitly refused in his adoption of an objective, chronicler's voice.

In directing the reader to the plague's symbolic importance through Tarrou's confession, Rieux subtly integrates within his chronicle the allegory to which he himself refuses all allusion. For, recounting the shock of his discovery that his fairly ordinary father, a magistrate, regularly requested the death penalty in the courtroom, Tarrou describes his resolution to refuse all that brings death, for whatever reason (*TRN*, 1425; *P*, 242). Suggesting that we are all complicit in the death of innocents, Tarrou asserts that we must nonetheless fight any force that brings death; and this includes maintaining vigilance, as well, against the potential each of us carries within ourselves for infection by such a plague, whatever form such evil might take. Tarrou describes the moral loneliness of his struggle, explaining that he knows he has no place in today's world: 'à partir du moment où j'ai renoncé à tuer, je me suis condamné à un exil définitif' (*TRN*, 1426) ('once I'd definitely refused to kill, I doomed myself to an exile that can never end' (*P*, 243)). By quoting Tarrou at length, Rieux implicitly invites us to read Oran's ordeal symbolically, as Tarrou himself does; in this way, Rieux's resolutely factual chronicle allows us access to the multiple layers of meaning that may be read into the plague.

Given these traces of strain within Rieux's chronicle – the tension between the singularity and pathos of the individual's (including Tarrou's) experience of the plague and Rieux's effort to provide an objective, historical chronicle, his conviction that he should speak for all (*TRN*, 1469; *P*, 291) – it is striking that he chooses to conclude with an account of one citizen for whom he could not speak, the maddened Cottard firing on the crowd. Rieux's own explanation for his choice to close his chronicle in this way is characteristically neutral, even enigmatic: 'Il est juste que cette chronique se termine sur lui qui avait un cœur ignorant, c'est-à-dire solitaire' (*TRN*, 1469) ('It is fitting that this chronicle should end with some reference to that man, who had an ignorant, that is to say lonely, heart' (*P*, 291)). Rieux's choice soberly emphasises the persistence of an undomesticated solitude despite his own experience of all that is noble, beautiful and resilient in human solidarity. And the presence of such perversion, scandalous to Rieux's demonstration, prepares his sober conclusion, following the description of a jubilant Oran: solidarity's victory can never be definitive, for the plague might always return (*TRN*, 1473–4; *P*, 297). *La Peste* thus warns us that the solitary and scandalous heart is always ready to awaken, like the plague, to test and threaten the collective. Solidarity's victory is at best fragile, as Rieux, listening from within Oran's closed gates to the 'terrible powerlessness' of far-away radio voices of solidarity (*TRN*, 1332; *P*, 134), had already realised: powerless voices perhaps suggestive, on a deeper level, of the essential fragility of even the most robust human solidarity.

Despite Rieux's sober conclusion; despite critical objections to the absence of indigenous, Algerian voices and experiences in the novel;[6] despite Camus's own despairing conviction, in 1946, 'je trouve ce livre manqué' ('I feel this book is a failure');[7] it was immensely successful upon its publication in 1947, selling 22,000 copies in just two weeks.[8] Its success has never waned. To date, over five million copies have been sold, in some thirty languages. As Camus himself asserted to Roland Barthes in 1955, the movement from *L'Etranger* to *La Peste* is that from solitude to solidarity.[9] In a France struggling to emerge from the trauma, humiliation and deprivation of World War II, Rieux's account of the triumph of human solidarity over oppression, the resistance of such solidarity to any evil that would destroy it, brought welcome solace and encouragement. Camus was to go on to develop the theme of revolt in his essay *L'Homme révolté*, published in 1951. In *La Peste*, however, as early as 1947, we already need to imagine Sisyphus no longer merely happy (as Camus argues in *Le Mythe de Sisyphe*), but in revolt against all that would crush, suffocate and dismantle the human.

NOTES

1. The epigraph to *La Peste* is taken from the preface to Volume III of Daniel Defoe's *Robinson Crusoe*.
2. Albert Camus, Letter to Francine Camus, 31 August 1944. Quoted in Olivier Todd, *Albert Camus, une vie* (Paris, Gallimard, 1996), p. 501.
3. The effort to resist such oppression, to speak out against that which would impose silence, was Camus's own, as journalist and ultimately editor of the Resistance newspaper *Combat* during the German occupation of France.
4. Albert Camus, *Journaux de voyage*, ed. Roger Quilliot (Paris, Gallimard, 1978), p. 42. English translation (modified) is by Hugh Levick, from Albert Camus, *American Journals* (New York, Paragon House, 1987), p. 45.
5. Raymond Quilliot, '"La Peste": Présentation' (*TRN*, 1942). Pointing to the 'Cas douteux' ('Questionable Case') diagnosis on Paneloux's death certificate, Edward Hughes extends this ambiguity to Paneloux's shaken faith; the uncertain pathology of Paneloux's death thus represents 'a final irony in the case of the once uncompromising preacher who had traded so happily in theological certainties', *Albert*

Camus: Le Premier Homme/La Peste (Glasgow, University of Glasgow French and German Publications, 1995), p. 69.

6. Conor Cruise O'Brien, among other critics, has pointed to the absence of indigenous voices and experiences in *La Peste* in his *Albert Camus of Europe and Africa* (New York, Viking, 1970).

7. Albert Camus, Letter to Patricia Blake, 8 July 1946, quoted in Todd, *Albert Camus*, p. 569.

8. Todd, *Albert Camus*, p. 603.

9. Albert Camus, Letter to Roland Barthes, 11 January 1955 (*TRN*, 1973–5).

13

DAVID R. ELLISON

Withheld identity in *La Chute*

Following upon four years of near silence after the controversy with Sartre in *Les Temps modernes* surrounding the disputed philosophical claims of *L'Homme révolté*, the publication in 1956 of *La Chute* dispelled any premature notion that Camus might have lost his considerable talents and intellectual relevance as a writer. In a tightly structured imaginative fable centred in an examination of human duplicity remarkable for its mixture of lucidity and ferocious wit, Camus made his return to centre stage both assertive and enigmatic. Of all Camus's texts, and in contradistinction to the outspoken straightforward presentation of *Le Premier Homme* which was to follow it, *La Chute* is the most resistant to our understanding as readers, for two essential reasons: (1) it is highly personal; its rhetorical mode is that of a monological confession; and (2) it eludes our grasp by alluding to numerous other works of literature in the Western tradition, from the Bible through Dante to Dostoyevsky, to such a degree that we have difficulty separating levels of meaning in an effort to attain the work's semantic core. Of all Camus's texts, *La Chute* has generated the broadest diversity of critical readings precisely because of the apparently uncontrollable multiple meanings that inhere within its personal and allusive potential.[1]

Plot, structure, themes

For readers familiar with the evolution of Camus's work until 1956, *La Chute* contains a number of surprises. The most striking of these is the setting of the novel – which is no longer the sun-infused landscape of North Africa, but the fog-enveloped watery horizon of Holland. Drawing in part on his own remembrances of a short trip to The Hague and Amsterdam in October 1954 and in part on literary and cultural artefacts, Camus chose to place the action of his ironical narrative in a location that represented for him the antithesis of the stark geographical and aesthetic sobriety he found dominant in the Mediterranean world. Inevitably, the reader who comes to *La Chute* with a clear memory of *L'Homme révolté* and especially of its lyrical conclusion on the notions of 'mesure' ('measure', 'moderation') and 'pensée solaire' ('solar' or enlightened thought) will find in the setting of the novel – a tobacco- and gin-filled sailors' bar in the red-light district of Amsterdam – a conscious and studied reversal of the values Camus had sought to define in his philosophical treatise of 1951. In the simplest of definitions, we say that irony is a figure of speech whereby one says the opposite of what one means: in the case of *La Chute*, it would seem that the entirety of the text is ironical, in that it says the opposite of what Camus had asserted in a philosophically discursive mode in *L'Homme révolté*.

At a first level, it is possible to see in *La Chute* a belated and textually complex 'reading' of *L'Homme révolté* in which Camus, instead of criticising modern man for not recognising his limits and for denying his double nature as beast and moral being, creates in the novel's duplicitous protagonist an alter ego who revels in unlimited self-indulgence and in the inauthentic proclamation of his essential superiority. Whereas in the final pages of his philosophical treatise Camus had stated that all equivocal language, every misunderstanding could lead to violence and death, that 'le langage clair, le mot simple, peut seul sauver de cette mort' (*Ess*, 687) ('only clear language, the simple word, can save us from this death'), in his novel he portrays an anti-hero whose language is consistently ambiguous, whose ironical circumlocutions weave a dizzying and obscuring web around the notions of innocence and justice that lie, tantalising in their near-absence, at the centre of the text.

Unlike *La Peste*, in which the voice of Dr. Rieux was that of a chronicler speaking in the name of his fellow citizens, *La Chute* is constructed as a dialogue in which only one voice is heard, as a dialogue that may be the imaginary projection of one monomaniacal consciousness. The chatty protagonist calls himself Jean-Baptiste Clamence and introduces himself to his silent interlocutor with polite ceremony in an Amsterdam bar exotically named 'Mexico-City'. As a whole, the narrative is a chronologically complicated, unfolding development on the career and personality of Clamence. The more we read of the novel, the more we know about its protagonist, the more we understand why a materially successful Parisian lawyer who enjoyed the admiration of his colleagues and the adulation of his clients gradually became disillusioned with his profession, lost all self-esteem, and moved to Amsterdam to become 'judge-penitent' in a meeting-place for the exiled and disinherited of the modern world. In order to gain a preliminary understanding of *La Chute*, we need to determine who Clamence is and how he evolved from his Paris identity to his masked persona at the 'Mexico-City'. This task is made difficult by the fact that the narrative as a whole functions as a constant and consistent withholding of the protagonist's identity. Just as in Nietzsche's late aphoristic writings a veil does not conceal the truth but merely another series of veils, in the universe of *La Chute* a mask seems merely to hide more masks.[2]

The narrative is organised into six chapters of moderate length, each of which contributes cumulatively to a jagged, fragmented portrait of Clamence. In the first chapter, we meet the protagonist in his bar and discover him talking to an unnamed interlocutor in the second-person formal form. When Clamence, in the first sentence of the text, says: 'Puis-je, monsieur, vous proposer mes services, sans risquer d'être importun?' (*TRN*, 1477) ('May I, Monsieur, offer my services without running the risk of intruding?' (*F*, 5)), the reader has the impression that he or she is being addressed; indeed, Camus has constructed his text in such a way that the 'you' (*vous*) to whom Clamence speaks might be any person who picks up a copy of *La Chute*. This impression is dispelled somewhat later on when the interlocutor begins to assume his own traits of identity and character, when he becomes more particularised as a specific partner in the dialogue, but it is important to the dynamic of the novel that the reader be placed in the sometimes uncomfortable position of directly participating listener.

In the first two chapters of the novel, the picture Clamence paints of his past life shows a man in possession of intelligence, wit, charm and just the right dose of cynicism for the managing of a comfortable existence in a decadent European capital. Yet at one point in his confident story a chink in the armour appears: he remembers an evening when, after a particularly satisfying day, precisely when he had begun to exult in a feeling of power and domination, he suddenly heard an explosion of inexplicable laughter at his back (*TRN*, 1495; *F*, 30). It turns out that the repressed origin of this laughter occurred some two or three years previously, when he was crossing the Pont des Arts over the Seine river. Having noticed a lone woman leaning over the bridge's parapet, and briefly aware of her sensual charm, Clamence continued on his way until he heard 'le bruit, qui, malgré la distance, me parut formidable dans le silence nocturne, d'un corps qui s'abat sur l'eau' (*TRN*, 1511) ('the sound – which, despite the distance, seemed dreadfully loud in the midnight silence – of a body striking the water' (*F*, 52)). Moments later, he heard a repeated cry that grew gradually fainter, but despite these signs of distress and of impending disaster, he did not turn around, but regained the isolated comfort of his Paris apartment. Immediately after the telling of this central, all-determining event, Clamence and his interlocutor conclude their evening walk and arrive at the protagonist's Amsterdam residence, which the latter describes, significantly, as an *abri*, or 'refuge' (*TRN*, 1511; *F*, 53). We begin to understand, at the midpoint of *La Chute*, that the complex histrionics of the protagonist are, on one level, a strategy of avoidance: his verbose assertions of a generalised human guilt constitute an attempt to hide from his own guilt, which is specific, concrete, and real.

In chapters 4 and 5, after the account of Clamence's inaction on the bridge, we learn how the Parisian lawyer transforms himself into 'judge-penitent'. This crucial turn or reversal occurs once Clamence decides that absolute innocence is an impossibility, that all people are guilty, that even Jesus Christ falls short of perfection and thereby deserves our forgiveness. As we reach the end of chapter 5, Clamence's remarks become increasingly bitter and devastatingly ironical:

> Dès lors, puisque nous sommes tous juges, nous sommes tous coupables les uns devant les autres, tous christs à notre vilaine manière, un à un crucifiés, et toujours sans savoir . . . Dans la solitude, la fatigue aidant, que voulez-vous, on se prend volontiers pour un prophète. Après tout, c'est bien là ce que je suis, réfugié dans un désert de pierres, de brumes et d'eaux pourries, prophète vide pour temps médiocres, Elie sans messie, bourré de fièvre et d'alcool, le dos collé à cette porte moisie, le doigt levé vers un ciel bas, couvrant d'imprécations des hommes sans loi qui ne peuvent supporter aucun jugement.   (*TRN*, 1535)

> Wherefore, since we are all judges, we are all guilty before one another, all Christs in our cheap way, one by one crucified, always without knowing . . . In solitude and when fatigued, one is inclined, after all, to take oneself for a prophet. When all is said and done, that's really what I am, having taken refuge in a desert of stones, fogs, and stagnant waters – an empty prophet for shabby times, Elijah without a messiah, stuffed with fever and alcohol, my back up against this mouldy door, my finger raised towards a threatening sky, showering imprecations on lawless men who cannot endure any judgement.
> (*F*, 86)

In the sixth and final chapter, Clamence receives his interlocutor at home, in the 'refuge' of his apartment. Here, he continues his reflections on the generalised guilt that envelops humankind in the century of world wars and concentration camps, but now describes that guilt in unmistakably religious terms, borrowing from Christian imagery for the development of his theories. At the beginning of the chapter, he alludes to an episode in his past that is farthest removed from the narrative present – a period during World War II in which he was interned in a North African prison camp. He explains that his fellow prisoners, in a desire to create a form of societal order within their group, elected him their 'pope'. His role was not only that of prisoner-representative to the authorities, but also that of leader and exemplar who incorporated the values of his small society. He assumed his duties playfully at first, but soon began to take himself seriously. One day, he drank the water of a dying comrade, justifying this action to himself as follows: 'les autres avaient besoin de moi, plus que de celui-ci qui allait mourir de toute façon, et je devais me conserver à eux. C'est ainsi, cher, que naissent les empires et les églises, sous le soleil de la mort' (*TRN*, 1541) ('the others needed me more than this fellow who was going to die anyway . . . I had a duty to keep myself alive for them. Thus, *mon cher*, empires and churches are born under the sun of death' (*F*, 93)). With this episode we learn that Clamence's own guilt extends farther into the past than the dramatically presented bridge sequence. At the same time we discover in his own personal adventure an allegory of the political process whereby one individual, in proclaiming his own superiority over others, begins the process of dictatorial domination.

The Christian imagery introduced by the ironical use of the word 'pope' in a context of misery and duplicity is expanded upon in a further development in chapter 6 that is fraught with religious symbolism. Clamence asks his listener to open a cupboard that contains a panel from the Van Eyck altarpiece called *The Adoration of the Lamb*. This panel had been stolen in 1934 from the cathedral of Saint-Bavon in Ghent (Belgium), had occupied a conspicuous place on the walls of the 'Mexico-City' for a while, then was removed to its current location in Clamence's room. The one panel in the protagonist's possession is generally referred to as 'The Just Judges': it depicts famous and morally irreproachable judges on horseback who have come to admire the Mystic Lamb, who stands in the adjoining centre panel and who figures the innocence of Jesus Christ. Since the panel of the Just Judges is no longer in proximity to the Mystic Lamb, Clamence exults in his own private achievement – which consists of having separated justice from innocence. It is this separation that allows him to exercise his duplicitous 'profession' of judge-penitent.

Assuming the multiple masks of a false and pretentious penitence, Clamence not only conceals his identity in an only apparently revealing confessional discourse, but also implicates his interlocutor in a game of guilt and deceit. At the very end of the novel, the protagonist discovers that his listener is also a Parisian lawyer. What Clamence has been saying throughout his narrative can be considered an echo of what his interlocutor could have said, and might now say if he decides to accept Clamence's invitation to confess his own past guilty actions. The narrative structure of *La Chute* is circular. Clamence has related a story that can now be repeated by his listener, who, in telling his story, can invite another person to confess, ad infinitum. Words engender more words, and guilt is infinite. At the same time, of course, since the interlocutor has never spoken in the text, he may be a figment of Clamence's imagination (the 'other' lawyer may be the verbose protagonist's own mirror image) – in which case the supposed dialogue collapses into a ceaseless self-engendering monologue. Doubtless we shall never know which of these stagings – the monological or the dialogical – is the 'true' one, since, as Clamence says (truthfully): 'il est bien difficile de démêler le vrai du faux dans ce que je raconte' (*TRN*, 1537) ('it's very hard to disentangle the true from the false in what I'm saying' (*F*, 88)).

Interpretative Issues

Until now, I have emphasised certain key elements of the novel's overt narrative organisation and highlighted some of its salient themes. But *La Chute* is an enigmatic text that cannot be reduced to simple schemas and that invites interpretative labour. In what follows, without any pretence to exhaustiveness, I shall raise some interpretative issues in three distinct areas: the novel's elaborately constructed setting; the unusual (for Camus) preponderance of religious motifs; and the narrative complexity of *La Chute* as it compares to Camus's previous fictions.

The setting and its connotations

In choosing Amsterdam as the location for *La Chute*, Camus capitalised on historical and literary connotations that necessarily surround the city in the mind of a cultivated European reader. The novelist emphasises two periods of Amsterdam's history – its colonial period (the era extending from the seventeenth until the early nineteenth century when Holland administered the Dutch East Indies) and the years of World War II. In the first case, Camus reminds us that the commerce linking Holland to the Indies included trade not just in spices, exotic foodstuffs and aromatic wood, but also in slaves. When Clamence and his interlocutor take their evening walk through the city streets, the former points out two ornamental carved heads on a particularly elegant house: these heads represented 'Negro slaves' (*F*, 34), and the house belonged to a man who owed his considerable wealth to the selling of these people. With typical irony, Clamence explains that the only important difference between the colonial period and our modern age is that our rich ancestor had the courage to proclaim directly and emphatically 'Voilà, j'ai pignon sur rue, je trafique des esclaves, je vends de la chair noire' (*TRN*, 1498) ('You see, I'm a man of substance; I'm in the slave trade; I deal in black flesh' (*F*, 34)), whereas today the successful entrepreneur has more liberal views (he will sign manifestos against man's inhumanity to man), but institutes the equivalent of slavery in his dehumanising factories.

Just as one is surrounded by evidence of Amsterdam's colonial past, by visual representations of the sins of the City Fathers, in the same way one is necessarily reminded of the more immediate past – the years of World War II in which the Jewish population of the city (and of the Netherlands as a whole) was subject to persecution, deportation and ultimate death in Nazi prison camps. At the very beginning of his story, Clamence tells us that he lives in the Jewish quarter of the city (*TRN*, 1481; *F*, 10), and on several occasions he uses the terms 'liquidation' and 'clean-up' (*lessivage*) in alluding to the tenets of Nazi ideology, whereby the 'impure' non-Aryan elements of European society were to be flushed out of the continent in a massive 'cleansing' operation. Naturally, the numerous canals of Amsterdam (a city often called 'the Venice of the North') played a role in Camus's emphasis on liquid imagery as such, including the unpleasant metaphors of *liquidation* and *lessivage*.

Water dominates as the single most important symbol in *La Chute*, not only through its own connotative potential, but also in its opposition to other elements and symbols. Thus, when Clamence asserts that the concentric circles of Amsterdam's canals resemble the circles of Hell, he alludes to Dante's *Inferno*, but replaces the imagery of fire used by the Italian poet with his own water imagery (*TRN*, 1483; *F*, 13). Later on in the narrative, in describing the 'negative landscape' of the Zuyderzee with its blending of grey sky and flat grey sea, the protagonist speaks of 'un enfer mou' ('a flabby hell') in which 'l'espace est incolore, la vie morte' ('space is colourless and life dead') (*TRN*, 1512; *F*, 54). Unlike classical Christian emblems of hell, which rest on the clear illuminating power of flame, Camus's personal rewriting of our fallen state accentuates the blurring of boundaries, the mental and spiritual confusion of the modern human being, who, abandoned by God and by all transcendence, does not know, in a fundamental sense, where he or she is. Unlike the Christians, for whom an almighty deity has established the frontiers of good and evil, and unlike the ancient Greeks, who navigated among islands whose 'échine sans arbres traçait la limite du ciel, leur rivage rocheux tranchait nettement sur la mer' (*TRN*, 1525) ('treeless backbone marked the limit of the sky and their rocky shore contrasted sharply with the sea' (*F*, 72)), the inhabitants of the modern world make their voyage in liquid imprecision, unaware of all frontiers, unable to find their way against a nebulous horizon.

Religion

La Chute is unique among Camus's novels in that it makes consistent use of a religious vocabulary. In the first place, the name of the protagonist is

Jean-Baptiste Clamence – a double allusion to St John the Baptist, the New Testament figure who prepares the way for Jesus Christ. Not only is the first name transparently that of the saint, but the last name, Clamence, plays on the Latin present participle *clamans*, meaning 'crying', which is to be found in the legendary expression that describes John's arduous wanderings and preachings: *vox clamantis in deserto* – that is, the voice of one crying in the wilderness. From the very beginning of the novel, Camus ironically equates the disabused ruminations of his protagonist with the act of prophecy. But what separates Clamence from the prophets of the Bible is his own emptiness of character, his moral vacancy, as well as the fact that his prophecy announces nothing concrete or real. There is further irony in Camus's choice of Clamence/*clamans* as a name for his hero. The epithet of 'Baptist' was chosen for John for obvious and literal reasons: his role was to purify, in the act of baptism by water, those people who awaited the Messiah. Clamence, however, is not only impure in a general sense (that is, morally unadmirable), but the moment at which he could have demonstrated the courage of a genuine moral choice occurs when he does *not* jump into the water to save a drowning woman from death. The plunge into water that promises purification for the Christian is the plunge not taken by Clamence.

The essential role of Jean-Baptiste Clamence is to reverse the values on which Christian morality is constructed. Whereas the actions of St John and Jesus exemplified the notion of *agape* – that is, brotherly love or charity wherein all humans demonstrate their essential equality and oneness – the actions and the mad fantasies of Clamence centre in dreams of power and domination. Thus, when he imagines his own beheading (in an allusion not just to the end of *L'Etranger*, but to the end of the life of St John, whose severed head was presented on a silver platter by Salome to King Herod), it is not as a sacrifice in the name of Christian charity, but rather as a devious method for obtaining the subservient admiration of his 'public': 'Au-dessus du peuple assemblé, vous élèveriez alors ma tête encore fraîche, pour qu'ils s'y reconnaissent et qu'à nouveau je les domine, exemplaire. Tout serait consommé, j'aurais achevé, ni vu ni connu, ma carrière de faux prophète qui crie dans le désert et refuse d'en sortir' (*TRN*, 1551) ('Above the gathered crowd, you would hold up my still warm head, so that they could recognise themselves in it and I could again dominate – an exemplar. All would be consummated; I should have brought to a close, unseen and unknown, my career as a false prophet crying in the wilderness and refusing to come forth' (*F*, 107)).

Clamence's self-debasement emerges in a strategy of confessional discourse that aims at the humiliation of his interlocutor. Clamence's genius consists in his discovery that one can humiliate one's opponent at least as effectively by beginning below his level as by reigning above it. Penitence as practised by Clamence is merely a step towards the attainment of judgemental superiority.

The importance of Christian imagery in Camus's novel begins, of course, with the title of the volume. In naming his work *The Fall*, Camus alludes to the episode in Genesis in which Adam and Eve, the original human inhabitants of Eden, are driven out of their earthly paradise. The Biblical episode describes the human being's fall from grace, and his/her fall into the hardships and constraints of life in the natural and social worlds. Camus plays with the notion of the fall: first, when Clamence, in describing his early, self-satisfied Paris days, admits: 'libre de tout devoir, soustrait au jugement comme à la sanction, je régnais, librement, dans une lumière édénique' (*TRN*, 1489) ('free of any duty, shielded equally from judgement as from penalty, I freely held sway bathed in a light as of Eden' (*F*, 22)); later, when the unknown woman falls from the bridge (*TRN*, 1511; *F*, 52–3); and finally, when, discovering his own duplicity, Clamence begins to fall, literally and inexplicably, in public places (*TRN*, 1515; *F*, 58). In Clamence's case, falling relates to the important and pervasive theme of laughter in the novel. To fall in front of one's fellow humans is to lose face, to cease being superior and to become the mere object of someone else's amusement. Camus recognises that cruelty is never very far from laughter, since both laughter and cruelty derive from the superiority of one person over another. As Clamence progresses towards his final status as judge-penitent, he understands that he can regain his mastery over others by laughing at himself. By becoming a strategic ironist, by forcing his listener(s) to identify with his narrative, he eventually reverses the situation and regains control of his staged dialogue. In his essay 'De l'Essence du rire', Baudelaire asserted that Christ never laughed, that the comical as such, being based on a very non-charitable discrepancy in power between the person who laughs and the object of his merriment, was therefore 'Satanic' in mode.[3] It was Satan, disguised as a serpent, who caused the fall of humankind. In his use of mordant irony, in his efforts to undermine innocence and separate it from justice, Clamence aligns himself with his tortuous predecessor.

Narration

If Camus's three novels retain the attention of the reading public today, it is not just because of the ideas they express but also because of their subtle and appropriate narrative forms. Camus heightened the dramatic tension of *L'Etranger* by constructing it symmetrically around three deaths (that of the protagonist's mother at the beginning, that of the Arab in the middle of the story and that of Meursault himself at the end). The central placement of the murder scene at the beach calls attention to the centrality of the act within the text; form and content coincide and illuminate each other in this one theatrical moment. For *La Peste*, a work that depicts not the struggle of an individual against his fate but the plight of an entire community, Camus chose the form of a chronicle in which the personality of the narrator is not allowed to intervene. What Dr Rieux tells of the epidemic and its effects is not in his own name, but in the name of Oran's citizenry. The action of the novel builds slowly and gradually, and has the overall structure of a five-act classical tragedy.

In composing *La Chute*, Camus faced a delicate balancing act. On the one hand, his protagonist being representative of the excesses and unreason of our time, the novelist needed to give him free rein to express himself with appropriate hyperbole. The discourse of Clamence could not appear controlled from the outside lest it lose its power of disorientation and dislocation of the reader's sensibilities. On the other hand, however, for an ironical tale to exercise maximum rhetorical power, it must be tightly constructed and concentrated in its effects. Camus managed to reconcile these two opposite demands through an astute manipulation of the text's formal potential. By structuring *La Chute* as a conversation in which only the 'unhinged' protagonist speaks, and by allowing the conversation to seem interminable in its labyrinthine meanderings as it stretches over several days and several landscapes, the author draws his reader into Clamence's web, into the dizzying perverse logic of his duplicitous arguments. At the same time, however, underneath the simple chronological progression of the conversation (from the initial meeting in the 'Mexico-City' through the evening walk in the city to the excursion on the Zuyderzee to the final meeting in Clamence's room), Camus has created a subterranean temporal archaeology that the reader gradually excavates as he or she moves towards the conclusion of the book. It is the subtle and complex layering of temporal levels that gives *La Chute* its density and that allows the narrative to say so much elliptically.

Although Camus does not intend his novel to be 'realistic' or narrowly mimetic (for this reason, very few specific dates are to be found in the text), nevertheless he makes it possible for the reader to reconstruct five separate narrative levels, which I shall designate by number, moving from present to most remote past:

1. Current conversation: the dialogue between Clamence and his interlocutor that begins in the 'Mexico-City' one evening and concludes just a few days later in Clamence's room. We are in post-war Europe, most likely in the late forties or early fifties.

2. Clamence's recent past in Amsterdam: in various rapid allusive comments, the protagonist relates his early days in the Dutch city and his assumption of the role of judge-penitent. It is during this period that the Van Eyck painting appears, first on the wall of the 'Mexico-City', then in Clamence's apartment.

3. Clamence's life as lawyer in Paris: this period includes the early days of self-satisfaction as well as the uncomfortable episodes on the bridges of the city. We can assume that a good part of what is described at this level occurs immediately after 1945.

4. Clamence's life in prison camp: this episode takes place during World War II after 1942 (we know this because the narrator alludes briefly to the Allies' occupation of North Africa via 'Operation Torch'). From this temporal layer subsists only the one crucial remembrance of Clamence as 'pope'.

5. The theft of the Van Eyck painting: this is an actual historical event that took place in 1934 (the 'Just Judges' panel of the altarpiece was indeed stolen and its unknown location was a matter of speculation for years). Clamence is, of course, not the original thief, but is depicted by Camus as participating in the process whereby the painting remains removed from its rightful place and hidden from public view.

Like *L'Etranger*, *La Chute* is constructed around a central point. Just as it is necessary to grasp the importance of the murder scene in the first novel, in the same way our interpretation of *La Chute* as an aesthetic whole will depend on the way in which we read the scene on the bridge in which Clamence does not act. In a fundamental sense, the dramatic centre of *La Chute* occurs at the deepest remove of level three, the original bridge scene that splits the protagonist's life into a 'before' of unquestioning egocentric pleasure in a kind of Eden and an 'after' of duplicity in the self-chosen role of judge-penitent. Level five remains outside the essential narrative frame and relates to level two; level four adds depth to our understanding of Clamence's human weakness and lends resonance to the pervasive theme of political domination, but it does not have the central causative status of the episode on the bridge.

In a curious way, *La Chute* appears to be a studied rewriting of *L'Etranger*. Both texts centre on an individual, on a central moment in which he acts in a criminal fashion and on the problem of his guilt and moral responsibility. In *L'Etranger*, the entirety of the novel hinges on the murder scene and on the way in which the reader chooses to judge the protagonist's involuntary, dream-like killing of the Arab. In *La Chute*, the central event is not a violent action, but a passive avoidance of human intervention. In the eyes of the law (of society) Clamence would appear to be less guilty than Meursault; after all, the law does not prescribe that we must jump off bridges to save people we do not know. Nevertheless, the rhetoric of the text has us believing, from the very beginning, in the guilt of the protagonist. There is no question that Clamence is not only guilty of a specific crime of passivity, but that he incorporates and exemplifies the moral nullity of his time. Between the writing of *L'Etranger* and the appearance of *La Chute* lies World War II – its violence, its wholesale destruction, its prison camps, its carefully planned and plotted *lessivages*. Gone is the Romantic pathos with which Camus portrayed Meursault as pursued by a blind fate and misunderstood by a hypocritical society. As he demonstrated in *La Peste*, evil is not conveniently located in an exterior social or political entity, but lies dormant within us all. *La Chute* moves beyond the sober expository clarity of *La Peste* and manifests the ubiquitous presence of evil within logic and within language itself.

With *La Chute*, in an explosion of formal and rhetorical brilliance, Camus wrote his most allusive, most demanding, and most complex work. In his last completed novel, he diagnosed the ills of the age but offered no solutions, no prescriptions for an improving of the human condition. In *La Chute* Camus gave literary form to the excesses (*démesure*) he had criticised in *L'Homme révolté*. Unlike the serious philosophical treatise, however, the ironical novel remains within the foggy confusion of northern climes. Ironically, it may be that by sinking into this darkness Camus achieved a higher clarity of perception and judgement than in his nostalgic solar myth of a disappearing Mediterranean unity.

NOTES

1. For a subtle discussion of *La Chute* as 'disdainful confession' and as rhetorically devious monologue, see Maurice Blanchot, '*La Chute*: La Fuite', in *L'Amitié* (Paris, Gallimard, 1971), pp. 228–35. For a psychoanalytical approach to the narrator as witness, see Shoshana Felman, 'Camus' "The Fall", or The Betrayal of the Witness', in Shoshana Felman and Dori Laub, *Testimony: Crises of Witnessing in Literature, Psychoanalysis and History* (New York, Routledge, 1992), pp. 165–203. On the literary intertexts of the novel (particularly Dante, Baudelaire and Dostoyevsky), see F. W. Locke, 'The Metamorphoses of Jean-Baptiste Clamence', *Symposium* 21 (1967), 306–15, and David Ellison, 'Camus and the Rhetoric of Dizziness: *La Chute*', *Contemporary Literature* 24.3 (Autumn 1983), 322–48. On the importance of Van Eyck's 'Just Judges' panel of *The Adoration of the Lamb* as iconic intertext for the novel, see Jeffrey Meyers, 'Camus' *The Fall* and Van Eyck's *The Adoration of the Lamb*', *Mosaic* 7.3 (1974), 43–51, and Margaret Gray, 'Les

"Juges Intègres" de Clamence: Une lecture psychanalytique de *La Chute*', in Lionel Dubois (ed.), *Albert Camus entre la misère et le soleil* (Poitiers, Pont-Neuf, 1997), pp. 73–80.

2. For an ironical development on the deluded impulse to unveil the truth, see the fourth paragraph of the Preface to the second edition of Nietzsche, *The Gay Science, With a Prelude in Rhymes and an Appendix of Songs*, trans. Walter Kaufmann (New York, Vintage Books, 1974), p. 38.

3. Charles Baudelaire, 'De l'essence du rire et généralement du comique dans les arts plastiques', *Œuvres complètes*, ed. Claude Pichois, 2 vols. (Paris, Gallimard (Bibliothèque de la Pléiade, 1976), vol. II, pp. 525–43.

14

DEBRA KELLY

Le Premier Homme and the literature of loss

Ce qu'ils n'aimaient pas en lui, c'était l'Algérien.
(PH, 318)

What they did not like in him was the Algerian.
(FM, 253)

The focus of this final chapter will be Camus's unfinished text *Le Premier Homme*, published posthumously in 1994, and the exploration of his relationship to Algeria in a narrative concerned with personal origins, family, and the history and the present of a community.

Born into the poor *pied-noir* community in Algeria in 1913, Camus in his literary exploration of identity necessarily engages not only with a personal history, but also with the collective histories of North Africa and of European colonialism, and specifically with the political, social and cultural configuration of 'French Algeria'. Those collective histories are integral to an understanding of the plural nature of the Maghreb. In those short stories in *L'Exil et le Royaume* (1957) which explicitly take the country of his birth as their context, an increasingly troubled relationship with the Algeria of the period is already evident. The emphasis here will be on *Le Premier Homme* as a work of the imagination. Just as Camus's imagination was haunted in the late 1950s by the increasing violence of the Algerian War of Independence and the political polarisation it brought, so this literary expression of impossible return and potentially irretrievable loss continues to haunt the imagination of readers, critics and writers. This 'return to Camus' took various forms in the 1970s, 1980s and especially the 1990s following the immense international publishing success of *Le Premier Homme* in 1994, and of Olivier Todd's biography in 1996.[1]

Recent readings, influenced by postcolonial theory and its emphasis on the power relations between formerly colonised regions and the colonising powers, have put Camus 'in the dock' to answer for a list of offences ranging from overt racism, for example in *L'Etranger*, to 'special pleading' in the defence of 'French Algeria' in *Le Premier Homme*.[2] I want to argue that the ambiguities of Camus's writing and of the representation of memory in the Algerian context are more complex and intense than trial by political conviction allows.

Read within a framework extending beyond postcolonial theory to memory studies, *Le Premier Homme* is a text of 'mediation' in the sense that Avery Gordon defines 'haunting' as a particular form of mediation: 'As a concept, mediation describes the process that links an institution and an individual, a social structure and a subject, and history and a biography.'[3] The narrative of *Le Premier Homme* is haunted by the silences of the past (the dead father and other war dead; the almost silent mother; the deaf uncle; the incuriosity about the past manifested by the poor; the dead of the cemetery of Solferino) and of the present that will soon become a past (the Algerian War of Independence will efface the collective history of the French Algerians). The act of writing involves various forms of mediation: between the individual and the institution that is the French colonial system, including the notion of 'French Algeria'; between the subject and the social structures of the family and of the poor settler community into which Camus was born; and between the history of French colonialism and personal biography.

This chapter aims, in addition, therefore, to enable us 'to appreciate Camus's very real contribution to an understanding of the traumas of colonisation and decolonisation'.[4] Indeed, Camus's text shares many of the preoccupations of North African postcolonial writing in French which includes several autobiographical texts published from the period of the independence struggles in the 1950s onwards. These texts engage not only with the question of individual self-expression and identity, but also with collective social, ideological and historical contexts in the wake of European colonialism. Yet, as the prominent Arabo-Berber Algerian woman writer Assia Djebar notes, while she is currently perceived as the embodiment of an 'Algeria-woman', and is solicited within the Western literary and critical establishment as such, Camus's claim to an Algerian identity has become suspect at this point in the history of colonialism and postcolonialism.[5]

Historical ambiguities

Vieux cimetière des colons, l'immense oubli. (*PH*, 303)

Old settler cemetery, immense oblivion. (*FM*, 244)

The accusation that Camus's narrative mythologises not just himself but also the way in which Algeria was colonised, and the lives of its poor settler community, would appear to damn the book from the start. Emily Apter sums it up: 'For critics steeped in postcolonial perspectives, Camus's name triggers not only a deplorable record on the Algerian War that rightly cost him friendships on the left, but also his systematic nullification of Arab characters, particularly evident in *L'Etranger*, *La Peste* and the short stories in *L'Exil et le Royaume*.' Yet she also notes the recent recuperation and re-appropriation of Camus as a 'universal freedom-fighter' by Algerian exiles and dissidents as part of a wider reaction against the rise of fundamentalism in Algeria in the 1990s.[6]

The aim here is not to re-tread ground that has been comprehensively covered by several critics concerning the historical and political circumstances of France and Algeria in the second half of the 1950s, and Camus's position as a very public intellectual.[7] There were evident contradictions between Camus's political stance on the condition of the Arab and Kabyle populations of Algeria and his calls for reforms, for example in *Misère de la Kabylie* (1939) and 'Crise en Algérie' (1945), and his fictions, which omit any reference to the colonial system and its oppression, and in which the indigenous characters lack individual identity. Camus is accused of de-historicising the colonial past and privileging his loyalty to the European settler community at the expense of the values of justice that he championed elsewhere in his political writings. Such accusations focus especially on chapter 7 of *Le Premier Homme* and Jacques Cormery's visit to the old settler, Veillard. The attack on Camus for his idealised image of colonial Algeria has a lineage that can be traced back to Albert Memmi's analysis, in *The Coloniser and the Colonised*, of coloniser–colonised relations and of the privileged position of even the poor *pieds-noirs* compared to the majority of the indigenous populations.[8]

The facts of the colonial situation in Algeria have been analysed from a number of perspectives. Sociological research, for instance, has shown that in 1954 the *pieds-noirs* constituted 11 per cent of the population of Algeria, while holding 50 per cent of all available jobs in industry. However, the lives of the various sectors of the population varied widely, as Assia Djebar's own working through of her childhood as the daughter of an educated Arab primary schoolteacher in the French education system during the 1930s and 1940s makes clear. In many readings of *Le Premier Homme*, the issue of poverty that destines the working-class settler to anonymity is evaded. Yet as Camus insists, it is not only the war that threatens his community, for its state has been and continues to be one of oblivion; the poor mark only 'les traces vagues du chemin de la mort' (*PH*, 79) ('faint traces on the path to death' (*FM*, 62)). The critic David Carroll has argued that Camus's notion of an Algeria in which there would be justice for both European and Arab Algerians is very different from the French state's version of 'French Algeria' (as it is from that of Algerian nationalists).[9] And following Cruise O'Brien's argument closely while arriving at a very different conclusion, Nancy Wood argues that *Le Premier Homme* shows Camus trying to come to terms with a legacy that he knows to be implicated in colonial oppression but that cannot be reduced to that alone. For Wood, Camus is engaged in the construction of a historical memory that includes all the 'ambivalences, but moderates the extremes', attempting to 'invent for himself and his community a historical memory that could be invoked as part of Algeria's collective heritage'. Wood's counter-argument also takes up the idea that *Le Premier Homme* is more complex than Cruise O'Brien's reading allows, and locates the key site of this complexity in Camus's research into Algeria's colonial history (evident in the notes for the unfinished novel): 'however, these memories take on such a hallucinatory and ambivalent character', Wood notes, that they undermine rather than secure any patrimonial claim and the project constitutes finally a defensive historical memory.[10]

'Hallucinatory' is a term used by Cruise O'Brien to describe Camus's version of colonial Algeria devoid of a past before the arrival of the Europeans; it is also a term used by Freud to describe an element of the process of mourning to which I will return. Carroll concludes that Camus writes his short stories and his last novel to express a history that he knows already to be lost, indirectly revealing in his fiction what he could not admit or accept in his politics: Algerian independence and the departure and exile of French Algerians from the country. Camus counters, then, Memmi's analysis of suffering in the colonial system (although Memmi did recognise the poor settler as victim also), and thereby sets about collapsing the binary opposition of coloniser and colonised. This is not to deny the differences between cultures violently oppressed by colonialism and a culture created by the colonial system, and whose fate is therefore inextricably bound up with its defeat. Yet it is clear that for Camus, his community, its way of life and his own identity are being denied by both sides in the struggle of the colony for independence – to return to the epigraph at the beginning of this chapter, what *they* did not like in him was the Algerian. The *they* certainly means the 1950s Parisian left-wing intelligentsia opposed to continuing colonisation; it could also encompass various elements in the local nationalist struggle uncomfortable with Camus's claims to be Algerian. Furthermore, while it is true that in the state of the text as we have it, the commemoration of the *pied-noir* community can be read at the expense of the Arab who remains largely anonymous as in colonialist discourse, there are equally plans for the elaboration of a native Algerian character – a rebel often referred to as Saddok – in the 'Notes and Sketches' appended to the main body of *Le Premier Homme*. The various sketches of dialogues between Cormery and Saddok give a voice to Algerian nationalist discourse, and Camus's plan for what he referred to as the last part of the work was to see Jacques explaining to his mother 'la question arabe, la civilisation créole, le destin de l'Occident' (*PH*, 307) ('the Arab question, Creole civilisation, the fate of the West' (*FM*, 246)). Apter arrives at a similar conclusion to that of Carroll: the text is written in the knowledge of the defeat of French Algeria.[11] Historical rupture brought about by defeat leads to loss on both the personal and collective levels.

Textual ambiguities

Je vais raconter l'histoire d'un monstre. L'histoire que je vais raconter . . .

(*PH*, 300)

I am going to tell the story of an alien. The story that I'm going to tell . . .

(*FM*, 241)

Political, economic and cultural loss, therefore, are all evident, yet in the act of writing there is the restoration of a memory, defensive or otherwise, destined to be lost, but which, through its inscription in *Le Premier Homme*, endures. Assia Djebar perceives *Le Premier Homme* (in direct opposition to Cruise O'Brien's analysis of it as a text that indulges in nostalgia, a melodrama of the self by a writer who has regressed) to be rather 'the first novel by a new forty-six year old writer called Camus'.[12] While not experimental in the way of other texts of the 1950s (for example those of 'new novelists' such as Alain Robbe-Grillet, Robert Pinget and Michel Butor), there is in the quest to configure the 'mythical homeland' the need to create a particular set of figures, signs and symbols, and in so doing an embryonic poetics of loss and of love is elaborated.[13] The text's ambiguity and complexity is not solely political and historical. The project of *Le Premier Homme* is firstly a 'writerly' one, which is not to suggest that such a life-writing project (like others of its type) is merely an intellectual project that takes little account of, and makes no impact on, the realities of a postcolonial (but not post-imperial) world. The difficulty lies in tolerating the tension between the text's historical context and its status as a work of the imagination that cannot be judged solely on political sensibilities. Ambiguity and complexity reside in the text's form and its processes, as in its politics. As in the textual dynamics of North African autobiographical projects of diverse origins from the 1950s to the present day, there is a focus on the present of the act of writing, on the act of creation as well as on recollection and the retrieval of history, asking what it means to be a colonised or previously colonised subject.

Camus poses the question of what it means to be a 'French Algerian' through the figure of Jacques Cormery. The difference from the 'French from France' is insisted upon, and the relationship with the metropolitan 'centre' is troubled. France is 'une terre inconnue de l'autre côté des mers' (*PH*, 31) ('a strange land on the other side of the seas' (*FM*, 21)) in which his father died, but has little meaning for Jacques. While the cultural space of Camus's text is not a shared one, remaining 'alien' to the indigenous cultures around it, *Le Premier Homme* is a mediating text within the contradictions and ambiguities which constitute the postcolonial world. It shares several of the themes that recur in the work of North African writers: poverty and exclusion, and their accompanying shame; the realities of everyday life in colonial and postcolonial systems; interactions in the home and with the outside world; the experience of school and social-class differences; education and alienation from the family and the community; working lives; injustice; racism; poverty; the relationship of the individual to history, to power, to the Other; the struggle for the expression of a politics of self-determination for the individual, the community, the nation.[14] Colonialism distorts the identity of the colonised subject; it has equally made a 'monster' of Cormery. Cormery is a 'monster' on a personal level, created by an education that alienates him from his background; on the collective level, the French Algerian is a 'monster' created by the colonial system. A quest for the origins of the creation of the monster goes well beyond 'nostalgia', and comes to involve personal and political risk. This is a further characteristic shared with North African autobiographical writing, where risk takes many forms, and where the image of sacrifice frequently provides a pervasive metaphor. The creative process becomes a testimony to a way of living and writing a necessary intervention despite the political and personal cost. Camus's remembrance is subjective certainly – it is socially constructed as is history. Yet a multiplicity of memories must be held side by side, as must a multiplicity of histories, if we are to make sense of the postcolonial world.

Loss, love and the inscriptions of history

En somme, je vais parler de ceux que j'aimais. Et de cela seulement. Joie profonde.   (*PH*, 312)

In short, I wanted to speak of those I loved. And of that only. Intense joy.
                                                                                    (*FM*, 250)

Le Premier Homme embodies other knowledge than solely that of history, a knowledge provoked in Cormery by the experience in 'le vaste champ des morts' (*PH*, 29) ('the vast field of the dead' (*FM*, 20)) in the Saint-Brieuc cemetery when 'le temps se disloqu(e)' (*PH*, 317) ('time goes out of joint' (*FM*, 253)). This new course of time demands a new expression: a poetics that is at once one of love and of loss, 'grounding history in love' and creating a text where 'ultimately knowledge was to defer to love'.[15]

From the very beginning of the text, the main character is presented as belonging both to Europe and to Africa, born into the world in a narrative of Biblical dimensions. Read alongside texts by other North African writers, this recourse to a set of what I have termed 'preferred myths' in order to elaborate an individual selfhood is a recurrent feature of those who have endured the multiple effects of colonisation and then tried to come to terms with these in writing. Camus writes of the impact of colonisation, resulting in loss for all those involved, even if subsequently some retrieval and reconciliation with fractured identities is possible. The loss of generations is symbolised in the double scenes of the cemeteries at Saint-Brieuc and Solferino. The power of inscriptions lost and found provides a recurring dynamic in the narratives of writers such as Khatibi and Djebar, as it does in some of the writing of Jacques Derrida, an Algerian Jew who likewise imagines the 'language of an indecipherable history' and who sees writing and effacement as inextricably linked: 'to meditate on writing, which is to say also on effacement . . . is to meditate constantly on what renders unreadable or what is rendered unreadable'.[16] Sarocchi reads the tomb at Saint-Brieuc as revealing the vanity of any inscription, and the tombs at Solferino as undermining the possibility of making anything endure in writing, yet the narrative of *Le Premier Homme* persists in its elaboration of an inscription in history.[17] The self of the writer is in the present of writing, not only in the accumulation of autobiographical 'facts' or in the rewriting of a history either erased or appropriated by others. If the postcolonial state is one of becoming, in which a new relationship is opened up with time and space, Camus's unfinished novel seems to anticipate the need for the writer to engage with this process.

Loss takes many forms in the text, each time bound up with *love*: love for the father (and in the end, the quest for the father – the 'recherche du père' of the title of Part One of the novel – leads not to retrieval, but to irredeemable loss); love for the mother, who is lost to the child and to the adult in her silence and illiteracy when 'ce qu'il désirait le plus au monde, (c')était que sa mere lût tout ce qui était sa vie et sa chair' (*PH*, 292) ('what he wanted most was for his mother to read everything that was his life and his being' (*FM*, 238)); love for the uncle who represents the 'tribe' that Cormery has left behind; love for the grandmother – even though she is the incarnation of authority – who looks at him with 'une sorte de tendresse désespérée' (*PH*, 153) ('a sort of hopeless love' (*FM*, 127)); love for Monsieur Bernard, mediator between Jacques and the French educational system, between Jacques and his family, both living and dead, and between Jacques and those lost in the First World

War, both Arab and French; love for Malan; love for the forgotten dead in the Solferino cemetery; love for the land of Algeria itself. Is this 'nostalgia'? Since a large part of memory studies has focussed on traumatic memory – the Holocaust, the effects of colonisation on the colonised – any more positive role for nostalgia has been deemed suspect, despite the fact that in its etymological sense, it evokes not only the return, but also pain, and a pain that may be forever unresolved. Mieke Bal has delineated a space for nostalgia between 'ordinary' and 'traumatic' memory, and ascribes to it an empowering role if it is 'critically tempered and historically informed'; nostalgia is 'a structure of relation to the past, not false or inauthentic in essence'.[18] If *Le Premier Homme* is written in the full understanding of the consequences of the Algerian War of Independence, this is not a surrender to nostalgia, but part of the work of mourning and loss. The aim of the elaboration of a collective memory – which is arguably Camus's purpose in *Le Premier Homme* – is to create 'a useable past' for the creation of a group identity. In contrast to history, this reflects a 'committed perspective', belonging to one group and not to others: 'Collective memory tends to be impatient with ambiguity and to represent itself as representing an unchanging reality, so it provides a particular textual resource for creating a particular kind of community.'[19] Yet since the French Algerians have no future, rather than expressing 'an unchanging reality', *Le Premier Homme* is a book of mourning. In Freudian terms, nostalgia is a substitute for mourning and prevents any coming to terms with loss. The 'work of mourning' is the struggle of the ego to detach itself finally from the loved object so as to become free again, a process to which *Le Premier Homme* points. Mourning is a kind of remembering and, unlike nostalgia, will end in letting go. Contemporary writers, however, have not yet let go of Camus, as will be explored in the concluding section.

Le Premier Homme, mourning and the haunting of modern memory

> Il n'y avait plus sous cette dalle que cendres et poussières. Mais, pour lui, son père était de nouveau vivant . . . (*PH*, 32)

> Under that slab were left only ashes and dust. But, for him, his father was again alive . . . (*FM*, 22)

To return to the notion of haunting invoked at the beginning of this chapter, Avery Gordon writes: 'The ghost is not simply a dead or missing person, but a social figure, and investigating it can lead to that dense site where history and subjectivity make social life.'[20] Cormery is haunted by his father and by the forgotten in the graves of Solferino; Camus is haunted by events in Algeria, and all the more intensely in the writing of *Le Premier Homme* from 1958 onwards, which coincided with his public silence on the country of his birth; writers, critics and readers continue to be haunted by Camus. The recurrence of the metaphor of spectres and ghosts is striking in the critical discourse on writings not only by Camus but also by others with reference to the Algerian War in general. For Sarocchi, *Le Premier Homme* is a 'spectrographie' ('spectrography') of French Algeria; it provides 'a spectral analysis', not a political one, of Cormery's destiny and of that of his community; and this spectre is always that of the father.[21]

It is on the creative aspects of such haunting that I wish to end. Camus and his fictions haunt contemporary North African writing, especially by women, recurrently in the case of Assia Djebar.[22] Djebar makes the point that consciousness of loss is paradoxically almost restorative and that the consciousness itself therefore must be preserved: 'Il y a deux sortes de perte: il y la perte qui vous hante et la perte que vous oubliez, l'oubli de la perte ... Le terrible c'est l'oubli de la perte' ('There are two sorts of loss. There is the loss that haunts you and the loss you forget, the forgetting of loss . . . The terrible thing is the forgetting of loss').[23] Camus shares with these women writers a meditation on personal and collective loss, to the point where it is possible to speak of a poetics of loss in contemporary North African writing. Are women attempting to reconcile the opposition between coloniser and colonised, and to identify with a man who would have been excluded from full participation in the Algeria constructed by nationalist discourse after independence, just as they have been obliged as women to take up ambiguous positions ever since? In addition to Assia Djebar, loss is also a dynamic of the writing of the Algerian Jewish *pied-noir* Hélène Cixous, her 'Algériance' as she calls it. In Nina Bouraoui's autobiographical *Garçon manqué (Tomboy)* (2000), the writer describes herself as 'made of the land of Algeria'. In a vocabulary that clearly echoes *L'Etranger*, the 'violent sun' of Algeria reveals that she is not a 'real' Algerian, and yet she cannot go back to France. In a short story by Maïssa Bey, a young Algerian male narrator remembers reading *L'Etranger* in school. The narrative is at once critical of the implicit colonialist discourse that removes the Arab's subjectivity – Meursault fires at the Arab 'with a capital A as if it was his name' – and of the violence of contemporary Algerian society: 'Only the blokes here don't blame the sun.'[24]

The haunting is more sustained in Assia Djebar's *La Disparition de la langue française (The Disappearance of the French Language)*, in which the protagonist Berkane, almost fifty years old and an exile from Algeria for twenty years, returns to his country and overtly acknowledges the memory of Camus.[25] Berkane too is haunted by his father's shadow, a father who fought in the Second World War for France and dies soon after independence. After disappearing in a car crash in Kabylia on his way to a camp where he was imprisoned by the French in 1962, Berkane leaves behind an unfinished autobiographical project entitled *L'Adolescent* (*The Adolescent*), written in French, his 'langue de mémoire' ('memory language'). Berkane's death is also 'unfinished', in the way that Assia Djebar has described that of Camus; his return has become a disappearance, and his ghost returns to haunt his French lover, Marise. The unfinished text is the one that the reader has just read, written against the violent background of the 'disappearance of the French language' as the professional classes exile themselves from 1990s Algeria and the rise of fundamentalism. Another community is now threatened with effacement and the consequences of violence in Algeria continue to haunt.

At a time when issues of national identity are increasingly discussed in terms of cultural and collective memory rather than in terms of the identity of the nation state, and when struggles for minority rights are also organised around questions of cultural memory, a reading of *Le Premier Homme* leaves us with another apparition of the 'first man'. The 'turn to memory' is at once a response to, and a symptom of, rupture, lack and absence. The discourse of cultural memory can 'mediate and modify difficult and tabooed moments of the past'. The problem is that the appeal to memory over history may 'displace analysis by empathy, politics by sentiment'.[26] On any site of conflict there is equally a struggle for memory, and it is certain that memory makes claims that will not be acceptable to everyone. The point is not to blame or exonerate Camus 'as a coloniser'; it is rather, as Sarocchi expresses it, to see how successfully or otherwise he interprets a 'political ambiguity'.[27] The colonisation of Algeria by France and Camus's relationship to it is rather more than a 'political ambiguity', although Sarocchi's point regarding blame or exoneration is important. A work of literary imagination that engages with memory work, *Le Premier Homme* is an interpretation of history and personal experience that haunts and continues to tell us much about the anxieties of contemporary postcolonial cultures.

NOTES

1. N. Wood, 'Colonial Nostalgia and *Le Premier Homme*', *Vectors of Memory. Legacies of Trauma in Postwar Europe* (Oxford, Berg, 1999), pp. 143–4; O. Todd, *Albert Camus, une vie* (Paris, Gallimard, 1996).

2. A. Haddour, *Colonial Myths. History and Narrative* (Manchester, Manchester University Press, 2000); P. Dunwoodie and E. J. Hughes (eds.), *Constructing Memories: Camus, Algeria and 'Le Premier Homme'* (Stirling, Stirling French Studies, 1998); N. Harrison, *Postcolonial Criticism. History, Theory and the Work of Fiction* (Cambridge, Polity, 2003).

3. A. F. Gordon, *Ghostly Matters. Haunting and the Sociological Imagination* (Minneapolis, University of Minnesota Press, 1997), p. 19.

4. E. J. Hughes, *Le Premier Homme/La Peste* (Glasgow, University of Glasgow French and German Publications, 1995), p. 87.

5. A. Djebar, *Ces voix qui m'assiègent* (Paris, Albin Michel, 1999), p. 224. See, for example, autobiographical texts by Mouloud Feraoun, Albert Memmi and Abdelkébir Khatibi.

6. E. Apter, 'Out of Character: Camus's French Algerian Subjects', *Modern Language Notes* 112.4 (1997), 502, 500.

7. C. Cruise O'Brien, *Albert Camus of Europe and Africa* (New York, The Viking Press, 1970); 'The Fall', *The New Republic*, 19 October 1995; E. Said, 'Camus and the French Imperial Experience', in *Culture and Imperialism* (London, Vintage, 1994 (1993)), pp. 204–24.

8. *Portrait du colonisé* précédé de *Portrait du colonisateur* (Paris, Gallimard, 1985 (1957)) has been arguably the North African Jewish writer Albert Memmi's most famous text.

9. D. Carroll, 'Camus's Algeria: Birthrights, Colonial Injustice and the Fiction of a French Algerian People', *Modern Languages Notes* 112.4 (1997), 522.

10. Wood, 'Colonial Nostalgia', pp. 153, 155, 160.

11. Apter, 'Out of Character', 514, 516.

12. Djebar, *Ces voix*, p. 232.

13. J. Sarocchi, *Le Dernier Camus ou 'Le Premier Homme'* (Paris, Nizet, 1995), p. 163.

14. D. Kelly, *Autobiography and Independence. Selfhood and Creativity in North African Postcolonial Writing in French* (Liverpool, Liverpool University Press, 2005).

15. T. Garfitt, 'Le Premier Homm(ag)e: Grounding History in Love' and D. Walker, 'Knowing the Place for the First Time?', in Dunwoodie and Hughes (eds.), *Constructing Memories*, pp. 1, 20.

16. J. Derrida, *Points . . . Interviews. 1974–1994* (Stanford, Stanford University Press, 1995), p. 119; Haddour, *Colonial Myths*, p. 170.

17. Sarocchi, *Le Dernier Camus*, p. 120. Sarocchi notes the Biblical dimensions of the narrative, p. 28.

18. M. Bal, J. Crew and L. Spitzer, *Acts of Memory. Cultural Recall in the Present* (Hanover NH and London, University Press of New England, 1999), p. xi.

19. J. V. Wertsch, *Voices of Collective Remembering* (Cambridge, Cambridge University Press, 2002), pp. 31, 66.

20. Gordon, *Ghostly Matters*, p. 8.

21. Sarocchi, *Le Dernier Camus*, pp. 96, 149.

22. Djebar, *Ces voix*, pp. 224–32, where she meditates on Camus's 'unfinished' text and on his 'unfinished' death; *Le Blanc de L'Algérie* (Paris, Albin Michel, 2003), pp. 103–4. In the case of Djebar, it is clear that her reading of *Le Premier Homme*

has facilitated what could be termed a reconciliation with Camus. Earlier in *Ces voix qui m'assiègent*, she writes that she took a considerable time to recognise her relationship to him (p. 221).

23. A. Djebar, 'Le Territoire des langues', in L. Gauvin (ed.), *L'Ecrivain francophone à la croisée des langues: entretiens* (Paris, Karthala, 1997), p. 30.
24. N. Bouraoui, *Garçon manqué* (Paris, Stock, 2000), p. 36; M. Bey, 'Un jour de juin', *Nouvelles d'Algérie* (Paris, Grasset, 1998), pp. 46–7.
25. A. Djebar, *La Disparition de la langue française* (Paris, Albin Michel, 2003), p. 92.
26. These arguments summarise the ideas of several critics in the field of memory studies: A. Huyssens, *Twilight Memories: Marking Time in a Culture of Amnesia* (London, Routledge, 1995), p. 5; Bal et al., *Acts of Memory*, p. vii; K. Hodgkin and S. Radstone (eds.), *Contested Pasts. The Politics of Memory* (London, Routledge, 2003), pp. 11–12.
27. Sarocchi, *Le Dernier Camus*, p. 44.

EDWARD J. HUGHES

Postface

Who reads Camus? Were we to focus on the admittedly narrow world of academic publications and interest, we might well conclude that Camus has come to be an author more written about outside France than inside it. It was in France in the early 1970s that he was notoriously dismissed as an author whose philosophy is only suitable for sixth-form study.[1] Long before that, as Olivier Todd reminds us, Sartre was decidedly patronising about the philosophical shortcomings of Le Mythe de Sisyphe, although somewhat more approving in his response to L'Etranger when these texts appeared in 1942.[2] Yet Camus's ability to attract mass audiences both within the hexagon and beyond is undisputed. Jeanyves Guérin reported in the 1990s that statistically speaking, Camus remained the author most widely read by school pupils and university students in France.[3] In a recent survey for French television, Camus was placed fifty-ninth in a poll to establish 'les plus grands Français de tous les temps' ('the greatest French people of all time'), above Sartre, who occupied ninety-fifth place.[4] In the English-speaking world, his work regularly features on undergraduate reading lists for courses on twentieth-century French literature, politics and philosophy.

How we approach a text like Le Mythe de Sisyphe is arguably important for any approach to Camus's work more generally. We can, as Sartre did, dismiss the essay as philosophically unconvincing, just as we can criticise L'Homme révolté as a rough and ready history of European ideas, as a patchwork of that continent's cultural, philosophical and political history. David Carroll makes the important point that the author of Le Mythe is less interested in any wisdom about the ultimate meaning of life that might arrive via great philosophy than in the visceral feeling, experienced by ordinary people, that life may abruptly lose meaning: 'Le sentiment de l'absurdité au détour de n'importe quelle rue peut frapper à la face de n'importe quel homme' (Ess, 105), warns Camus ('At any street corner, the feeling of absurdity can strike any man in the face' (MS, 10–11)). Moreover, for Carroll, Camus's take on the Sisyphus myth and his refusal of any big narrative marks an early phase in a career-long battle against ideological certainties, whether philosophical, political or religious. In a related way, Colin Davis demonstrates (as we saw in chapter 8) how the vain quest for secure ultimate values in Camus's reflection on the Absurd anticipates the debate about ethical value central to what we conveniently label postmodernity.

In Camus's work generally, we regularly find the same conscious lowering of philosophical horizons identified in *Le Mythe*. He views sceptically the promise of longer-term salvation held out by both Christianity and Marxism, preferring to situate many of his heroes in a here and now that will not mutate into some transcendent, redemptive order. This insistence on a banal present, on limits, is central to Camus. The Everyman he constructs from this ordinariness forms a key dimension of his appeal to generations of readers. In the seductive portrait of Meursault that he paints in his preface to the American edition of *The Outsider* published in 1958, he evokes his protagonist's run-of-the-mill lifestyle, his typicality as he wanders, 'en marge, dans les faubourgs de la vie privée, solitaire, sensuelle' (*TRN*, 1928) ('in the margins, in the *faubourgs* of private, solitary, sensuous life'). For the general reader, the appeal is one of recognition. Meursault's unexceptional biography seems to map readily on to a familiar style of urban living in the modern world characterised less by community and kinship than by isolation and alienation; on to a cultural landscape denied the consolation of religious or political certainties; on to a world of mundaneness (it is not coincidental that Camus should choose the unfashionable, working-class *faubourg*, the inner suburb with its connotations of social ordinariness, as the locus of Meursault's confrontation with the everyday; or indeed that a bar in Amsterdam's red-light district should be where Clamence holds court in *La Chute*, a meeting-place, as David Ellison remarks, for 'the exiled and disinherited of the modern world' (see above, p. 179). Yet in *L'Etranger* we find an arresting transition from this obscurity to a position of social prominence. For however marginal a figure he cuts, Meursault leads a private life that delivers its own drama by catapulting him into a public sphere. Indeed, the declamatory tone in the closing lines of the novel when he expresses the wish that his execution be an occasion for antagonistic public spectacle confirms the paradox whereby the figure of social marginality and singularity becomes not only an object of public hate but also a point of cultural identification for millions of readers.

Camus regularly works this cusp between social anonymity and the spotlight, between private and public lives. His use of the confessional style of narrative is particularly effective in drawing out the private and drawing in the reader. The dramatic opening line of *L'Etranger* disarms us with its forthright intimacy. In *La Peste*, as Margaret Gray explains, Tarrou's confession forms a counterpoint to Rieux's conscious adoption of the more neutral chronicler's tone when called upon to bear witness to more collective suffering. And as David Ellison identifies in his analysis of *La Chute*, the dynamic of that novel requires the reader to occupy the uncomfortable position of being directly embroiled in Clamence's phoney world. Clamence's duplicitous verbosity implicates us and destabilises our value systems. His inauthenticity contrasts powerfully with Meursault's untutored candour, with Tarrou's anguished self-examination, with Janine's uncontrollable floods of tears at the end of 'La Femme adultère'.

Social anonymity and the crushing burden of life's ordinariness find specifically generational expression in *L'Exil et le Royaume*, where Camus conveys an acute, palpable feeling of mid-life unfulfilment. To the inarticulate dissatisfaction of the manual worker Yvars in 'Les Muets', we can add Janine's struggle to extricate herself from a sense of deep private desperation in 'La Femme adultère'. Janine may experience a fleeting, ecstatic release from her situation in her communion with the desert; more pessimistically, Yvars, on strike and faced with his own diminishing physical strength, contends with a knowing resignation unmitigated by any prospect of collective syndicalist triumph. Both protagonists have long since been estranged from the sensuous exuberance of youth that is given such free rein in Camus's early collection of lyrical essays, *Noces*. Yet as Danielle Marx-Scouras observes in chapter 10, Janine's private desperation can be mapped on to a more generalised, French Algerian sense of disconnection, the dawning awareness, felt keenly by Camus's woman protagonist, of unredeemed exclusion from the Algeria of Algerians. A redemptive contrast to this tale of exile lived in the colony is provided when, in the last story in the collection, 'La Pierre qui pousse', set in a significantly exotic location away from North Africa, D'Arrast's peripheral position in relation to a tribe living in the South American jungle is transformed as he is ushered into the hub of community life (*TRN*, 1686; *EK*, 152).

Returning to the strand of social ordinariness (and by implication to the bond between author and reader that this helps solder), we see the very conscious cultivation of the everyday in Camus's work. His turning away from the high-flown and the cerebral is strategic. In a brief late text entitled 'De l'insignifiance' ('On Insignificance') published in 1959 (*TRN*, 1903–6), Camus writes ironically of his desire to compile an anthology of insignificance. While noting the mocking tone in Camus's piece, Roger Quilliot explains that the basis for his essay was in fact a much more serious draft on the same subject to be found in the *Carnets* in early 1945 (*TRN*, 1903). Quilliot reminds us that Camus used the motif of insignificance extensively in both *L'Etranger* and *La Peste*, where the routine and the quotidian form the bedrock of experience for the likes of Meursault and Grand. As Camus argues in *L'Homme révolté*, characters in a novel inhabit a world that is neither more beautiful nor more edifying than our own (*Ess*, 666; *R*, 229). In his defence of the nineteenth-century French Algerians in *Le Premier Homme*, by contrast, Camus stresses the arduous material conditions confronting the newly arrived *petits colons* for different strategic ends (see chapter 7 of Part I of the novel). For by representing the material, physical reality of early colonial life as a form of hell on earth, Camus helps construct a form of settler martyrology.

Camus's fictional work connects powerfully with his own world. It forms a bridge between France and its most important colonial possession, Algeria, a connection which he sets out matter-of-factly (some might say incongruously) in his Nobel address when he speaks of 'la plupart d'entre nous, dans mon pays et en Europe' (*Ess*, 1073) ('most of us, in my country and in Europe'). He can write about France as an outsider, as when he complains in *Le Premier Homme* of the country's soot-filled northern cities, where the proliferation of plastic and nylon goods and drab, discoloured advertising posters discourage the alienated Mediterranean visitor (*PH*, 26; *FM*, 17). Yet as a war-time journalist often based in France, he writes as an insider, both capturing and helping to shape the national mood. Indeed, for generations of Western readers, Camus's Frenchness was as mainstream as Western colonial dominance was unproblematical. The history of the reception of *L'Etranger* bears this out. For as Peter Dunwoodie explains, Meursault remained for decades a universalised Everyman, with his status as 'colonial man' either blindly overlooked or conveniently occluded.

Dunwoodie's inferred paradigm of generational readings of the novel prompts us to think further about 'colonial man' and about modes of reading in a postcolonial frame of reference and beyond. To that end, and by way of a somewhat serpentine conclusion, I want to speculate about a tiny pocket of *L'Etranger* where we are able to see retrospectively the interconnectedness of Algerians and French Algerians. The moment occurs during the prison scene early in Part II of the novel when Marie visits Meursault. She is surrounded, and outnumbered, by Moorish women visiting their menfolk. Camus depicts the local Arab-speaking families as literally providing a background murmur as they squat while European inmates and their visitors shout to be heard: 'Malgré le tumulte, ils parvenaient à s'entendre en parlant très bas. Leur murmure sourd, parti de plus bas, formait comme une basse continue aux conversations qui s'entrecroisaient au-dessus de leurs têtes' (*TRN*, 1178) ('In spite of the din, they were managing to make themselves heard by talking in very low voices. Their muffled murmuring, coming from lower down, formed a kind of continuo for the conversations going backwards and forwards above their heads' (*O*, 72–3)). It is tempting to read the idea of the *basso continuo* as an emblem of Camus's ties to Algeria generally; as we have seen, the situation in his homeland was to be one of the great leitmotifs of his writing career. From the early campaigning journalism in 1939 when he highlighted the plight of the Kabyles in *Misère de la Kabylie* to what was to prove, in Camus's short life, the end-of-career campaigning in *Le Premier Homme*, this time on behalf of the French Algerian settlers, we see a tenacious, indeed obdurate engagement.

Four of the short stories in the *L'Exil et le Royaume* collection construct contrasting fictional situations which dramatise the European's engagement with North Africa. 'Les Muets' and 'La Femme adultère' we have already considered. Two others depict traumatic choices and the intimidating consequences of position-taking. In 'L'Hôte', the culturally liberal French Algerian schoolteacher Daru, forced to hold as prisoner overnight a native Algerian suspected of murder, can show his charge nothing but fraternal hospitality. Yet being cast in the role of jailer means that he is afterwards threatened with revenge from the prisoner's Arab brothers. In 'Le Renégat', the young European missionary sets out to conquer African resistance to Christianity, to see, as he would have it, good prevail over evil. Yet he ends up a literally mutilated, alienated subject, torn between Africa and Europe. Derangement is the consequence of his Manichean confrontation of these two cultural spaces. With his tongue cut out, he becomes the incarnation of inarticulacy and of crude cultural confusion and bigotry.

The fluctuations in Camus's own position in regard to French Algeria have been pored over and his position-taking dissected. A postcolonial reading of the prison-scene cameo from *L'Etranger* might well view with understandable suspicion the *basso continuo* attributed to the native women (taking it as a marker of cultural hierarchy in which North Africans are routinely and dismissively assigned a *'murmure sourd'*, a mere backdrop to European conversation). Certainly the narrative thread of *L'Etranger* suggests a form of social apartheid, dramatised in the stand-off between Meursault and his unnamed Arab adversary. That said, in the scene in the prison visiting room, North Africans are described as succeeding in communicating, whereas Europeans strain to do so. In positing this contrast, Meursault as narrator is arguably giving voice to an underlying European insecurity that persists in spite of obvious colonial supremacy. Yet new contexts prompt and legitimise new readings. Sixty years on, a number of Algerian women writers have adopted Camus as a fraternal figure, as we have seen in chapter 14. From the vantage point of hindsight, we might then revisit the page of *L'Etranger* that precedes the prison scene: here, at the beginning of his period of incarceration, Meursault explains to fellow inmates (most of whom are Arabs, to use Camus's mode of designation) the reason for his imprisonment. His untutored, frank account is greeted with silence but this then gives way to an exchange in which the prisoners explain to him how to arrange the matting to form a bed. The cell, and the shared misery it represents for its inhabitants, thus becomes a culturally plural space which North African and European prisoners occupy. However tenuously, the group scene enacts a provisional form of uneasy interethnic cohabitation, albeit on the periphery of society. It delivers a sharing of space, albeit parenthetically, in the regimented, punitive surroundings of the prison regime. Significantly, this tense configuration of issues and characters – homicide, fraternity, North African, European – forms the template also used by Camus in 'L'Hôte'. It suggests the author's abiding preoccupation with what is presented as the problematics of interethnic cohabitation. In today's postcolonial order, in which Western urban spaces often serve as the meeting ground for the once colonised and the once colonising, Camus's fictional portraits of 'colonial men' such as Meursault and Daru serve as a reminder of historical divisions and mindsets.

One critic has referred to *L'Etranger* as a 'cool, elegant and startling book . . . the creation of an author living in a precarious present and uncertain of his future'.[5] The precariousness in question encompassed Camus's ill-health and the dire situation of the Second World War, not forgetting the volatility of the situation in Algeria (the bloody colonial massacres at Sétif in May 1945 served as a reminder of that). Camus was keenly aware of a fundamental conditionality facing the writer (as well, of course, as facing his generation more generally). As he remarked in his Nobel address in Stockholm in December 1957, the writer is 'obscur ou provisoirement célèbre, jeté dans les fers de la tyrannie ou libre pour un temps de s'exprimer' (*Ess*, 1072) ('obscure or provisionally famous, thrown into the shackles of tyranny or free for a time to express himself'). The unpredictable future facing the author of *L'Etranger* was to bring Camus both failure and fame: national and international celebrity as a novelist; the bitter public row with Sartre and *Les Temps modernes*, and beyond that the decolonisation debate, with, as Charles Forsdick draws out in chapter 9, the radically diverging affective and intellectual positions this engendered; a complicated private life involving numerous extra-marital relationships; self-imposed solitude as his position became increasingly isolated in the 1950s; the Nobel Prize, which, although he received it at the exceptionally early age of forty-four for what the Nobel committee saw as an 'authentic moral engagement' with the fundamental questions of his day (*Ess*, 1893), came ironically at a great low in Camus's life; the beginning of the end for French Algeria; and his own premature death. Writing in his preface to the *Chroniques algériennes* in 1958, Camus conceded that the long confrontation between an individual and a particular historical situation (he was referring to his engagement with Algeria) was not without errors, contradictions and hesitations (*Ess*, 900). Indeed, he sees his Algerian chronicles as the history of a failure (*Ess*, 899). Yet this sense of the author's fallibility, his acceptance that he has made errors of judgement and, above all, his call to tolerance provide us with not only good reasons to revisit his work but also potentially with good lessons to draw from it. In a memorial tribute in January 1960, John Cruickshank reminded his audience that, in Camus's words, 'every authentic work of art is a gift offered to the future'.[6] In the case of Camus, this proleptic giving entails a body of work to be read, understood, puzzled and argued over, both in relation to the circumstances in which he produced it and, no less importantly, within the conditions of our contemporary situation and beyond. 'Désintoxiquer les esprits et apaiser les fanatismes' (*Ess*, 899) ('To remove the toxins from people's minds, to assuage fanaticisms') was, as Jeanyves Guérin reminds us, Camus's sincerely uttered call to the intellectual.[7] The appeal of the prescription endures, as does the challenge of Camus's complicated legacy.

NOTES

1. J.-J. Brochier, *Albert Camus philosophe pour classes terminales* (Paris, Balland, 1970).
2. Olivier Todd, *Albert Camus, une vie* (Paris, Gallimard, 1996), p. 309.
3. Jeanyves Guérin, *Camus: Portrait de l'artiste en citoyen* (Paris, Bourin, 1993), p. 10.
4. See http//programmes.france2.fr/leplusgrandfrancais/8709130-fr.php).
5. G. V. Banks, *Camus: L'Etranger* (Glasgow, University of Glasgow French and German Publications, 1992), p. 1.
6. J. Cruickshank, *Albert Camus and the Literature of Revolt* (New York, Oxford University Press/Galaxy Books, 1960), p. xx.
7. Guérin, *Camus*, p. 281.

.

PRIMARY WORKS BY CAMUS

Albert Camus éditorialiste à 'L'Express' (mai 1955-février 1956) (Cahiers Albert Camus 6), ed. Paul Smets, Paris, Gallimard, 1987.

Caligula: texte établi d'après la dactylographie de février 1941: suivi de 'La poétique du premier Caligula' (Cahiers Albert Camus 4), ed. A. James Arnold, Paris, Gallimard, 1984.

Camus à 'Combat' (Cahiers Albert Camus 8), ed. Jacqueline Lévi-Valensi, Paris, Gallimard, 2002.

Carnets I, II, III, Paris, Gallimard, 1962–89.

Essais, ed. Roger Quilliot, Paris, Bibliothèque de la Pléiade, 1965.

Fragments d'un combat, 1938–1940 (Cahiers Albert Camus 3), eds. Jacqueline Lévi-Valensi and André Abbou, Paris, Gallimard, 1978.

Journaux de voyage, ed. Roger Quilliot, Paris, Gallimard, 1978.

'Lettre au directeur des *Temps modernes*', *Les Temps modernes* 82 (1952), 317–33.

La Mort heureuse (Cahiers Albert Camus 1), Paris, Gallimard, 1971.

Le Premier Camus, suivi de *Ecrits de jeunesse d'Albert Camus*, ed. Paul Viallaneix (Cahiers Albert Camus 2), Paris, Gallimard, 1973.

Le Premier Homme (Cahiers Albert Camus 7), Paris, Gallimard, 1994.

Théâtre, Récits, Nouvelles, ed. Roger Quilliot, Paris, Bibliothèque de la Pléiade, 1962.

Available in English translation

Albert Camus: Lyrical and Critical, trans. Philip Thody, London, Hamish Hamilton, 1967.

American Journals, trans. Hugh Levick, New York, Paragon House, 1987; London, Hamish Hamilton, 1989.

Between Hell and Reason, trans. Alexandre de Gramont, London, University Press of New England, 1991.

Caligula and Other Plays: Caligula, Cross Purpose, The Just, The Possessed, trans. Stuart Gilbert, London, Penguin, 1984.

Exile and the Kingdom, trans. Justin O'Brien, London, Penguin, 2002 (1962).

The Fall, trans. Justin O'Brien, London, Penguin, 2000 (1963).

The First Man, trans. David Hapgood, London, Penguin, 1996.

A Happy Death, trans. Richard Howard, London, Penguin, 2002 (1973).

Lyrical and Critical Essays, trans. Ellen Conroy Kennedy, New York, Vintage Books, 1967.

The Myth of Sisyphus, trans. Justin O'Brien, London, Penguin, 2000 (1975).

Notebooks I: 1935–1942, trans. Philip Thody, New York, Knopf, 1963.

Notebooks II: 1942–1951, trans. Justin O'Brien, New York, Knopf, 1966; New York, Marlowe and Company, 1995.

The Outsider, trans. Joseph Laredo, London, Penguin, 2000 (1983). Also translated as *The Stranger*, trans. Matthew Ward, New York, Knopf, 1988.

The Plague, trans. Stuart Gilbert, London, Penguin, 1963.

The Rebel, trans. Anthony Bower, London, Penguin, 1971; reprinted with a new introduction by Olivier Todd, London, Penguin, 2000.

Resistance, Rebellion, and Death (partial translation of *Actuelles I, II* and *III*), trans. Justin O'Brien, London, Hamish Hamilton, 1961.

Selected Essays and Notebooks, trans. Philip Thody, London, Penguin, 1979.

Selected Political Writings, trans. and ed. Jonathan H. King, London, Methuen, 1981.

Youthful Writings, trans. Ellen Conroy Kennedy, New York, Knopf, 1976.

Biography

Lottman, Herbert R., *Albert Camus: a Biography*, London, Weidenfeld and Nicolson, 1979; New York, Braziller, 1980; reprinted London, Axis, 1997. Also available in French translation, *Albert Camus*, trans. Marianne Véron, Paris, Seuil, 1978.

Todd, Olivier, *Albert Camus, une vie*, Paris, Gallimard, 1996; translated (in abbreviated form) as *Albert Camus, A Life*, trans. Benjamin Ivry, London, Chatto & Windus, 1997; New York, Carroll & Graf, 2000.

Correspondence

Correspondance Albert Camus/Jean Grenier, ed. Marguerite Dobrenn, Paris, Gallimard, 1981.

CRITICAL WORKS

Achour, Christiane, *L'Etranger si familier*, Algiers, EnAP, 1984.

Apter, Emily, 'Out of Character: Camus's French Algerian Subjects', *Modern Language Notes* 112.4 (1997), 499–516.

'Out of Character: Camus's French Algerian Subjects', in *Continental Drift: From National Characters to Virtual Subjects*, Chicago and London, University of Chicago Press, 1999, pp. 61–75.

Archambault, Paul, *Camus's Hellenic Sources*, Chapel Hill, University of North Carolina Press, 1972.

Arnold, A. J., *Caligula: texte établi d'après la dactylographie de février 1941: suivi de 'La poétique du premier Caligula'* (Cahiers Albert Camus 4), Paris, Gallimard, 1984.

Aron, Raymond, *Mémoires*, Paris, Julliard, 1985.

Aronson, Ronald, *Camus and Sartre: The Story of a Friendship and the Quarrel that Ended It*, Chicago and London, University of Chicago Press, 2004.

(Aronson, Ronald), 'Sartre, Camus, and the *Caliban* articles', *Sartre Studies International* 7.2 (2001), 1–11.

'The Third Man in the Story: Ronald Aronson discusses the Sartre-Camus conflict with Francis Jeanson', *Sartre Studies International* 8.2 (2002), 20–67.

Audisio, Gabriel, *Hommes au soleil*, Maupré, Le Mouton blanc, 1923.

Héliotrope, Paris, Gallimard, 1928.

Jeunesse de la Méditerranée, Paris, Gallimard, 1935.

Le Sel de la mer, Paris, Gallimard, 1936.

Ulysse ou l'intelligence, Paris, Gallimard, 1945.

Backan, Ahmed, *Camus et Sartre: deux intellectuels en politique*, Lille, ANRT, 2004.

Bal, M., J. Crew and L. Spitzer, *Acts of Memory. Cultural Recall in the Present*, Hanover, NH and London, University Press of New England, 1999.

Banks, G. V., *Camus: 'L'Etranger'*, Glasgow, University of Glasgow French and German Publications, 1992; first published: London, Arnold, 1976.

Barrat, Denise (ed.), *Espoir et parole*, Paris, Seghers, 1963.

Bartfeld, Fernande, *L'Effet tragique. Essai sur le tragique dans l'œuvre de Camus*, Geneva, Champion-Slatkine, 1988.

'Le Théâtre de Camus, lieu d'une écriture contrariée', in Jacqueline Lévi-Valensi (ed.), *Albert Camus et le théâtre: Actes du Colloque tenu à Amiens du 31 mai au 2 juin 1988*, Paris, IMEC, 1992, pp. 177–85.

'Anti-Méditerranée et lyrisme de l'exil', *Perspectives* 5 (1998), 213–25.

Barthes, Roland, 'La Peste' (1955), in *Œuvres complètes*, ed. Eric Marty, Paris, Seuil, 2002, 5 vols., vol. 1, pp. 540–5.

Le Degré zéro de l'écriture, Paris, Seuil, 1953.

Bartlett, Elizabeth Ann, *Rebellious Feminism: Camus's Ethic of Rebellion and Feminist Thought*, New York, Palgrave/Macmillan, 2004.

Beer (Capstick), Jill, '*Le Regard*: Face to Face in Albert Camus's "L'Hôte" ', *French Studies* 56.2 (2002), 179–92.

Béji, Hélé, 'Radicalisme culturel et laïcité', *Le Débat* 58 (January–February 1990), 45–9.

Bertrand, Louis, *Le Sang des races*, Paris, Ollendorf, 1899.

Les Villes d'or: Algérie et Tunisie romaines, Paris, Fayard, 1921.

Bey, Maïssa, *Nouvelles d'Algérie*, Paris, Grasset, 1998.

'Femmes au bord de la vie', *Albert Camus et les écritures algériennes. Quelles traces?*, Aix-en-Provence, Edisud, 2004, pp. 127–33.

Biondi, J.-P., *Les Anticolonialistes (1881–1962)*, Paris, Laffont, 1992.

Birchall, Ian, 'Camus contre Sartre: quarante ans plus tard', in David H. Walker (ed.), *Albert Camus: les extrêmes et l'équilibre*, Amsterdam, Rodopi, 1994, pp. 129–50.

Blanchot, Maurice, 'Le Mythe de Sisyphe', in *Faux Pas*, Paris, Gallimard, 1943, pp. 65–71.

'Tu peux tuer cet homme', *La Nouvelle Revue française* 3 (1954), 1059–69.

L'Entretien infini, Paris, Gallimard, 1969.

'*La Chute*: La Fuite', in *L'Amitié*, Paris, Gallimard, 1971, pp. 228–35.

Bloom, Harold (ed.), *Albert Camus*, Philadelphia, Chelsea House, 1989.

Albert Camus's 'The Stranger', Philadelphia, Chelsea House, 2001.

Bouraoui, Nina, *Garçon manqué*, Paris, Stock, 2000.

Braun, Lev, *Witness of Decline. Albert Camus: Moralist of the Absurd*, Rutherford, NJ, Fairleigh Dickinson University Press, 1974.

Brée, Germaine, *Camus*, New Brunswick, NJ, Rutgers University Press, 1959.

Camus and Sartre: Crisis and Commitment, London, Calder and Boyars, 1974.

Brée, Germaine (ed.), *Camus: A Collection of Critical Essays*, Englewood Cliffs, NJ, Prentice-Hall, 1962.

Brochier, J.-J., *Albert Camus philosophe pour classes terminales*, Paris, Balland, 1970.

Brodziak, Sylvie, et al. (eds.), *Albert Camus et les écritures du xxe siècle*, Arras, Artois Presses Université, 2003.

Bronner, Stephen Eric, *Camus: Portrait of a Moralist*, London, University of Minnesota Press, 1999.

Broyelle, Claudie and Jacques, *Les Illusions retrouvées: Sartre a toujours raison contre Camus*, Paris, Grasset, 1982.

Capstick, Jill, 'Mastery or Slavery: The Ethics of Revolt in Camus's "Les Muets"', *Modern and Contemporary France* 11.4 (2003), 453–62.

Carroll, David, 'Camus's Algeria: birthrights, colonial injustice and the fiction of a French Algerian people', *Modern Language Notes* 112.4 (1997), 517–49.

Albert Camus, The Algerian: Colonialism, Terrorism, Justice, New York: Columbia University Press, forthcoming.

Champigny, Robert, *Sur un héros païen*, Paris, Gallimard, 1959. Also available as *A Pagan Hero*, trans. Rowe Portis, Philadelphia, University of Pennsylvania Press, 1969.

Charbit, Denis, 'Camus et l'épreuve algérienne', *Perspectives* 5 (1998), 157–81.

Chaulet-Achour, Christiane (C. Achour), *Albert Camus, Alger: 'L'Etranger' et autres récits*, Paris, Séguier, 1999.

Albert Camus et l'Algérie, Algiers, Barzakh, 2004.

Chouaki, Aziz, *Les Oranges*, Paris, Mille et une nuits, 1998.

Clot, J.-P., *Fantômes au soleil*, Paris, Gallimard, 1949.

Cohen-Solal, Annie, 'Camus, Sartre et la guerre d'Algérie', in Jeanyves Guérin (ed.), *Camus et la politique*, Paris, L'Harmattan, 1985, pp. 177–84.

Coombs, Ilona, *Camus, homme de théâtre*, Paris, Nizet, 1968.

Costes, Alain, *Albert Camus et la parole manquante: étude psychanalytique*, Paris, Payot, 1973.

Cruickshank, John, *Albert Camus and the Literature of Revolt*, New York, Oxford University Press/Galaxy Books, 1959/1960.

Daniel, Jean, *Camus*, Paris, Hachette, coll. Génies et réalités, 1969.

'Le Suicide d'une nation', *Le Nouvel Observateur* (14–20 April 1994), 28–9.

Soleils d'hiver. Carnets 1998–2000, Paris, Grasset, 2000.

Davis, Colin, 'Interpreting *La Peste*', *Romanic Review* 85.1 (1994), 125–42.

Ethical Issues in Twentieth-Century French Fiction: Killing the Other, Basingstoke, Macmillan, 2000.

'The Cost of Being Ethical: Fiction, Violence, and Altericide', *Common Knowledge* 9.2 (2003), 241–53.

Davison, Ray, *Camus: The Challenge of Dostoevsky*, Exeter, Exeter University Press, 1997.

'Mythologising the Mediterranean: The Case of Albert Camus', *Journal of Mediterranean Studies* 10.1–2 (2000), 77–92.

de Beauvoir, Simone, *La Force des choses*, Paris, Gallimard, 1963.

Debout, Simone, 'Sartre et Camus, témoins de la liberté', *Modern Language Notes* 112 (1997), 600–7.

Deguy, Jacques, 'Sartre lecteur de *L'Etranger*', *Albert Camus* (La Revue des Lettres Modernes), 16 (1995), 63–83.

Deleuze, Gilles, 'L'Ile déserte' (1953), in David Lapoujade (ed.), *L'Ile déserte et autres textes*, Paris, Minuit, 2002.

Derrida, Jacques, *Force de loi*, Paris, Galilée, 1994.

Points . . . Interviews. 1974–1994, Stanford, Stanford University Press, 1995.

Dine, Philip, 'Fighting and Writing the War Without a Name: Polemics and the French-Algerian Conflict', *AURIFEX*, 2 (2002) (http://www.goldsmiths.ac.uk/aurifex/issue2/dine.html).

Djebar, Assia, 'Afterword', in *Women of Algiers in Their Apartment*, Charlottesville, University Press of Virginia, 1992, pp. 159–211.

Le Blanc de l'Algérie, Paris, Albin Michel, 1995.

'Le Territoire des langues', in L. Gauvin (ed.), *L'Ecrivain francophone à la croisée des langues: entretiens*, Paris, Karthala, 1997, pp. 17–34.

Ces voix qui m'assiègent, Paris, Albin Michel, 1999.

La Disparition de la langue française, Paris, Albin Michel, 2003.

Djemaï, Abdelkader, *Camus à Oran*, Paris, Michalon, 1995.

Dostoyevsky, F., *Notes from the Underground*, trans. Jane Kentish, Oxford, Oxford University Press (World's Classics), 1991.

Drake, David, 'Sartre, Camus and the Algerian War', *Sartre Studies International* 5.1 (1999), 16–32.

Dunn, Susan, 'From Burke to Camus: Reconceiving the Revolution', *Salmagundi* 84 (1989), 214–29.

Dunwoodie, Peter, *Camus: 'L'Envers et l'Endroit' and 'L'Exil et le Royaume'*, London, Grant & Cutler, 1985.

Une histoire ambivalente: Le dialogue Camus-Dostoïevski, Paris, Nizet, 1996.

Writing French Algeria, Oxford, Clarendon Press, 1998.

Francophone Writing in Transition: Algeria 1900–1945, Berne, Peter Lang, 2005.

Dunwoodie, Peter and Edward J. Hughes (eds.), *Constructing Memories: Camus, Algeria and 'Le Premier Homme'*, Stirling, Stirling French Publications, 1998.

El Houssi, M., 'Camus ou le désir de Méditerranée', *Africa, America, Asia, Australia* 15 (1993), 29–39.

Ellison, David R., 'Camus and the Rhetoric of Dizziness: *La Chute*', *Contemporary Literature* 24.3 (Autumn 1983), 322–48.

Understanding Albert Camus, Columbia, University of South Carolina Press, 1990.

Felman, Shoshana, 'Camus' "The Fall", or The Betrayal of the Witness', in Shoshana Felman and Dori Laub, *Testimony: Crises of Witnessing in Literature, Psychoanalysis and History*, New York, Routledge, 1992, pp. 165–203.

Fitch, Brian T., *The Narcissistic Text: A Reading of Camus's Fiction*, Toronto, University of Toronto Press, 1982.

Fouchet, M.-P., *Un jour, je m'en souviens . . . Mémoire parlée*, Paris, Mercure de France, 1968.

Freeman, E., *The Theatre of Albert Camus: A Critical Study*, London, Methuen, 1971.

Garfitt, (J. S.) Toby, 'Grenier, Malraux, Camus', *Europe* 897–8 (January–February 2004), 208–23.

Garfitt, J. S. T., 'Grenier and Camus: From *Les Iles* to *La Chute*', *Forum for Modern Language Studies* 17.3 (1981), 217–29.

'Le Premier homm(ag)e: Grounding History in Love', in Dunwoodie and Hughes (eds.), *Constructing Memories*, pp. 1–8.

Gay-Crosier, Raymond, *Les Envers d'un échec: étude sur le théâtre d'Albert Camus*, Paris, Minard, 1967.

Giles, J. (ed.), *French Existentialism: Consciousness, Ethics and Relations with Others*, Amsterdam, Rodopi, 1999.

Gordon, A. F., *Ghostly Matters. Haunting and the Sociological Imagination*, Minneapolis, University of Minnesota Press, 1997.

Gray, Margaret E., 'Les "Juges Intègres" de Clamence: Une lecture psychanalytique de *La Chute*', in Lionel Dubois (ed.), *Albert Camus entre la misère et le soleil*, Poitiers, Pont-Neuf, 1997, pp. 73–80.

Grenier, Jean, *Les Iles*, Paris, Gallimard, 1959 (1933).

Albert Camus. Souvenirs, Paris, Gallimard, 1968.

Sous l'occupation, Paris, Claire Paulhan, 1997.

Grenier, Roger, *Albert Camus. Soleil et ombre: une biographie intellectuelle*, Paris, Gallimard, 1987.

Guérin, Jeanyves, *Camus: Portrait de l'artiste en citoyen*, Paris, Bourin, 1993.

Guérin, Jeanyves (ed.), *Camus et la politique*, Paris, L'Harmattan, 1985.

Camus et le premier 'Combat', La Garenne-Colombes, Editions européennes Erasme, 1990.

Haddour, Azzedine, *Colonial Myths: History and Narrative*, Manchester, Manchester University Press, 2000.

'The Camus–Sartre Debate and the Colonial Question in Algeria', in Charles Forsdick and David Murphy (eds.), *Francophone Postcolonial Studies: A Critical Introduction*, London, Arnold, 2003, pp. 66–76.

Hargreaves, Alec, 'Caught in the Middle: the Liberal Dilemma in the Algerian War', *Nottingham French Studies* 25.2 (1986), 73–82.

'Camus and the Colonial Question in Algeria', *Muslim World* 77 (1987), 164–74.

Harrison, Nicholas, *Postcolonial Criticism. History, Theory and the Work of Fiction*, Cambridge, Polity, 2003.

Hart, Elisabeth, 'Face à face: l'éthique lévinasienne dans "L'Hôte" ', in Lionel Dubois (ed.), *Les Trois guerres d'Albert Camus*, Poitiers, Les Editions du Pont-Neuf, 1995, pp. 172–7.

Hénein, Georges, 'Lettre à Henri Calet, 16 avril 1948', *Grandes Largeurs* 2 (autumn/winter 1981), 66.

Hodgkin, K. and S. Radstone, *Contested Pasts*, London and New York, Routledge, 2003.

Horowitz, Louise, 'Of Women and Arabs: Sexual and Racial Polarization in Camus', *Modern Language Studies* 17.3 (Summer 1987), 54–61.

Hughes, Edward J., *Albert Camus: Le Premier Homme/La Peste*, Glasgow, University of Glasgow French and German Publications, 1995.

'Camus and the Resistance to History', in E. J. Hughes, *Writing Marginality in Modern French Literature: from Loti to Genet*, Cambridge, Cambridge University Press, 2001, pp. 102–34.

Huyssens, Andreas, *Twilight Memories: Marking Time in a Culture of Amnesia*, London, Routledge, 1995.

Isaac, Jeffrey C., *Arendt, Camus and Modern Rebellion*, London, Yale University Press, 1992.

Jeanson, Francis, 'Albert Camus, ou l'âme révoltée', *Les Temps modernes* 79 (1952), 2070–90.

'Pour tout vous dire', *Les Temps modernes* 82 (1952), 354–83.

Jones, Rosemarie, *Camus: 'L'Etranger' and 'La Chute'*, London, Grant & Cutler, 1994.

Judt, Tony, 'The Lost World of Albert Camus', *New York Review of Books* 41.16 (6 October 1994), 3–5.

The Burden of Responsibility, Chicago and London, University of Chicago Press, 1998.

Kelly, Debra, *Autobiography and Independence. Selfhood and Creativity in North African Postcolonial Writing in French*, Liverpool, Liverpool University Press, 2005.

Khatibi, Abdelkebir, *Maghreb pluriel*, Paris, Denoël, 1983.

King, Adele (ed.), *Camus's 'L'Etranger': Fifty Years on*, New York, St Martin's Press, 1992.

Knapp, Bettina L., *Critical Essays on Albert Camus*, Boston, MA, G. K. Hall & Co., 1988.

Knauss, P. R., *The Persistence of Patriarchy: Class, Gender and Ideology in Twentieth-Century Algeria*, New York, Praeger, 1987.

Koestler, Arthur, *Darkness at Noon*, London, Cape, 1940.

The Yogi and the Commissar, London, Cape, 1945.

Kouchkine, Eugène, '*Les Justes*: le tragique de l'amour et du renoncement', in Jacqueline Lévi-Valensi and Agnès Spiquel (eds.), *Camus et le lyrisme*, Paris, Editions SEDES, 1997, pp. 161–71.

Krapp, J., 'Time and Ethics in Albert Camus's *The Plague*', *University of Toronto Quarterly* 68.2 (1999), 655–76.

Kritzman, Lawrence D., 'Camus's Curious Humanism or the Intellectual in Exile', *Modern Language Notes* 112.4 (1997), 550–75.

Le Sueur, James D., 'The Unbearable Solitude of Being: the Question of Albert Camus', in *Uncivil War: Intellectuals and Identity Politics during the Decolonisation of Algeria*, Philadelphia, University of Pennsylvania Press, 2001, pp. 87–127.

Lévi-Valensi, Jacqueline, 'Terre faite à mon âme: pour une mythologie du réel', *Perspectives* 5 (1998), 185–97.

Lévi-Valensi, Jacqueline (ed.), *Albert Camus et le théâtre: Actes du Colloque tenu à Amiens du 31 mai au 2 juin 1988*, Paris, IMEC, 1992.

Camus à 'Combat', Paris, Gallimard, 2002.

Lévi-Valensi, Jacqueline and Denis Salas (eds.), *Albert Camus: Réflexions sur le terrorisme*, Paris, Nicolas Philippe, 2002.

Locke, F. W., 'The Metamorphoses of Jean-Baptiste Clamence', *Symposium* 21 (1967), 306–15.

Malraux, A., 'D'une jeunesse européenne', in André Chamson et al., *Ecrits*, Paris, Grasset, 1927.

Maougal, Mohamed Lakhdar (ed.), *Albert Camus. Assassinat post-mortem*, Algiers, Editions APIC, 2004.

Margerrison, Christine, 'Struggling with the Other: Gender and Race in the Youthful Writings of Camus', in J. Giles (ed.), *French Existentialism: Consciousness, Ethics and Relations with Others*, Amsterdam, Rodopi, 1999, pp. 191–211.

Masters, Brian, *Camus: a Study*, London, Heinemann, 1974.

McBride, William L., 'The Polemic in the Pages of *Les Temps modernes* (1952) Concerning Francis Jeanson's Review of Camus' *The Rebel*', in *Sartre and Existentialism*, 8 vols., Hamden, CT, Garland, 1997, vol. VIII, pp. 79–93.

McCarthy, Patrick, *Camus. A Critical Study of his Life and Work*, London, Hamish Hamilton, 1982.

'The First Arab in *L'Etranger*', *Revue CELFAN Review* 4.3 (1985), 23–6.

Albert Camus: 'The Stranger' (Landmarks of World Literature), Cambridge, Cambridge University Press, 1988; second edition 2005.

Memmi, Albert, 'Camus ou le colonisateur de bonne volonté', *La Nef*, 12 December 1957, 95–6.

Portrait du colonisé, précédé de *Portrait du colonisateur*, Paris, Gallimard, 1985 (1957).

Merleau-Ponty, Maurice, *Humanisme et terreur*, Paris, Gallimard, 1947.

Meyers, Jeffrey, 'Camus' *The Fall* and Van Eyck's *The Adoration of the Lamb*', *Mosaic* 7.3 (1974), 43–51.

Montgomery, Geraldine F., *Noces pour femme seule. Le féminin et le sacré dans l'œuvre d'Albert Camus*, Amsterdam/New York, Rodopi, 2004.

Murchland, Bernard, 'Camus and Sartre: the Anatomy of a Quarrel', in Michel-Antoine Burnier (ed.), *Choice of Action: The French Existentialists on the Political Front Line*, trans. Bernard Murchland, New York, Random House, 1968, pp. 175–94.

Nacer-Khodja, Hamid, *Albert Camus. Jean Sénac ou le fils rebelle*, Paris, EDIF, 2004.

O'Brien, Conor Cruise, *Albert Camus of Europe and Africa*, New York, The Viking Press, 1970.

Camus, Glasgow, Collins (Fontana), 1970.

'The Fall', *The New Republic*, 16 October 1995.

Orme, Mark, '*Retour aux sources*: Crisis and Reappraisal in Albert Camus's Final Pronouncements on Justice', *Modern and Contemporary France* 11.4 (2003), 463–74.

Oxenhandler, Neil, *Looking for Heroes in Postwar France. Albert Camus, Max Jacob, Simone Weil*, Hanover, NH, Dartmouth College/University Press of New England, 1996.

Pollmann, Leo, *Sartre and Camus: Literature of Existence*, trans. Helen and Gregor Sebba, New York, Ungar, 1970.

Rioux, Jean-Pierre, and Jean-François Sirinelli (eds.), *La Guerre d'Algérie et les intellectuels français*, Brussels, Complexe, 1991.

Rizzuto, Anthony, *Camus. Love and Sexuality*, Gainesville, University Press of Florida, 1998.

Roman, Joel, 'Histoire et utopie dans *Ni victimes ni bourreaux*', in Jeanyves Guérin (ed.), *Camus et le premier 'Combat'*, La Garenne-Colombes, Editions européennes Erasme, 1990, pp. 125–34.

Rousset, David, 'Au secours des déportés dans les camps soviétiques' (1949), in *Lignes* n.s. 2 (May 2000), 143–60.

Royle, Peter, *The Sartre–Camus Controversy: A Literary and Philosophical Critique*, Ottawa, University of Ottawa Press, 1982.

Saadi, Yacef, *La Bataille d'Alger*, vol. I, Algiers, Entreprise Nationale du Livre, 1984.

Said, Edward, *Orientalism: Western Conceptions of the Orient*, London, Routledge and Kegan Paul, 1978.

Culture and Imperialism, London, Vintage, 1994 (1993).

Sarocchi, J., *Le Dernier Camus ou 'Le Premier Homme'*, Paris, Nizet, 1995.

'La Méditerranée est un songe, Monsieur', *Perspectives. Revue de l'Université hébraïque de Jérusalem* 5 (1998), 109–29.

Sartre, Jean-Paul, 'Réponse à Albert Camus', *Les Temps modernes* 82 (1952), 334–53.

'Explication de *L'Etranger*', in *Situations I*, Paris, Gallimard, 1947, pp. 92–112. Also available as 'Camus' "The Outsider" ', in Jean-Paul Sartre, *Literary and Philosophical Essays*, trans. Annette Michelson, New York, Criterion Books, 1955, pp. 24–41.

Situations v, Paris, Gallimard, 1964; translated as *Colonialism and Neocolonialism*, trans. Azzedine Haddour, Steve Brewer and Terry McWilliams, London, Routledge, 2001.

Showalter, Jr, English, *Exiles and Strangers: A Reading of Camus's 'Exile and the Kingdom'*, Columbus, Ohio State University Press, 1984.

'The Stranger': Humanity and the Absurd, Boston, Twayne, 1989.

Siblot, Paul, and Jean-Louis Planche, 'Le 8 mai 1945: éléments pour une analyse des positions de Camus face au nationalisme algérien', in Jeanyves Guérin (ed.), *Camus et la politique*, Paris, L'Harmattan, 1986, pp. 153–75.

Sprintzen, David, *Camus: A Critical Examination*, Philadelphia, Temple University Press, 1988.

Sprintzen, David A., and Adrian van den Hoven (eds.), *Sartre and Camus: A Historic Confrontation*, Amherst, Humanity Books, 2004.

Stéphane, N., 'La Mer heureuse', *Europe* 77.846 (October 1999), 132–44.

Suther, Judith D., *Essays on Camus's 'Exile and the Kingdom'*, Jackson, MS, University of Mississippi Romance Monographs, 1980.

Tarrow, Susan, *Exile from the Kingdom: A Political Re-reading of Albert Camus*, Birmingham, University of Alabama Press, 1985.

Thody, Philip, *Albert Camus, 1913–1960*, London, Hamish Hamilton, 1961.

van der Poel, Ieme, 'Albert Camus, ou la critique postcoloniale face au "rêve méditerranéen"', *Francophone Postcolonial Studies* 2.1 (2004), 70–8.

Vanney, Philippe, 'A propos d'une lecture: *Ni victimes ni bourreaux* d'Albert Camus ou la problématique révolutionnaire dans les relations internationales', *Bulletin d'études françaises*, University of Tokyo, 17 (1986), 36–67.

'Albert Camus devant la guerre', *Bulletin d'études françaises*, University of Tokyo, 19 (1988), 19–55; and 21 (1990), 1–30.

Vulor, Ena C., *Colonial and Anti-Colonial Discourses: Albert Camus and Algeria*, Lanham, MD, University Press of America, 2001.

Walker, David (ed.), *Albert Camus: Les Extrêmes et l'Equilibre: Actes du colloque de Keele, 25–27 mars 1993*, Amsterdam, Rodopi, 1994.

'Knowing the place for the first time?', in Dunwoodie and Hughes (eds.), *Constructing Memories*, pp. 9–20.

Walzer, Michael, 'Albert Camus's Algerian War', in *The Company of Critics*, New York, Basic Books, 1988, pp. 136–52.

Wertsch, J. V., *Voices of Collective Remembering*, Cambridge, Cambridge University Press, 2002.

Weyembergh, Maurice, 'Ni victimes ni bourreaux: continuité ou rupture?', in Jeanyves Guérin (ed.), *Camus et le premier 'Combat'*, La Garenne-Colombes, Editions européennes Erasme, 1990, pp. 109–24.

Albert Camus ou la mémoire des origines, Brussels, De Boeck, 1998.

Williams, James S., *Camus: 'La Peste'*, London, Grant & Cutler, 2000.

Wood, N., 'Colonial Nostalgia and *Le Premier Homme*', in *Vectors of Memory: Legacies of Trauma in Postwar Europe*, Oxford, Berg, 1999, pp. 143–66.

Young, Robert J. C., *Postcolonialism. An Historical Introduction*, Oxford, Blackwell, 2001.

'Sartre: the "African" Philosopher', in Jean-Paul Sartre, *Colonialism and Neocolonialism*, trans. Azzedine Haddour, Steve Brewer and Terry McWilliams, London, Routledge, 2001, pp. vii–xxiv.

Cambridge Companions to

AUTHORS

Homer edited by Robert Fowler

Virgil edited by Charles Martindale

Ovid edited by Philip Hardie

Dante edited by Rachel Jacoff

Cervantes edited by Anthony J. Cascardi

Goethe edited by Lesley Sharpe

Dostoevskii edited by W. J. Leatherbarrow

Tolstoy edited by Donna Tussing Orwin

Chekhov edited by Vera Gottlieb and Paul Allain

Ibsen edited by James McFarlane

Flaubert edited by Timothy Unwin

Pushkin edited by Andrew Kahn

Proust edited by Richard Bales

Thomas Mann edited by Ritchie Robertson

Kafka edited by Julian Preece

Brecht edited by Peter Thomson and Glendyr Sacks

Walter Benjamin edited by David S. Ferris

Lacan edited by Jean-Michel Rabaté

Nabokov edited by Julian W. Connolly

Camus edited by Edward J. Hughes

Chaucer, second edition edited by Piero Boitani and Jill Mann

Shakespeare edited by Margareta de Grazia andStanley Wells

Christopher Marlowe edited by Patrick Cheney

Ben Jonson edited by Richard Harp and Stanley Stewart

John Donne edited by Achsah Guibbory

Spenser edited by Andrew Hadfield

Milton, second edition edited by Dennis Danielson

John Dryden edited by Steven N. Zwicker

Molière edited by David Bradby and Andrew Calder

Aphra Behn edited by Derek Hughes and Janet Todd

Samuel Johnson edited by Greg Clingham

Jonathan Swift edited by Christopher Fox

Mary Wollstonecraft edited by Claudia L. Johnson

William Blake edited by Morris Eaves

Wordsworth edited by Stephen Gill

Coleridge edited by Lucy Newlyn

Byron edited by Drummond Bone

Keats edited by Susan J. Wolfson

Shelley edited by Timothy Morton

Mary Shelley edited by Esther Schor

Jane Austen edited by Edward Copeland and Juliet McMaster

The Brontës edited by Heather Glen

Charles Dickens edited by John O. Jordan

Wilkie Collins edited by Jenny Bourne Taylor

George Eliot edited by George Levine

Thomas Hardy edited by Dale Kramer

Oscar Wilde edited by Peter Raby

George Bernard Shaw edited by Christopher Innes

W. B. Yeats edited by Marjorie Howes and John Kelly

Joseph Conrad edited by J. H. Stape

D. H. Lawrence edited by Anne Fernihough

Virginia Woolf edited by Sue Roe and Susan Sellers

James Joyce, second edition edited by Derek Attridge

T. S. Eliot edited by A. David Moody

Ezra Pound edited by Ira B. Nadel

W. H. Auden edited by Stan Smith

Beckett edited by John Pilling

Harold Pinter edited by Peter Raby

Tom Stoppard edited by Katherine E. Kelly

Brian Friel edited by Anthony Roche

Herman Melville edited by Robert S. Levine

TOPICS

CULTURE